Political Correctness:

A Deceptive and Dangerous Worldview

A Short History of an Ideology

Edited by William S. Lind and Richard W. Hawkins

November 2004

Updated, April 2020

Cover Art: Freedom's Battle by A.F. Branco

(used with permission)

Publisher

Nehemiah Institute, Inc.

800-948-3101

Copies available from Publisher www.nehemiahinstitute.com

Or

Amazon.com

PART 2 – IDENTIFYING CULTURAL MARXISM IN THE CULTURE

PART 3 – IDENTIFYING CULTURAL MARXISM IN EDUCATION

PART 4 – ENGAGING IN THE WORLDVIEW BATTLES

FOREWORD

Perhaps the single most important Bible verse for our time is:

"For as he thinketh in his heart, so is he:---." Proverbs 23:7 KJV

The book you have in hand may be the most important read in understanding who we are today and how we got here. It provides an accurate and much needed historical background of the Political Correctness movement. It is critical for the Christian to understand the strategies and the depth of what the Progressives have done over the past 100+ years in fundamentally erasing the Judeo-Christian worldview from our history and replacing it with a thoroughly humanistic worldview. In other words, how did the Cultural Marxists *change how we think*?

We cannot overstate the importance of seeing how the Political Correctness movement of the past few decades is simply the outgrowth of Marxist ideology which was imported from Germany to the U.S. in the 1930s (as told in this book). Only the name has changed.

It is this ideology which has become the foundation of government-run secular education (pre-K through higher education). Unless concerned Christians are willing to "expose the deeds of darkness," (Eph. 5:11) and educate their children and youth in God-honoring schools, there is truly no reason to expect God's favor on our efforts at the restoration of our Judeo-Christian heritage.

Dan Smithwick, President
Nehemiah Institute
dan@nehemiahinstitute.com

DISCLAIMER
This book comprises essays from several writers. We have used their essays, with permission, and copied them with no edits (except for adding obvious citations where missing from quotes and references contained therein). We may or may not be in full agreement with every position stated by the authors.

PREFACE

Political Correctness: A Deceptive and Dangerous Worldview
Its Pedigree, History and Practices

Richard W Hawkins

If you know the enemy and know yourself, you need not fear the result of a hundred battles. If you know yourself but not the enemy, for every victory gained you will also suffer a defeat. If you know neither the enemy nor yourself, you will succumb in every battle. – Sun Tzu, The Art of War [1]

What is a worldview? As the word itself suggests, a worldview is an overall view of the world. It's not a physical view of the world, but rather a philosophical view, an all-encompassing perspective on everything that exists and matters to us.[2]

I have been teaching worldviews and leading Focus on the Family's *The Truth Project* for many years. Through the years it became very apparent that most Christians are ill equipped to understand what a Christian worldview is let alone other worldviews that are competing against the Christian worldview. There are many fine books describing the Christian worldview but few describing its current major competitor, Political Correctness, which is causing chaos in this nation and around the world.

It is not just Christians that are in the dark about worldviews. I've also found that secular conservatives and liberals are ill equipped to understand our cultural chaos. They ask, "Why can't we just all get along?" They don't understand the incompatibility of worldviews which causes the conflicts. For the secular individuals they may recognize the battle is between traditional values and Political Correctness but not understand why this is so.

The purpose of this book is to equip Christians and conservatives to

---

[1] https://www.goodreads.com/work/quotes/3200649-s-nz-b-ngf
[2] Anderson, James, "What is a worldview?" https://www.ligonier.org/blog/what-worldview/, (Jun 21,2017)

more effectively engage in these worldview battles to help restore Western Civilization back to America. In addition, this may help liberals refrain from trying to destroy this nation by understanding what the Politically Correct agenda is about. This book will present in sufficient detail the who, what, when, where and why of Political Correctness so you will know the enemy. The enemy is not flesh and blood but rather a very deceptive and dangerous worldview that has taken many captive by its lies.

Political Correctness has become a divisive and ugly use of ad hominem attacks on decent Americans to shame them into silence and prevent public debate. The Politically Correct (aka Social Justice) warriors launch unwarranted attacks directed at traditional American institutions and values to marginalize or eliminate their influence in order to fundamentally transform America. It is a tyrannical worldview called by various names such as Western Marxism, neo-Marxism, transitional Marxism, transformational Marxism, post modernism, secular humanism and, most appropriately, cultural Marxism. This atheistic worldview is pervasive in our homes, in many churches, in almost all the media, in K-20 education, in business and the local, state and national civil governments. It is not politics but affects politics in a very profound way; centralized state government is one of its primary idols. It impacts our culture including the family, church, state, community and commerce. It's a full-fledged worldview that initiated a vicious spiritual war that few have been prepared to fight. This book provides the armor for you to contend for Truth and stand against the schemes of the devil.

Scripture counsels Christians to be prepared for and actively stand strong in this spiritual war.

> **Ephesians 6:10-12 (ESV)** [10] Finally, be strong in the Lord and in the strength of his might. [11] Put on the whole armor of God, that you may be able to stand against the schemes of the devil. [12] For we do not wrestle against flesh and blood, but against the rulers, against the authorities, against the cosmic powers over this present darkness, against the spiritual forces of evil in the heavenly places.

Some of these schemes of the devil are found in false philosophies (i.e., worldviews). We have to know what these false philosophies are to be able to recognize the devil's lies and not be deceived.

> **Colossians 2:8 (ESV)** [8] See to it that no one takes you captive by philosophy and empty deceit, according to human tradition, according to the elemental spirits of the world, and not according to Christ.

In addition, the true Church is gifted with pastors and teachers to equip believers for ministry and spiritual warfare:

> **Ephesians 4:11-14 (ESV)** [11] And he gave the apostles, the prophets, the evangelists, the shepherds and teachers, [12] to equip the saints for the work of ministry, for building up the body of Christ, [13] until we all attain to the unity of the faith and of the knowledge of the Son of God, to mature manhood, to the measure of the stature of the fullness of Christ, [14] so that we may no longer be children, tossed to and fro by the waves and carried about by every wind of doctrine, by human cunning, by craftiness in deceitful schemes.

Unfortunately, much of the American Church has failed these teachings and has conformed to this world.

> **Romans 12:2 (ESV)** [2] Do not be conformed to this world, but be transformed by the renewal of your mind, that by testing you may discern what is the will of God, what is good and acceptable and perfect.

I owe a debt of gratitude to William S. Lind for allowing me to build this anthology upon his book *Political Correctness; A Short History of an Ideology*. The book was found a number of years ago by this editor at the former Free Congress Foundation website and William S. Lind's works are now found at TraditionalRIGHT.com with daily blogs and some videos. Speaking with Mr. Lind about permission to reprint his book he made two strong recommendations for the readers:

1. View the YouTube video 'The History of Political Correctness

(Complete).'[3]   The video includes testimony from Martin Jay, Professor at UC Berkeley, who "established a correspondence and friendship with many of the members of the Frankfurt School. He was closest to Leo Lowenthal, who had provided him access to personal letters and documents for his research. Jay's work since then has explored Marxism, socialism, historiography, cultural criticism, visual culture, and the place of post structuralism and post-modernism in European intellectual history."[4]

2. Read <u>Adorno: A Political Biography</u> by Lorenz Jager, Stewart Spencer (Translator) – Theodor W. Adorno—philosopher, cultural critic, sociologist, and music theorist—was one of the most important German intellectuals of the twentieth century. This concise, readable life is the first attempt to look at his philosophical and literary work in its essential political context. This recent study of Theodor Adorno, the Frankfurt School's most important "creative spirit," offers a highly readable introduction to the origins of Political Correctness, perhaps the best available to the layman

I also owe a debt of gratitude to the many authors that have given permission to reprint their published works in this book. I trust you, the reader, will look upon each chapter and appendix as a piece of a puzzle that when assembled presents a very clear and understandable picture of what we are up against. Speaking of picture, I also owe many thanks to A. F. Blanco for his print on the cover of this book that perfectly illustrates the worldview war we are facing.

I want to thank Dan Smithwick of Nehemiah Institute for encouraging me to put this book together and for his tireless efforts to get it published.

Dr. David A. Noebel (Doc) and Summit Ministries gets an honorable mention for introducing me to comparative worldview studies via *Understanding the Times*.

Finally, I want to thank my loving wife, Pam, for her patience by allowing me the time to work on this book.

---

[3] https://www.youtube.com/watch?v=EjaBpVzOohs
[4] https://en.wikipedia.org/wiki/Martin_Jay

PART 1

POLITICAL CORRECTNESS IS CULTURAL MARXISM: AN OVERVIEW

Political Correctness was introduced throughout our university system by the Frankfurt School academics in the early 1950s. This part addresses the history and foundational roots of Political Correctness, the purpose for its creation and the cultural institutions it targets for destruction while some of its adherents attempt to obscure its existence.

Introduction

William S. Lind

As Russell Kirk wrote, one of conservatism's most important insights is that all ideologies are wrong. Ideology takes an intellectual system, a product of one or more philosophers, and says, "This system must be true." Inevitably, reality ends up contradicting the system, usually on a growing number of points. But the ideology, by its nature, cannot adjust to reality; to do so would be to abandon the system.

Therefore, reality must be suppressed. If the ideology has power, it uses its power to undertake this suppression. It forbids writing or speaking certain facts. Its goal is to prevent not only expression of thoughts that contradict what "must be true," but thinking such thoughts. In the end, the result is inevitably the concentration camp, the gulag and the grave.

While some Americans have believed in ideologies, America itself never had an official, state ideology – up until now. But what happens today to Americans who suggest that there are differences among ethnic groups, or that the traditional social roles of men and women reflect their different natures, or that homosexuality is morally wrong? If they are public figures, they must grovel in the dirt in endless, canting apologies. If they are university students, they face star chamber courts and possible expulsion. If they are employees of private corporations, they may face loss of their jobs. What was their crime? Contradicting America's new state ideology of "Political Correctness."

But what exactly is "Political Correctness?" Marxists have used the term for at least 80 years, as a broad synonym for "the General Line of the Party." It could be said that Political Correctness is the General Line of the Establishment in America today; certainly, no one who dares contradict it can be a member of that Establishment. But that still does not tell us what it really is.

This short book, which Free Congress has decided to make available free over its website, seeks to answer that question. It does so in the only way any ideology can be understood, by looking at its historical origins, its method of analysis and several key components, including its place in higher education and its ties with the Feminist movement. Finally, it offers an annotated bibliography for those who wish to pursue the subject in greater depth. [5]

Perhaps the most important question facing Americans today is, "Do we really want America to be an ideological state?" Because conservatives know where all ideologies lead, our answers resoundingly, is "NO!" But if we expect to prevail and restore our country to full freedom of thought and expression, we need to know our enemy. We need to understand what Political Correctness really is. As you will soon see, if we can expose the true origins and nature of Political Correctness, we will have taken a giant step toward its overthrow.

---

[5] Mr Lind's reference to "This short book," refers to the Introduction, chapters 1,2,8, 13, 15 and Appendix 4 in this book which were originally published via Free Congress Foundation and titled *Political Correctness; A Short History of an Ideology.*

Chapter 1

What is "Political Correctness"?

William S. Lind

One fundamental question motivated Antonio Gramsci throughout his life: Why had it proven so difficult for Marxists to promote revolution in Western Europe and America?

The answer to that question is simple: the majority of European and American workers didn't believe a word of what the Marxists had to say and neither did they want what they had to offer. [6]
[inserted by Editor]

Most Americans look back on the 1950s as a good time. Our homes were safe, to the point where many people did not bother to lock their doors. Public schools were generally excellent, and their problems were things like talking in class and running in the halls. Most men treated women like ladies, and most ladies devoted their time and effort to making good homes, rearing their children well and helping their communities through volunteer work. Children grew up in two–parent households, and the mother was there to meet the child when he came home from school. Entertainment was something the whole family could enjoy.

What happened?

If a man from America of the 1950s were suddenly introduced into America in the 2000s, he would hardly recognize it as the same country. He would be in immediate danger of getting mugged, carjacked or worse, because he would not have learned to live in constant fear. He would not know that he shouldn't go into certain parts of the city, that his car must not only be locked but equipped with an alarm, that he dare not go to sleep at night without locking

---

[6] Murphy, Paul Austin, "Antonio Gramsci: Take over the Institutions!," *American Thinker,* https://www.americanthinker.com/articles/2014/04/antonio_gramsci_take_over_the_institutions.html, (April 26, 2014)

the windows and bolting the doors – and setting the electronic security system.

If he brought his family with him, he and his wife would probably cheerfully pack their children off to the nearest public school. When the children came home in the afternoon and told them they had to go through a metal detector to get in the building, had been given some funny white powder by another kid and learned that homosexuality is normal and good, the parents would be uncomprehending.

In the office, the man might light up a cigarette, drop a reference to the "little lady," and say he was happy to see the firm employing some Negroes in important positions. Any of those acts would earn a swift reprimand, and together they might get him fired.

When she went into the city to shop, the wife would put on a nice suit, hat, and possibly gloves. She would not understand why people stared, and mocked.

And when the whole family sat down after dinner and turned on the television, they would not understand how pornography from some sleazy, blank-fronted "Adults Only" kiosk had gotten on their set.

Were they able, our 1950s family would head back to the 1950s as fast as they could, with a gripping horror story to tell. Their story would be of a nation that had decayed and degenerated at a fantastic pace, moving in less than a half a century from the greatest country on earth to a Third World nation, overrun by crime, noise, drugs and dirt. The fall of Rome was graceful by comparison.

Why did it happen?

Over the last forty years, America has been conquered by the same force that earlier took over Russia, China, Germany and Italy. That force is ideology. Here, as elsewhere, ideology has inflicted enormous damage on the traditional culture it came to dominate, fracturing it everywhere and sweeping much of it away. In its place came fear, and ruin. Russia will take a generation or more to recover from Communism, if it ever can.

The ideology that has taken over America goes most commonly by the name of "Political Correctness." Some people see it as a joke. It is not. It is deadly serious. It seeks to alter virtually all the rules, formal and informal, that govern relations among people and institutions. It wants to change behavior, thought, even the words we use. To a significant extent, it already has. Whoever or whatever controls language also controls thought. Who dares to speak of "ladies" now?

Just what is "Political Correctness?" Political Correctness is in fact cultural Marxism – Marxism translated from economic into cultural terms. The effort to translate Marxism from economics into culture did not begin with the student rebellion of the 1960s. It goes back at least to the 1920s and the writings of the Italian Communist Antonio Gramsci. In 1923, in Germany, a group of Marxists founded an institute devoted to making the transition, the Institute of Social Research (later known as the Frankfurt School). One of its founders, George Lukacs, stated its purpose as answering the question, "Who shall save us from Western Civilization?" The Frankfurt School gained profound influence in American universities after many of its leading lights fled to the United States in the 1930s to escape National Socialism in Germany.

The Frankfurt School blended Marx with Freud, and later influences (some Fascist as well as Marxist) added linguistics to create "Critical Theory" and "deconstruction." These in turn greatly influenced education theory, and through institutions of higher education gave birth to what we now call "Political Correctness." The lineage is clear, and it is traceable right back to Karl Marx.

The parallels between the old, economic Marxism and cultural Marxism are evident. Cultural Marxism, or Political Correctness, shares with classical Marxism the vision of a "classless society," i.e., a society not merely of equal opportunity, but equal condition. Since that vision contradicts human nature – because people are different, they end up unequal, regardless of the starting point – society will not accord with it unless forced. So, under both variants of Marxism, it is forced. This is the first major parallel between classical and cultural Marxism: *both are totalitarian ideologies*. The totalitarian nature of Political Correctness can be seen on campuses where "PC" has taken

11

over the college: freedom of speech, of the press, and even of thought are all eliminated.

The second major parallel is that both classical, economic Marxism and cultural Marxism have *single-factor explanations of history*. Classical Marxism argues that all of history was determined by ownership of the means of production. Cultural Marxism says that history is wholly explained by which groups – defined by sex, race, and sexual normality or abnormality – have power over which other groups.

The third parallel is that both varieties of Marxism *declare certain groups virtuous and others evil a priori*, that is, without regard for the actual behavior of individuals. Classical Marxism defines workers and peasants as virtuous and the bourgeoisie (the middle class) and other owners of capital as evil. Cultural Marxism defines blacks, Hispanics, Feminist women, homosexuals and some additional minority groups as virtuous and white men as evil. (Cultural Marxism does not recognize the existence of non-Feminist women, and defines blacks who reject Political Correctness as whites).

The fourth parallel is in means: *expropriation*. Economic Marxists, where they obtained power, expropriated the property of the bourgeoisie and handed it to the state, as the "representative" of the workers and the peasants. Cultural Marxists, when they gain power (including through our own government), lay penalties on white men and others who disagree with them and give privileges to the groups they favor. Affirmative action is an example.

Finally, both varieties of Marxists employ a method of analysis *designed to show the correctness of their ideology in every situation*. For classical Marxists, the analysis is economic. For cultural Marxists, the analysis is linguistic: deconstruction. Deconstruction "proves" that any "text," past or present, illustrates the oppression of blacks, women, homosexuals, etc. by reading that meaning into words of the text (regardless of their actual meaning). Both methods are, of course, phony analyses that twist the evidence to fit preordained conclusions, but they lend a 'scientific" air to the ideology.

These parallels are neither remarkable nor coincidental. They exist because Political Correctness is directly derived from classical

Marxism, and is in fact a variant of Marxism. Through most of the history of Marxism, cultural Marxists were "read out" of the movement by classical, economic Marxists. Today, with economic Marxism dead, cultural Marxism has filled its shoes. The medium has changed, but the message is the same: a society of radical egalitarianism enforced by the power of the state.

Political Correctness now looms over American society like a colossus. It has taken over both political parties – recent Republican conventions were choreographed according to its dictates, while cultural conservatives were shown the door – and is enforced by many laws and government regulations. It controls the most powerful element in our culture, the entertainment industry. It dominates both public and higher education: many a college campus is a small, ivy-covered North Korea. It has even captured the higher clergy in many Christian churches. Anyone in the Establishment who departs from its dictates swiftly ceases to be a member of the Establishment.

The remainder of this short book will explore the subject of Political Correctness further: its history, its method of analysis (deconstruction), and the means by which it has attained its influence, especially through education.

But one more question must be addressed at the outset, the most vital question: how can Americans combat Political Correctness and retake their society from the cultural Marxists?

It is not sufficient just to criticize Political Correctness. It tolerates a certain amount of criticism, even gentle mocking. It does so through no genuine tolerance for other points of view, but in order to disarm its opponents, to let itself seem less menacing than it is. The cultural Marxists do not yet have total power, and they are too wise to appear totalitarian until their victory is assured.

Rather, those who would defeat cultural Marxism must defy it. They must use words it forbids, and refuse to use the words it mandates; remember, sex is better than gender. They must shout from the housetops the realities it seeks to suppress, such as the facts that violent crime is disproportionately committed by blacks and that most cases of AIDS are voluntary, i.e., acquired from immoral sexual acts. They must refuse to turn their children over to public schools.

Above all, those who would defy Political Correctness must behave according to the old rules of our culture, not the new rules the cultural Marxists lay down. Ladies should be wives and homemakers, not cops or soldiers, and men should still hold doors open for ladies. Children should not be born out of wedlock. Open homosexuality should be shunned. Jurors should not accept race as an excuse for murder.

Defiance spreads. When other Americans see one person defy Political Correctness and survive – and you still can, for now – they are emboldened. They are tempted to defy it, too, and some do. The ripples from a single act of defiance, of one instance of walking up to the clay idol and breaking off its nose, can range far. There is nothing the Politically Correct fear more than open defiance, and for good reason; it is their chief vulnerability. That should lead cultural conservatives to defy cultural Marxism at every turn.

While the hour is late, the battle is not decided. Very few Americans realize that Political Correctness is in fact Marxism in a different set of clothes. As that realization spreads, defiance will spread with it. At present, Political Correctness prospers by disguising itself. Through defiance, and through education on our own part (which should be part of every act of defiance), we can strip away its camouflage and reveal the Marxism beneath the window-dressing of "sensitivity," "tolerance," and "multi-culturalism." Who dares, wins.

Chapter 2

The Historical Roots of "Political Correctness"

Raymond V. Raehn

Cultural hegemony refers to domination or rule maintained through ideological or cultural means. It is usually achieved through social institutions, which allow those in power to strongly influence the values, norms, ideas, expectations, worldview, and behavior of the rest of society.

Cultural hegemony functions by framing the worldview of the ruling class, and the social and economic structures that embody it, as just, legitimate, and designed for the benefit of all, even though these structures may only benefit the ruling class. This kind of power is distinct from rule by force, as in a military dictatorship, because it allows the ruling class to exercise authority using the "peaceful" means of ideology and culture. [7]   *[inserted by Editor]*

America is today dominated by an alien system of beliefs, attitudes and values that we have come to know as "Political Correctness." Political Correctness seeks to impose a uniformity of thought and behavior on all Americans and is therefore totalitarian in nature. Its roots lie in a version of Marxism which seeks a radical inversion of the traditional culture in order to create a social revolution.

Social revolution has a long history, conceivably going as far back as Plato's *Republic*. But it was the French Revolution of 1789 that inspired Karl Marx to develop his theories in the nineteenth century. In the twentieth century, the success of the Bolshevik Revolution of 1917 in Russia set off a wave of optimistic expectation among the Marxist forces in Europe and America that the new proletarian world of

---

[7] Cole, Nicki Lisa, Ph.D, "What is Cultural Hegemony," https://www.thoughtco.com/cultural-hegemony-3026121 (1/6/2020)

equality was finally coming into being. Russia, as the first communist nation in the world, would lead the revolutionary forces to victory.

The Marxist revolutionary forces in Europe leaped at this opportunity. Following the end of World War I, there was a Communist "Spartacist" uprising in Berlin, Germany led by Rosa Luxemburg; the creation of a "Soviet" in Bavaria led by Kurt Eisner; and a Hungarian communist republic established by Bela Kun in 1919. At the time, there was great concern that all of Europe might fall under the banner of Bolshevism. This sense of impending doom was given vivid life by Trotsky's Red Army invasion of Poland in 1919.

However, the Red Army was defeated by Polish forces at the battle of the Vistula in 1920. The Spartacist, Bavarian Soviet and Bela Kun governments all failed to gain widespread support from the workers and after a brief time they were all overthrown. These events created a quandary for the Marxist revolutionaries in Europe. Under Marxist economic theory, the oppressed workers were supposed to be the beneficiaries of a social revolution that would place them on top of the power structure. When these revolutionary opportunities presented themselves, however, the workers did not respond. The Marxist revolutionaries did not blame their theory for these failures. They blamed the workers.

One group of Marxist intellectuals resolved their quandary by an analysis that focused on society's cultural "superstructure" rather than on the economic substructures as Marx did. The Italian Marxist Antonio Gramsci and Hungarian Marxist Georg Lukacs contributed the most to this new cultural Marxism.

Antonio Gramsci worked for the Communist International during 1923-24 in Moscow and Vienna. He was later imprisoned in one of Mussolini's jails where he wrote his famous "Prison Notebooks." Among Marxists, Gramsci is noted for his theory of cultural hegemony as the means to class dominance. In his view, a new "Communist man" had to be created before any political revolution was possible. This led to a focus on the efforts of intellectuals in the fields of education and culture. Gramsci envisioned a long march through the society's institutions, including the government, the judiciary, the military, the schools and the media. He also concluded that so long as the workers had a Christian soul, they would not respond to revolutionary appeals.

Georg Lukacs was the son a wealthy Hungarian banker. Lukacs began his political life as an agent of the Communist International. His book *History and Class Consciousness* gained him recognition as the leading Marxist theorist since Karl Marx. Lukacs believed that for a new Marxist culture to emerge, the existing culture must be destroyed. He said, "I saw the revolutionary destruction of society as the one and only solution to the cultural contradictions of the epoch," and, "Such a worldwide overturning of values cannot take place without the annihilation of the old values and the creation of new ones by the revolutionaries."

When he became Deputy Commissar for Culture in the Bolshevik Bela Kun regime in Hungary in 1919, Lukacs launched what became known as "Cultural Terrorism." As part of this terrorism he instituted a radical sex education program in Hungarian schools. Hungarian children were instructed in free love, sexual intercourse, the archaic nature of middle-class family codes, the out-datedness of monogamy, and the irrelevance of religion, which deprives man of all pleasures. Women, too, were called to rebel against the sexual mores of the time. Lukacs's campaign of "Cultural Terrorism" was a precursor to what Political Correctness would later bring to American schools.

In 1923, Lukacs and other Marxist intellectuals associated with the Communist Party of Germany founded the Institute of Social Research at Frankfurt University in Frankfurt, Germany. The Institute, which became known as the Frankfurt School, was modeled after the Marx-Engels Institute in Moscow. In 1933, when Nazis came to power in Germany, the members of the Frankfurt School fled. Most came to the United States.

The members of the Frankfurt School conducted numerous studies on the beliefs, attitudes and values they believed lay behind the rise of National Socialism in Germany. The Frankfurt School's studies combined Marxist analysis with Freudian psychoanalysis to criticize the bases of Western culture, including Christianity, capitalism, authority, the family, patriarchy, hierarchy, morality, tradition, sexual restraint, loyalty, patriotism, nationalism, heredity, ethnocentrism, convention and conservatism. These criticisms, known collectively as Critical Theory, were reflected in such works of the Frankfurt School as Erich Fromm's *Escape from Freedom* and *The Dogma of Christ*, Wilhelm's Reich's *The Mass Psychology of Fascism* and Theodor Adorno's *The Authoritarian Personality*.

The Authoritarian Personality, published in 1950, substantially influenced American psychologists and social scientists. The book was premised on one basic idea, that the presence in a society of Christianity, capitalism, and the patriarchal-authoritarian family created a character prone to racial prejudice and German fascism. *The Authoritarian Personality* became a handbook for a national campaign against any kind of prejudice or discrimination on the theory that if these evils were not eradicated, another Holocaust might occur on the American continent. This campaign, in turn, provided a basis for Political Correctness.

Critical Theory incorporated sub-theories which were intended to chip away at specific elements of the existing culture, including "matriarchal theory," "androgyny theory," "personality theory," "authority theory," "family theory," "sexuality theory," "racial theory," "legal theory," and "literary theory." Put into practice, these theories were to be used to overthrow the prevailing social order and usher in social revolution.

To achieve this, the Critical Theorists of the Frankfurt School recognized that traditional beliefs and the existing social structure would have to be destroyed and then replaced. The patriarchal social structure would be replaced with matriarchy; the belief that men and women are different and properly have different roles would be replaced with androgyny; and the belief that heterosexuality is normal would be replaced with the belief that homosexuality is equally "normal."

As a grand scheme intended to deny the intrinsic worth of white, heterosexual males, the Critical Theorists of the Frankfurt School opened the door to the racial and sexual antagonisms of the

18

Trotskyites. Leon Trotsky believed that oppressed blacks could be the vanguard of a communist revolution in North America. He denounced white workers who were prejudiced against blacks and instructed them to unite with the blacks in revolution. Trotsky's ideas were adopted by many of the student leaders of the 1960s counterculture movement, who attempted to elevate black revolutionaries to positions of leadership in their movement.

The student revolutionaries were also strongly influenced by the ideas of Herbert Marcuse, another member of the Frankfurt School. Marcuse preached the "Great Refusal," a rejection of all basic Western concepts, sexual liberation and the merits of feminist and black revolution. His primary thesis was that university students, ghetto blacks, the alienated, the asocial, and the Third World could take the place of the proletariat in the Communist revolution. In his book *An Essay on Liberation*, Marcuse proclaimed his goals of a radical transvaluation of values; the relaxation of taboos; cultural subversion; Critical Theory; and a linguistic rebellion that would amount to a methodical reversal of meaning. As for racial conflict, Marcuse wrote that white men are guilty and that blacks are the most natural force of rebellion.

Marcuse may be the most important member of the Frankfurt School in terms of the origins of Political Correctness, because he was the critical link to the counterculture of the 1960s. His objective was clear: "One can rightfully speak of a cultural revolution, since the protest is directed toward the whole cultural establishment, including morality of existing society…"

His means was liberating the powerful, primeval force of sex from its civilized restraints, a message preached in his book, *Eros and Civilization*, published in 1955. Marcuse became one of the main gurus of the 1960s adolescent sexual rebellion; he himself coined the expression, "make love, not war." With that role, the chain of Marxist influence via the Frankfurt School was completed: from Lukacs' service as Deputy Commissar for Culture in the Bolshevik Hungarian government in 1919 to American students burning the flag and taking over college administration buildings in the 1960s. Today, many of these same colleges are bastions of Political Correctness, and the former student radicals have become the faculties.

One of the most important contributors to Political Correctness was Betty Friedan. Through her book *The Feminine Mystique,* Friedantied Feminism to Abraham Maslow's theory of self-actualization. Maslow was a social psychologist who in his early years did research on female dominance and sexuality. Maslow was a friend of Herbert Marcuse at Brandeis University and had met Erich Fromm in 1936. He was strongly impressed by Fromm's Frankfurt School ideology. He wrote an article, "The Authoritarian Character Structure," published in 1944, that reflected the personality theory of Critical Theory. Maslow was also impressed with the work of Wilhelm Reich, who was another Frankfurt School originator of personality theory.

The significance of the historical roots of Political Correctness cannot be fully appreciated unless Betty Friedan's revolution in sex roles is viewed for what it really was – a manifestation of the social revolutionary process begun by Karl Marx. Friedan's reliance on Abraham Maslow's reflection of Frankfurt School ideology is only one indicator. Other indicators include the correspondence of Friedan's revolution in sex roles with Georg Lukacs' annihilation of old values and the creation of new ones, and with Herbert Marcuse's transvaluation of values. But the idea of transforming a patriarchy into a matriarchy – which is what a sex-role inversion is designed to do – can be connected directly to Friedrich Engels book *The Origin of the Family, Private Property, and the State.* First published in 1884, this book popularized the now-accepted feminist belief that deep-rooted discrimination against the oppressed female sex was a function of patriarchy. The belief that matriarchy was the solution to patriarchy flows from Marx's comments in *The German Ideology,* published in 1845. In this work Marx advanced the idea that wives and children were the first property of the patriarchal male. The Frankfurt School's matriarchal theory and its near-relation, androgyny theory, both originated from these sources.

When addressing the general public, advocates of Political Correctness – or cultural Marxism, to give it its true name – present their beliefs attractively. It's all just a matter of being "sensitive" to other people, they say. They use words such as "tolerance" and "diversity," asking, "Why can't we all just get along?"

The reality is different. Political Correctness is not at all about "being nice," unless one thinks gulags are nice places. Political Correctness is Marxism, with all that implies: loss of freedom of expression, thought control, inversion of the traditional social order, and, ultimately, a totalitarian state. If anything, the cultural Marxism created by the Frankfurt School is more horrifying than the old, economic Marxism that ruined Russia. At least the economic Marxists did not exalt sexual perversion and attempt to create a matriarchy, as the Frankfurt School and its descendants have done.

This short essay has sought to show one critical linkage, that between classical Marxism and the ingredients of the "cultural revolution" that broke out in America in the 1960s. The appendices to this paper offer a "wiring diagram" which may make the trail easier to follow, along with a more detailed look at some of the main actors. Of course, the action does not stop in the '60s; the workings of the Frankfurt School are yet very much with us, especially in the field of education. That topic, and other present-day effects of Frankfurt School thinking, will be the subjects of other chapters in this book.

Profiles

Georg Lukacs

- He began his political life as a Kremlin agent of the Communist International.

- His *History and Class-Consciousness* gained him recognition as the leading Marxist theorist since Karl Marx.

- In 1919 he became the Deputy Commissar for Culture in the Bolshevik Bela Kun Regime in Hungary. He instigated what become known as "Cultural Terrorism."

- Cultural Terrorism was a precursor of what was to happen in American schools.

- He launched an "explosive" sex education program. Special lectures were organized in Hungarian schools and literature was printed and distributed to instruct children about free love, the nature of sexual intercourse, the archaic nature of the bourgeois family codes, the outdatedness of monogamy, and the irrelevance of religion, which deprives man of all pleasure. Children were urged to reject and deride paternal authority and the authority of the Church, and to ignore precepts of morality. They were easily and spontaneously turned into delinquents with whom only the police could cope. This call to rebellion addressed to Hungarian children was matched by a call to rebellion addressed to Hungarian women.

- In rejecting the idea that Bolshevism spelled the destruction of civilization and culture, Lukacs stated: "Such a worldwide overturning of values cannot take place without the annihilation of the old values and the creation of new ones by the revolutionaries."

- Lukacs' state of mind was expressed in his own words:
  - "All the social forces I had hated since my youth, and which I aimed in spirit to annihilate, now came together to unleash the First Global War."
  - "I saw the revolutionary destruction of society as the one and only solution to the cultural contradictions of the speech."
  - "The question is: Who will free us from the yoke of Western Civilization?"
  - "Any political movement capable of bringing Bolshevism to the West would have to be 'Demonic'."
  - "The abandonment of the soul's uniqueness solves the problem of 'unleashing' the diabolic forces lurking in all the violence which is needed to create revolution."

- Lukacs' state of mind was typical of those who represented the forces of Revolutionary Marxism.

- At a secret meeting in Germany in 1923, Lukacs proposed the concept of inducing "Cultural Pessimism" in order to increase the state of hopelessness and alienation in the people of the West as a necessary prerequisite for revolution.

- This meeting led to the founding of the Institute for Social Research at Frankfurt University in Germany in 1923 – an organization of Marxist and Communist-oriented psychologists, sociologists and other intellectuals that came to be known as the Frankfurt School, which devoted itself to implementing Georg Lukacs's program.

Antonio Gramsci

- He was an Italian Marxist on an intellectual par with Georg Lukacs who arrived by analysis at the same conclusions as Lukacs and the Frankfurt School regarding the critical importance of intellectuals in fomenting revolution in the West.

- He had traveled to the Soviet Union after the Bolshevik Revolution of 1917 and made some accurate observations that caused him to conclude that a Bolshevik-style uprising could not be brought about by Western workers due to the nature of their Christian souls.

- Antonio Gramsci became the leader of the Italian Communist Party, which earned him a place in one of Mussolini's jails in the 1930s, where he wrote *Prison Notebooks* and other documents.

- These works became available in English to Americans.

- His advice to the intellectuals was to begin a long march through the educational and cultural institutions of the nation in order to create a new Soviet man before there could be a successful political revolution.

- This reflected his observations in the Soviet Union that its leaders could not create such a new Soviet man after the Bolshevik Revolution.

- This blueprint for mind and character change made Gramsci a hero of Revolutionary Marxism in American education and paved the way for creation of the New American Child in the schools by the education cartel.

- The essential nature of Antonio Gramsci's revolutionary strategy is reflected in Charles A. Reich's *The Greening of America*: "There is a revolution coming. It will not be like revolutions in the past. It will originate with the individual and the culture, and it will change the political structure as its final act. It will not require violence to succeed, and it cannot be successfully resisted by violence. This is revolution of the New Generation."

Wilhelm Reich

- In his 1933 book entitled *The Mass Psychology of Fascism*, he explained that the Frankfurt School departed from the Marxist sociology that set "Bourgeois" against "Proletariat." Instead, the battle would be between "reactionary" and "revolutionary" characters.

- He also wrote a book entitled *The Sexual Revolution* which was a precursor of what was to come in the 1960s.

- His "sex-economic" sociology was an effort to harmonize Freud's psychology with Marx's economic theory.

- Reich's theory was expressed in his words: "The authoritarian family is the authoritarian state in miniature. Man's authoritarian character structure is basically produced by the embedding of sexual inhibitions and fear in the living substance of sexual impulses. Familial imperialism is ideologically reproduced in national imperialism...the authoritarian family...is a factory where reactionary ideology and reactionary structures are produced."

- Wilhelm Reich's theory, when coupled with Georg Lukacs' sex education in Hungary, can be seen as the source for the American education cartel's insistence on sex education from kindergarten onwards and its complete negation of the paternal family, external authority, and the traditional character structure.

- Reich's theory encompassed other assertions that seem to have permeated American education:

    o The organized religious mysticism of Christianity was an element of the authoritarian family that led to Fascism.

    o The patriarchal power in and outside of man was to be dethroned.

    o Revolutionary sexual politics would mean the complete collapse of authoritarian ideology.

    o Birth control was revolutionary ideology.

    o Man was fundamentally a sexual animal.

- Reich's *The Mass Psychology of Fascism* was in its ninth printing as of 1991 and is available in most college bookstores.

Erich Fromm

- Like Wilhelm Reich, Fromm was a social psychologist of the Frankfurt School who came to America in the 1930s.

- His book *Escape from Freedom*, published in 1941, is an ideological companion to Wilhelm Reich's *The Mass Psychology of Fascism*.

- Fromm asserted that early capitalism created a social order that resulted in Calvin's Theory of Predestination, which reflected the principle of the basic inequality of men which was revived in Nazi ideology.

- He asserted the authoritarian character experiences only domination or submission and "differences, whether sex or race, to him are necessarily of superiority or inferiority."

- He asserted that "Positive Freedom" implies the principle that there is no higher power than the unique individual self; that man is the center and purpose of life; that the growth and realization of man's individuality is an end that can be subordinated to purposes which are supposed to have a greater dignity.

- Fromm made the real meaning of this "Positive Freedom" clear in another of his many books – *The Dogma of Christ* - wherein he describes a revolutionary character such as himself as the man who has emancipated himself from the ties of blood and soil, from his mother and father, and from special loyalties to state, race, party or religion.

- Fromm makes his revolutionary intent very clear in *The Dogma of Christ*..."We might define revolution in a psychological sense, saying that a revolution is a political movement led by people with revolutionary characters, and attracting people with revolutionary characters."

Herbert Marcuse

- Like Wilhelm Reich and Erich Fromm, Marcuse was an intellectual of the Frankfurt School who came to America in the 1930s.

- He has often been described as a Marxist philosopher, but he was in fact a full-blooded social revolutionary who contemplated the disintegration of American society just as Karl Marx and Georg Lukacs contemplated the disintegration of German society: "One can rightfully speak of a cultural revolution, since the protest is directed toward the whole cultural establishment, including the morality of existing society...there is one thing we can say with complete assurance: the traditional idea of revolution and the traditional strategy of revolution has ended. These ideas are old-fashioned...What we must undertake is a type of diffuse and dispersed disintegration of the system."

- Marcuse published *Eros and Civilization* in 1955, which became the founding document of the 1960s counterculture and brought the Frankfurt School into the colleges and universities of America.

- He asserted that the only way to escape the one-dimensionality of modern industrial society was to liberate the erotic side of man, the sensuous instinct, in rebellion against "technological rationality."

- This erotic liberation was to take the form of the "Great Refusal," a total rejection of the capitalist monster and its entire works, including technological reason and ritual-authoritarian language.

- He provided the needed intellectual justifications for adolescent sexual rebellion and the slogan "Make Love, Not War."

- His theory included the belief that the Women's Liberation Movement was to be the most important component of the opposition, and potentially the most radical.

- His revolutionary efforts would blossom into a full-scale war by revolutionary Marxism against the European white male in the schools and colleges.

Theodor Adorno

- He was another Marxist revolutionary and a member of the Frankfurt School who came to America in the 1930s.

- Along with others, Adorno authored *The Authoritarian Personality*, which was published in 1950.

- Adorno's book was inspired by the same kind of theoretical assertions revealed in the works of Wilhelm Reich, Erich Fromm, and Herbert Marcuse based on analytical studies of German society that were begun in 1923.

- The basic theme was the same. There was such a thing as an authoritarian character that was the opposite of the desired revolutionary character. This authoritarian character was a product of capitalism, Christianity, conservatism, the patriarchal family and sexual repression. In Germany, this combination induced prejudice, anti-Semitism and fascism according to Frankfurt School theory.

- It so happened that most Americans were products of capitalism, Christianity, conservatism, the patriarchal family, and sexual repression in their youth. So Theodor Adorno and other members of the Frankfurt School had a golden opportunity to execute Georg Lukacs' and Antonio Gramsci's program for creating social revolution in America instead of Germany.

- They would posit the existence of authoritarian personalities among Americans with tendencies toward prejudice, and then exploit this to force the "scientifically planned re-education" of Americans with the excuse that it was being done in order to eradicate prejudice.

- This scientifically-planned re-education would become the master plan for the transformation of America's system of fundamental values into their opposite revolutionary values in American education so that school children would become replicas of the Frankfurt School revolutionary characters and thus create the New American Child.

- This can be confirmed by noting that *The Authoritarian Personality* is the key source of the affective domain of Benjamin Bloom's *Taxonomy of Educational Objectives* of 1964, which guided the education cartel thereafter.

Chapter 3

Political Correctness and the Assault On Individuality

Ward Parks [8]

In the culture wars now raging on, around, and in relation to our university campuses, the leading weapon in the arsenal of the new radical establishment is the ad hominem attack. Critics of political correctness are routinely castigated for the racism, sexism, and homophobia that allegedly impels them; thus reasoned arguments are demolished not through reasoned rebuttal but through imputations of personal wickedness. Now a peculiarity of these accusations is that their moralism stands at odds with the relativism and even nihilism that academic radicals exhibit in other contexts. If all views and values are equal, what's wrong with racism in the first place? Yet radicals do indeed condemn racism, thus appealing to the moral sensibility of the American public at large that continues to believe that there is such a thing as right and wrong; yet at the same time they have been engaged in a programmatic undermining of traditional ethics and common sense. This strange collaboration between nihilism and moral puritanism, between the assertion that nothing is really good and true and the assertion that there are evils so absolute as to justify the sacrifice of a world of lesser goods to the task of combatting them, has been the key to success for academic radicals. It has enabled them to seem virtuous while maintaining commitment to no identifiable virtue. Yet academic radicals have a commitment nonetheless. They are committed to an ideology of power. The triumph of this ideology entails the demolition of the individual as the seat of conscience and moral authority. Thus the strategy of ad

---

[8] Ward Parks was a Bradley Resident Scholar at The Heritage Foundation. He spoke at The Heritage Foundation on January 29, 1993. ISSN 0272-1155. ©1993 by The Heritage Foundation

hominem attack is consistent with the greater aim of political correctness.

The Strategy of Personal Attack. Ad hominem attack takes many forms, and it will not be my task today to enumerate these, nor even to concentrate on the worse cases. If it were, I would be talking about the politicization of hiring and firing, the ideological exploitation of sexual harassment charges, and the reliance on guilt inducement and humiliation of scapegoats in sensitivity training sessions. But more subtle, and therefore more revealing, are the modes of personal attack that political correctors bring to bear on their most visible opponents. One such public figure is Lynne Cheney, whose most recent publication, *Telling the Truth*, provided a moderate, balanced, and well-documented description of the state of political coerciveness that now holds sway in many academic arenas. Yet defenders of the academic establishment have replied that Cheney herself has been politicizing the National Endowment for the Humanities and, through the NEH, trying to politicize academe.

This is an astonishing criticism, emanating as it does from the mouths of the very people who for years have been proclaiming that all discourse is political and that the classroom ought therefore to be used by radical professors as a vehicle for social transformation. This was, indeed, the very kind of claim that Cheney had been quoting in *Telling the Truth*. [9] And yet – and here we come to the second leading countercharge – Cheney herself, or so allege her critics, has not been telling the truth. But apart from the fact that these critics do not deal with Cheney's evidence, their recourse to the idea of "truth" is itself surprising, since sophisticated academics of a poststructuralist stripe hold no truck with "truth" nor with any other such term that smacks of transcendence and disinterestedness. In short, the radical orthodoxy seems suddenly to have decided that politicization and prevarication are vices after all, and having thus reversed itself, has proceeded to indict Cheney ethically for what are really its

---

[9] Cheney, Lynne V, *Telling the Truth*, (New York, NY, Simon and Shuster, 1995)

own offenses.

Attacking Motivation. The same tactic of substituting moral indictment of adversaries in place of reasoned rebuttal of claims has been evident in the response of the academic establishment not just to individuals like Cheney but to groups like the National Association of Scholars. The major NAS statements, "Is the Curriculum Biased" [10] and "The Wrong Way to Reduce Campus Tensions," [11] are, whether or not one agrees with them, principled responses to current academic conditions, and a number of the articles in *Academic Questions,* the NAS journal, present important evidence bearing on the political correctness controversy. But again, defenders of the new academic establishment do not respond to what NAS scholars actually say but to what allegedly motivates them. To Paul Bove, the NAS pretense that "some abstraction called 'free speech' has been violated" and its hypocritical defense of professional "decorum" merely serve to "mask violence"; such commitments induce **"NAS** types to support racist professors in their 'decorous' because 'scientific' assaults on nonwhite people."

Bove is referring, presumably, to Michael Levin and Philippe Rushdan; yet apart from the complexities of and differences between these two controversies, what is being brushed aside here is nothing less than the case for academic freedom. A scholar needs to be free to follow the logic of his argument wherever it leads because truth often violates against the conventional wisdom of a particular time and community; the examples of Socrates, Galileo, Darwin, and many others can be adduced on this point. One marvels that this argument needs to be made at all; yet Bove either cannot or will not differentiate between the defense of free inquiry and the defense of the unsavory conclusions which free inquiry sometimes brings to birth. Thus he does not hesitate to

---

[10] National Association of Scholars, "Is the Curriculum Biased?" https://www.nas.org/blogs/statement/is_the_curriculum_biased , (Nov 8, 1989)
[11] National Association of Scholars, "The Wrong Way to Reduce Campus Tensions," https://www.nas.org/blogs/statement/the_wrong_way_to_reduce_campus_tensions, (Jan 1, 1991)

label the NAS membership "NAS'ies," implying an affinity between the organization and the Nazi movement. The sweeping reductionism in charges like this make reasoned discussion impossible. When an ideological professor can proceed to the moral indictment of a whole class of opponents without feeling obliged to make even a gesture towards acknowledging what they actually say, the cause of intellectual totalitarianism is far advanced.

The Contradictions of Deconstruction. Now the use of moral indictment in place of reasoned rebuttal makes a certain sense, as a rhetorical strategy anyway, in the context of a politicized discourse; but I feel it is noteworthy that this same device was much in evidence in literary studies ten or fifteen years ago when the ruling critical methods were not so overtly political but rather linguistic and philosophical. I became acquainted with this personally at the School of Criticism and Theory in 1981, when deconstruction was in its heyday. Those of us who resisted deconstruction were retrograde in a number of respects; "fascist," as I recall, was the epithet of choice, though subsequent disclosures about the early career of Paul de Man, the leading American deconstructionist, prompted his disciples thereafter to turn to other evils of ours.

Now it struck me at the time that there is something innately peculiar about a deconstructive moralism. For moral indictment makes no sense without moral agency; yet Derrida and his followers have been relentlessly warring against the idea of agency for a quarter of a century. The attack on the author is a special case of this. The belief that a text should be read as an expression of the intentions of the author, say the deconstructionists, is based on the fallacy that the author is a plenitude of meaning from which the text derives and that, further, he is able to control the play of signification in his text. But to the deconstructionist, the act is radically dissociated from the actor, and the actor himself has no real integrity, since the very limitations and circumscriptions that define him project those exclusions through which he can be deconstructed. This is to say that deconstruction holds no truck with the idea of identity. The human subject is himself a logocentric illusion. But if the individual does not exist, and if he is not the cause of his own actions, what could possibly be the sense of indicting him morally?

Radical Relativism. Further, even if the idea of the human individual could somehow be recuperated as a moral agent, it's hard to see how deconstructionists could affirm any moral principle that could serve as a basis for moral judgment. For it is to deconstruction, more than to any other thread in the current web of political correctness, that the charge of "radical relativism" best applies. Deconstructive relativism is actually a kind of radical negationalism whose logic runs like this. Any assertion defines itself through an act of exclusion, and that exclusion projects a supplement. That supplement is both the antithesis of the assertion and its co-condition. The idea of "man," for example, defines itself by casting "woman" out from its nature, and in this way "man" becomes dependent on the "woman" who has been excluded.

Left-Wing Moral Puritanism. Now while deconstructionists would never use a term like "ethical imperative," it remains true that the ethical imperative governing their critical practice is that what is marginalized ought to be brought back into the center. That is how deconstruction proceeds: it identifies what a literary text, for example, has excluded, and then it shows how this excluded content is actually central to the project of this literary text. Such an imperative is indifferent to the moral content of what is in that center and what is in the margins. Deconstructionists have tried to cast their theory in a favorable light by representing as marginalized what is also in their perception victimized; thus a politicized deconstructive reading would identify as marginalized contents that are in some way associated with women or minorities. But nothing in the logic of deconstruction itself would stand in the way of the very accurate perception that Klansmen and Nazi sympathizers are exceedingly marginalized in the typical literature department today and that a proper deconstructive reading of the sociological "text" of such a department ought to mainstream them. My point is that deconstruction is innately amoral and cannot serve as the basis for moral judgment without serious contradiction. Of course, no one here will be surprised to learn that political correctors contradict themselves. My question is, why did deconstruction arise in the same intellectual environment that gave birth to left-wing moral puritanism, and through what mechanism have the two been able to function so complicitously?

My construction of what has happened grows out of my belief that human nature has an inborn and irrepressible moral component; no matter how badly people are actually behaving, they cannot keep from orienting themselves, whether positively or negatively, towards some conception of the good. Even criminals do this; street gangs, for example, have codes of loyalty and vengeance not unlike those of warlike tribal societies.

The Assault on the Individual. It is precisely through controlling the moral function that our political correctors have attained their current position of ascendancy, both in the universities and in the nation at large; and we need to understand the mechanism that has been involved. What deconstruction provided was a method for systematically embarrassing traditionalists whenever they tried to affirm and build judgments on the basis of ordinary and sane ethical principles. But this suppression of the normal operation of the ethical function created a vacuum which the morality of the radical Left could fill. Deconstructive and politically leftist rhetorical and logical moves continue to operate in this mutually supportive relationship: deconstruction levels and keeps the space open, and political radicalism fills the space with its new idols. But the change cannot be described simply as the substitution of one set of moral principles or value terms for another. In the process the individual has been eradicated, at least in a certain sense. No longer is moral assertion conceived as an appeal to the individual conscience. Rather, morality has been collectivized, and the role of the individual is to offer his assent. The good individual is he who has accepted that good which the collective has decreed, not he who has found good within his own heart.

This is ethics reconstituted within an ideology of centralization and power, since it demands that individuals surrender their own judgment of what is right and wrong and put determination of ends in the hands of those who define the ruling moral paradigms. Now deconstruction is fundamentally an instrument for destabilization and decentering, so at this stage its usefulness becomes more limited. Thus it is that, over the past few years, deconstructionists have yielded center stage to a new assortment of critics and critical methods. Perhaps the most important of these has been Michel Foucault, whose peculiar talent lay in the bleak gaze which he turned to social and institutional history, a gaze in which all nuances and intimacies and reciprocities of human interchange were reduced to power relations. This work was continued and extended in literary studies by a group called the new historicists, who are essentially soft Marxists uninterested in economics but addressing themselves instead to a history of cultural production. At the same time, hard Marxists such as Fredric Jameson were reestablishing coherence amid the chaos that deconstruction had wrought.

Marxist Theory. With Jameson and company a historical dialectic becomes the agent and mover, and human subjectivity and consciousness are seen as epiphenomenal, shaped rather than shaping, moving within limits always circumscribed by forces that they never fully grasp. Structures of will and intention unfold in spaces defined now by the political unconscious. Conventional ethics, in such a view, is essentially trivial; what matters are history's grand designs, which individual actors, embroiled in their own petty dramas, can rarely discern. Marxist professors, however, seem to be miraculously free from the limitations that bedevil the rest of us with respect to the historical and political determination of our consciousness; and so they are the ones who will define for us what our roles should be in the new world order that is revealing itself, naturally, as described in their theories.

Political Sins. Again, it is not the usual practice of Marxists, new historicists, and other fellow travelers to speak of ethics as such; yet movements of condemnation and proscription perform a crucial function within their work. The ethical operator within the essentially neo-Marxist program that is political correctness is the idea of oppression. By accentuating oppression, political correctors appeal to the moral sensibilities of the general public, since most of us would agree that genuine oppression is much to be deplored. But neo-Marxist oppression, as we have seen, is not located within the structure of intention and subjectivity, but within the political unconscious. We can, and routinely do, perpetrate oppression without knowing it. Thus we stand in need of perpetual consciousness-raising, chastisement, and confession. This is the format of the contemporary sensitivity training session. The demand that young people apologize for sins that they are unaware of ever having committed profoundly undermines the confidence they might otherwise develop in the voice of their own conscience. Yet political correctors cannot permit individuals to learn to rely on their own inner sense of truth, since the dogmas of political correctness are thoroughly counterintuitive. Therefore the sin of oppression, inaccessible to individual self-awareness yet the source of individual guilt, becomes the club with which they break the back of the human spirit.

"Oppression" is by nature a political sin, since it occurs between people in the context of relations. A moral system that is oriented around "oppression" as its defining evil does not will the moral or spiritual upliftment of individuals as its final end; rather, individual transformation is instrumental towards ulterior political purposes. Traditional ethics too registers concern for community well-being; thus it encodes such needful social virtues as respect for legitimate authority and sacrifice for others. Yet the underlying goal of traditional ethical culture – and here I am attending particularly to the religious sphere that has been the source of our most enduring ethical systems – is higher self-knowledge and an approach to the divine. Salvation remains an individual affair, whether one is a Christian, Muslim, Hindu, or Buddhist. By the same token, the root "sins" in traditional moral culture are flaws of character, not political infelicities. In the Christian Middle Ages, for example, the seven deadly sins (pride, greed, envy, etc.) are aspects of that selfishness which block the outpouring of the grace of God into the heart of the individual man or woman. The dignity of individuals is inscribed in such a conception, for it is through individual sanctification that the highest good is made known in human life. Such a process demands the cultivation of conscience, since conscience is the arbiter within the arena of the individual human soul. By contrast, a politicized conception of sin demands a locus of judgment in the political sphere, where the free exercise of conscience is liable to be stifled amid the charges and countercharges that get bandied about when power is at stake.

Race-Class-Gender. Oppression as unconscious political sin requires a sociological model that can assign guilt to large classes of people without providing these people with a way of knowing what in personal terms they are guilty of. It is here that the race-class-gender trinity becomes a useful tool in the neo-Marxist project of tearing apart traditional community and reconstituting it on ideological foundations. American society has come to believe that no person should be discriminated against on basis of race and gender; at the same time, race and gender are sites of intense social conflict. By magnifying and inflating these conflicts, radicals can contribute to the atomizing of our society. Racial conflict promotes tribal loyalty at the expense of law and so weakens the national covenant; conflict between the sexes slices the tissue of human intimacy and asserts the priority of the political over the natural. Once society has been atomized and the traditional bonds that tied people together have been sufficiently weakened, then the assault on the individual is particularly devastating, since the individual person is without effective support. When he is now accused of a racism and sexism that resides in a socio-political analysis of the world at large to which his personal behavior is irrelevant, he is being pressured to give up the right to assess the world and himself in terms of the moral content that he himself finds there. What political correctors want of individuals, in other words, is ideological and moral surrender.

Race, class, and gender provide the major instruments in the assault; but other kinds of grouping provide natural sites of resistance to political correctness and so have been the targets of unrelenting denunciation. My emphasis on the individual in this

37

talk should not be taken as a denial of the human need to form associations; to the contrary, individuals fulfill themselves in large part through the ties that bind them. Left to their own devices, people naturally affiliate with groups of different types. Race, class, and gender are indeed variables relevant to group formation; but they are not the only such variables. Three other group principles are family (or more generally, kinship), nation, and religion. A sociological analysis concerned with group identity ought to attend to all of these categories; but it is race, class, and gender that the academic Left harps on. For family and religion constitute themselves on grounds that are not originally political at all, whereas the particular nation in which we live – the United States -- is founded on universal principles that the radical Left is trying to undermine. This antipathy is not new; socialists and revolutionaries have been waging war on family, nation, and religion for more than a hundred years, and the sad condition of these institutions is in part reflective of the battering they have had to take.

Resisting Totalitarians. The hostility towards family and religion is particularly interesting; for while these two institutions are oriented towards opposite ends of the human experience, in traditional societies they have consistently been friendly to each other. For family is constituted through ties of blood and engages that aspect of our humanity which is most incarnated in the world of materiality. Sexual relations between man and woman and the nursing which a mother gives to her infant are probably the most intimate of shared human experiences in the physical sense. On the other hand, communion with God, or whatever other names are given to states of spiritual exaltation in the various religious traditions, satisfies that urge in the human spirit to rise above the materiality of its form and circumstances and to attain to that which is supreme. The alliance between family and religion poses a formidable obstacle to ideologues who wish not merely to govern the state but to possess the human soul. I am speaking, of course, of totalitarians, for that is what our political correctors are. Deconstruction, Marxism, and feminism are all relentlessly anti-transcendental, and thus strike at what is central to religious experience; at the same time, the politically correct alliance is waging open war against the traditional heterosexual family. We have seen this phenomenon before. Communist governments throughout this century have engaged in the same basic campaign.

An Ideology Against Humanity. Political correctness has enjoyed its success because it has managed to convince the public that it speaks on behalf of virtue. My purpose has been to analyze the mechanism by which conscience has been snared and the power of the moral function coopted for radical purposes. In truth, there is nothing virtuous about political correctness. It is an ideology of power, or a kind of failed religion; it appeals to human aspiration, but turns the force of idealism destructively against human ordinariness, instead of learning to discover the wisdom and greatness that is to be found in simple things. The human spirit cannot permanently be kept captive to creeds of this type. There is a dignity within humanity that always reasserts itself, whatever depravity men may descend to for spans of time. We should not forget this. Truth retains its power, and the human conscience its inextinguishable spark. Political ideologues who think that they can rewrite reality and the human character doom themselves not only to eventual defeat, but to ignominy as well.

I am reminded, in closing, of J.R.R. Tolkien's great saga, *The Lord of the Rings,* where the power of Sauron is overthrown not by mighty warriors but by simple hobbits who have no pretensions about themselves and prefer a smoke and a good meal to glory and dominion. Now is a time for a heroism of ordinariness, for small acts rightly performed even though they seem in the short run to be unavailing. I am sure that in the end these efforts will not be in vain.

CHAPTER 4

THE TYRANNY OF POLITICAL CORRECTNESS

J.P. Thackway,   July 2007 [12]

Cultural Marxism is a Western Civilization plague; you won't find it just in America as you'll discover Rev J P Thackway addresses the same problems the British face as Americans face. Britain is just ahead of America in criminalizing outspoken opponents of cultural Marxism – Editor

Around twenty years ago, we began to hear a new phrase – "Politically Correct" – or PC for short. Since then it has entered everyday speech and life, and is never far from us. Some dictionary definitions give the flavour of it:

> *"Language or conduct that deliberately avoids giving offence, for example on the basis of ethnic origin or sexual orientation."*

> *"Conforming to a belief that language and practices which could offend political sensibilities (as in matters of sex or race) should be eliminated."*

> *"Of, relating to, or supporting broad social, political, and educational change, especially to redress historical injustices in matters such as race, class, gender, and sexual orientation."*

Put like this, PC seems almost reasonable. But then, as someone has pointed out, many dictionaries are PC too.

EXAMPLES

When we come to examples of PC, we see it as it is. Consider the female police recruit in 2006. This 19-year old, who had passed her written tests, was asked during her interview what she would do if she needed advice. She replied, "I would go to my sergeant and ask

---

[12] Thackway, J.P., "The Tyranny of Political Correctness," https://www.bibleleaguetrust.org/the-tyranny-of-political-correctness/

him for help." She then failed the interview for referring to the sergeant as "him," thus revealing her lack of "gender awareness."(!)

Other examples abound. A hospital manager bans Easter hot cross buns because they might offend Muslim patients. A nursery tells its children no longer to say "Baa, baa, black sheep" but "Baa, baa, grey sheep," out of consideration for black children. In school, "blackboard" is called some other name for the same reason. "Nitty-gritty" is out because of its supposed association with the slave trade (new for the 2007 anniversary of its abolition).

Gender-specific words are neutralised to no longer offend or exclude women. Therefore, headmaster/headmistress becomes head teacher; policeman is changed to police officer, fireman to firefighter, chairman to chair or chairperson. Mankind is deemed sexist and becomes humankind or humanity. Police Force is Police Service – as if the hint of authority is unacceptable. "Positive discrimination" bypasses suitable candidates for jobs in favour of women, ethnic minorities, disabled people, etc.

In addition, to prevent the least hint of anything pejorative, PC changes job titles. Vision Clearance Executive is a window cleaner, Education Centre Nourishment Production Assistant is a dinner lady, Waste Removal Officer is a dustman, Domestic Engineer is a housewife and Stock Replenishment Adviser is a shelf stacker.

How should we interpret PC? Is it as ludicrous as it seems – or is there a more sinister and dangerous dimension to this? Does it impinge upon the truth of God and the spread of the gospel? What ought to be our response to its challenges in our generation?

1. SOME THINGS ABOUT PC CAN BE WELCOMED.

In its concern to avoid epithets that offend and upset people, it encourages us to consider others. This in principle is scriptural: "having compassion one of another … be pitiful, be courteous" (1 Peter 3:8). This applies "especially unto them who are of the household of faith" but also "unto all men" (Galatians 6:9).

Who would deny that it is much kinder to refer to a child at school as having "special needs" rather than as "educationally sub-normal"?

And not to label someone who suffers from mental problems as an "idiot"? Moreover, any labels that arise from prejudice and cruelty are better removed from our vocabulary in order to love our neighbour as ourselves.

Wounding names that stigmatise disadvantaged people are the language of a fallen and heartless world. Where greater care is taken and sensitivity is shown, this must be acknowledged as right by Christians who are exhorted to "be kind one to another, tenderhearted..." (Ephesians 4:32). Regarding ethnic minorities who are here legally, we must "do no wrong, do no violence to the stranger" (Jeremiah 22:3). All this is seeing PC at its best.

However, PC is clearly more than calling for respect and good manners. It goes far beyond this into another realm that should cause us deep concern. That those who offend PC receive no forgiveness alerts us to something more in it. For instance, in 2004, when Robert Kilroy-Silk criticised Arabs in a newspaper column he had to resign from his job with the BBC – probably the most PC institution in Britain today. We hear of cases where the Police, with remarkable swiftness, have followed up complaints against good people who question the suitability of homosexuals to adopt children, and even a child at school playfully calling another child "Gay."

What, then, is the true face of PC?

2. PC HAS A REVEALING HISTORY.

Historians tell us that PC has its roots in Marxism. It was developed at the Institute for Social Research in Frankfurt, Germany. Founded in 1923, this became the Frankfurt School – a group of thinkers who aimed to dismantle the Christian basis of the West because it prevented the spread of Communism. Agustin Blazquez expresses this succinctly,

> *"What was the problem with Western Civilization? Its belief in the individual, that an individual could develop valid ideas. At the root of Communism was the theory that all valid ideas come from the effect of the social group of the masses. The individual is nothing. And they believed that the only way for Communism to advance was to help (or force, if necessary)*

*Western Civilization to destroy itself. How to do that?
Undermine its foundations by chipping away at the rights of
those annoying individuals.*

*One way to do that? Change their speech and thought patterns
by spreading the idea that vocalizing your beliefs is
disrespectful to others and must be avoided to make up for past
inequities and injustices. And call it something that sounds
positive: 'Political Correctness…'[13]*

*Political Correctness remains just what it was intended to be: a
sophisticated and dangerous form of censorship and oppression,
imposed upon the citizenry with the ultimate goal of
manipulating, brainwashing and destroying our society.[14]*

Communism largely collapsed in the late 1980s, but PC may well be
its continuance in a more subtle form. During the Cold War era, the
West feared a Communist takeover – in God's mercy that never came.
And yet the agenda, techniques and aims of "the New Left" are very
much with us in PC.

3. MOST PC IS NEEDLESS AND FARCICAL.

This is clear because the zealous minority behind PC do not represent
those they claim to represent. The helpful Campaign against Political
Correctness website makes this shrewd point, "… those spouting
political correctness assume that they have the right to give opinions
for people they perceive to be from 'minorities' without usually first
consulting the people they purport to speak for. E.g., people say that
you should not use the term 'Brainstorming' as it could be offensive to
people with epilepsy. Epilepsy Action, however, say, 'We are often
asked about the word "brainstorming" and whether its use is
acceptable. If the word is being used to describe a meeting where
participants are suggesting ideas, then its use is not offensive to

---

[13] Blazquez, Agustin, "POLITICAL CORRECTNESS: THE SCOURGE OF OUR
TIMES," http://amigospais-guaracabuya.org/oagaq088.php
[14] https://www.newsmax.com/Pre-2008/Political-CorrectnessThe-
Scourge/2002/04/04/id/666560/

people with epilepsy' ... people (are) using political correctness where it was not asked for, not needed and certainly not wanted." [15]

In the case of the female police recruit mentioned above – Laura Midgley of CAPC said, "In the 43 police forces in the country, there are 17,679 male sergeants and 2,671 female sergeants. Is it really a lack of gender awareness to say the word 'him' when, according to the police's own official figures, over 86% of sergeants are men?" [16]

Another example. In October 2006, Greater Manchester police advised officers not to issue arrest warrants against Muslims at prayer times during Ramadan. The Manchester-based Muslim group, the Ramadan Foundation, criticised this policy. Mohammed Shafiq said, "It's stupid, lunacy, that police could even consider not arresting Muslims during Ramadan. I don't know where they get these ideas from and I'm glad an officer was clearly angry enough to leak the memo. Police shouldn't hesitate to arrest any Muslims they had planned to during Ramadan. We must all be equal under the law. If people think Muslims are immune from the law, it will only stir up tensions within the community." [17]

This response begs the question why the decision was made. As Mr. Shafiq said, "I don't know where they get these ideas from." Yet get them they do, and so do so many other bodies and authorities in the UK and beyond. Apparently, 80% of people in the UK are fed up with PC, yet we are continually monitored, intimidated, corrected – and drip-fed Newspeak PC words like a catechism. But by whom? A respondent to a newspaper asked,

> *"Who are these people who have nothing better to do with their time than analyze and then criticise every word a public (or even semi-private) figure says? What a pity these do-gooders can't get a life, or even an occupation where they could actually do some good? Almost every phrase that is in current usage today has some kind of questionable background ...!"*

[15] Epilepsy Action, "Is the word 'brainstorming' offensive to people with epilepsy?" https://www.epilepsy.org.uk/press/facts/brainstorming-offensive

[16] https://web.archive.org/web/20040615070925/http://www.capc.co.uk/

[17] BBC News, "Ramadan arrest advice 'is lunacy'," http://news.bbc.co.uk/2/hi/uk_news england/manchester/6074186.stm, (Oct 22, 2006)

The answer may well lie in the agenda behind PC. What is happening is that a militant, atheistic and unrepresentative minority are busily indoctrinating the rest of us to revise how we speak, what we believe, and how we view others.

4. PC HAS A HIDDEN TARGET.

The stupidity of PC tends to mask the fact that its real aim is at biblical Christianity. If PC wants to destroy the Christian foundation of British society (Psalm 11:3), then its target will be Christianity itself. It hates our message, and that is behind its pretended concern about it offending others who do not share its views – in reality it is because it does not share our views. The rugged doctrines of our message fall foul of PCs approved words and allowed vocabulary.

Although we see PC as an expression of atheistic, secular humanism or postmodernism, its inspiration is from a deeper source. It is the spirit of the age, under the control of "the god of this world" (2 Corinthians 4:4). It is the age-old concerted rebellion "against the Lord, and against his Christ" (Psalm 2:1-3; Acts 4:26). In seeking to break down the biblical and moral bulwarks, PC is really the guilty party.

a] It turns morality on its head.

PC makes the guilty innocent and the innocent guilty. It says it is "OK to be Gay" but not OK for a Christian Bed and Breakfast owner to refuse a Gay couple a stay in his own home. More than "not OK," such a man would now be classed a criminal for simply acting according to conscience and protecting his family.

The recent case of Scottish firemen threw this into relief. In conscience, they refused to distribute community safety advice at a Gay festival. All were disciplined and sent on a "diversity training" course. upside down values. In its view, sin is right and righteousness is wrong.

b] It has created double standards.

PC would make the teaching of scriptural morality taboo. Biblical words that brand wrong behaviour and that make value judgments are replaced with bland and meaningless alternatives. Thuggish pupils are not expelled from school but "excluded." There is even a call to drop the term "yob" [British for yobbo, hoodlum, lout] as it allegedly stigmatises young people. And yet, Christians who smack their disobedient children are "hitting" them and are guilty of "violent assault." It is tragic to see the way children's charities have jumped on the PC bandwagon and joined to call to have parents' right to smack banned.

Some nursery children must not be called "naughty" but showing "unacceptable behaviour." Yet, PC is perfectly happy to sanction course, vulgar, foul and blasphemous language that transgress every one of God's commandments. It has one law for the righteous and another law for everybody else. It says it hates censorship and yet would censor everybody who fails its litmus test.

c] It outlaws freedom of speech and expression.

For its agenda to prevail it polices our words and even our thoughts. An unwritten law governs what we can say or think, and people feel intimidated, looking over their shoulders. The implications for evangelism and contending for issues of national righteousness are clear. On the pretext of not offending other religions in our "multicultural society," our exclusive gospel is anathema. Since Christianity has supposedly caused past injustices to women and various minorities, its call for biblical values is called a return to Victorian, repressive values. PC demands liberty for itself but would gag those who disagree with it. It is wonderfully tolerant with the feckless and the deviant but incredibly intolerant with the upright and biblical who venture to speak for the truth. PC would silence every voice except its own.

5. OUR DUTY IN THE LIGHT OF PC IS CLEAR.

It is largely to ignore it. In the small area where it confirms scriptural niceties and thoughtfulness, Christians have always been PC. In all the rest, with its evil origin and perverse application, we must see it for what it is.

1] PC has always been with us.

Philip Atkinson has a further definition of PC,

"The communal tyranny that erupted in the 1980s. It was a spontaneous declaration that particular ideas, expressions and behaviour, which were then legal, should be forbidden by law, and people who transgressed should be punished ... It started with a few voices but grew in popularity until it became unwritten and written law within the community. With those who were publicly declared as being not politically correct becoming the object of persecution by the mob, if not prosecution by the state."[18]

Put like this, perpetrators of PC are the enemies of God and the church. We find it condemned in the Scriptures, "Woe unto them that call evil good, and good evil; that put darkness for light, and light for darkness; that put bitter for sweet, and sweet for bitter!" (Isaiah 5:20).

We also find those insisting upon their perverted protocol bravely resisted. The Hebrew midwives defied Pharaoh when his ethnic cleansing policy became PC (Exodus 1:17). Nebuchadnezzar's PC decree about praying was ignored by Daniel (Daniel 6:10). It was PC to say that the disciples had stolen Jesus' body (Matthew 28:11-15), but the apostles preached Christ and the resurrection because ""we ought to obey God rather than men" (Acts 5:29). Let us do the same in our day, not causing needless offence, but not shunning the offense of the cross.

2] PC BEHOVES US TO CONTEND FOR THE FAITH IN CERTAIN KEY AREAS.

a] "Gender issues," fuelled [sic] by Feminism,

Those who marry, and become a family consisting of father and mother and their children feel almost victimised these days. They apparently discriminate against "families that come in all shapes and sizes." This is PC euphemism for unmarried mothers with children of multiple partners, same sex couples with adopted offspring, cohabiting couples and their illegitimate children. The confusion, blight, crime and expense this has caused our society is obvious. What

---

[18] Atkinson, P., "Political Correctness," https://www.ourcivilisation.com/pc.htm, (Dec 17, 2002)

is just as obvious is that it destroys manhood and womanhood, marriage, and the family – all that gives cohesion to society.

However, it is really Holy Scripture that is under attack: "he which made them at the beginning made them male and female" … "For the husband is the head of the wife, even as Christ is the head of the church" … "That he might seek a godly seed. Therefore take heed to your spirit, and let none deal treacherously against the wife of his youth" (Matthew 19:4; Ephesians 5:25; Malachi 2:15). Instead of denouncing these other family models as immortality and sodomy, we are warned against being sexist, homophobic and committing "hate crime." However, let us not be cowed but courageous as we serve our generation by the will of God.

b] Crime and punishment.

This vexed issue has been a headache for successive governments. But PC has coined new phrases designed to intimidate those calling for traditional (biblical) ways of dealing with it. People are not sent to jail as punishment but for punishment – the subtle distinction means rehabilitation is the main goal. The word "punishment" is nearly taboo now. Therefore, prisons become almost like hotels, inmates can be called "Mr." and some must be allowed to vote. Many judges pass soft sentences in the first place – "the sword" (Romans 13:4) has become a slap on the wrist. What does God's word say to this PC? "Submit yourselves … unto governors, as unto them that are sent by (the Lord) for the punishment of evildoers, and for the praise of them that do well" (1 Peter 2:13, 14).

c] Homosexuality.

PC invents euphemisms to protect sodomites. It has hijacked the harmless word "gay" – originally meaning merry, light-hearted, brightly coloured, carefree – to mean this brand of moral wickedness. Perversion is now "orientation" instead. "Equality and diversity" ensure that the rights of such people are respected and their lifestyle never criticised. One word against it and an individual could find himself visited by police and warned about "hate crime," as some high-profile cases show. Therefore, PC is very selective when it comes to human rights and minority interests. It comes down on the side of those who are on the opposite side of biblical Christianity.

However, God showed His abhorrence of this vile practice in the overthrow of Sodom and Gomorrah (Genesis 19:24, 25; 2 Peter 2:6). This is "an abomination" (Leviticus 18:22) – next only to sex with a beast (verse 23). Moreover, in Romans chapter one Paul declares such behaviour being given up by God to vile affections and "receiving in themselves that recompense of their error" (verses 26, 27) – solemnly in our day the AIDs epidemic. We must not shrink from holding these convictions, and where necessary, saying so.

d] False religion.

Since the 1960s, Britain has seen its colonial past come home in waves of immigration. This has brought to us representatives of religions foreign to these shores – Hinduism, Sikhism, Islam, and more recently from Eastern Europe... This is an excellent opportunity for home mission work – as numbers of Christians have found. However, with a nigh-apostate Established Church, and a weak, divided nonconformity, the gospel of Christ is not making conquests in its homeland that it might have done.

Moreover, it hands PC an opportunity to level the field in the name of respect and toleration. "Our multi-cultural society" is a buzzword for silencing the gospel. Which is why we hear of local councils banning Bibles from hospitals and hotels, university student unions rejecting Christian Unions because of their exclusive basis of faith, and some over-zealous policemen warning open-air preachers not to preach about hell – who in turn should be reminded that they have no mandate to make the law, only to enforce it.

However, false religion is false because it worships "other gods" (Exodus 20:3) and makes "graven images" (Exodus 20:4, 5), is "anathema" even if an angel from heaven preached another gospel (Galatians 1:8, 9), and men "should turn from these vanities unto the living God, which made heaven, and earth, and the sea, and all things that are therein" (Acts 14:15). Let us be as bold as the apostles were, since the same Lord is with us "always" (Matthew 28:20).

e] In the Church of God.

The spirit of the age has infiltrated the church in our day. And with it has come a PC that operates even in reformed circles. In our last magazine, we mentioned this in connection with the new role of women in today's churches. The most glaring example was the Today's New International Version – "the PC Bible" because it is full of "gender neutral" renderings instead of the generic "man," "brethren," etc.

Even among those who know better, PC has crept in. Certain issues are not discussed among us because they are deemed "secondary issues" or divisive. Matters like Bible translations, character of worship, the role of women in church, the pope as the Antichrist are studiously avoided in ministers fraternals and publications. It is noteworthy that although we sent review copies of Alan Macgregor's Three Modern Versions to certain leading reformed papers and magazines, they have never reviewed it.

This is tragic because it creates "no go" areas in issues vital to our day. Fellowship tends to be shallow because it feels it has to observe the party line and keep to safe areas. Happy is that church, however, where openness to "all the counsel of God" prevails, and not Political Correctness but scriptural awareness governs all that we believe and do (Acts 2:42; 2 Timothy 3:16, 17).

May God help us to discern these issues and "have understanding of the times." Let us carry on as we have ever done, and never submit to the tyranny of Political Correctness. It is nothing other than the tyranny of Satan himself, the prince of darkness and the father of lies. Let us avowedly "be blameless and harmless, the sons of God, without rebuke, in the midst of a crooked and perverse nation, among whom ye shine as lights in the world" (Philippians 2:15). We do not depend upon a sympathetic climate to live out the Christian life and serve God. We rely upon the Lord of hosts who is with us. "Ye are of God, little children, and have overcome them: because greater is he that is in you, than he that is in the world" (1 John 4:4).

Chapter 5

Cultural Marxism and Its Conspirators

Paul G. Kengor, 2019 [19]

<u>The American Spectator</u>

> *Above all, this is as much a lesson in the power of an enormously influential source like Wikipedia (and the Internet generally) to be abused and to spread bad information that ends up hurting people. Unfortunately, millions if not billions rely on Wikipedia, and what you thus have online is, ironically, the creation of a conspiracy theory about the "conspiracy theory" of cultural Marxism. – Paul G. Kengor*

Last week I did one of my routine exercises in my Marxism course at Grove City College. In that class, we scour everything on Marx and various strains and offshoots of Marxism. We read all sides — true liberal learning, real diversity, genuine academic pursuit of truth. At this conservative college, we look at all sides, which is what liberal universities claim to do but, under the flag of "diversity" and "tolerance," frequently shun opposing viewpoints that conflict with leftist orthodoxy. My Marxism course is an interactive class in which we pull up the big computer screen and openly Google terms, ideas, websites, and organizations. We do not shy away, ever, from daily checking Marxists.org, the website of Communist Party USA, *The Jacobin*, *The Militant*, you name it. We don't fear and censor opposing viewpoints. My students will not be left ignorant of what the other side thinks.

Last week, as I do at some point every semester, I Googled the words "cultural Marxism." I was shocked when the first thing that appeared on the page was this boxed definition:

---

[19] Kengor, Paul, Dr., "Cultural Marxism and its Conspirators," https://spectator.org/cultural-marxism-and-its-conspirators/, (April 3, 2019)

Cultural Marxism conspiracy theory. In contemporary usage, the term **Cultural Marxism** refers to an anti-Semitic conspiracy theory which claims that the Frankfurt School is part of a continual academic and intellectual effort to undermine and destroy Western **culture**.

Frankfurt School – Wikipedia
https://en.wikipedia.org/wiki/Frankfurt_School

Whoa. Seriously? After years of looking up "cultural Marxism," I had not seen that whopper. An "anti-Semitic conspiracy theory"? Says who? That's not a definition; it's an *ad hominem*. Actually, it's a cheap smear. And it's a smear that countless millions will see daily as their go-to definition for "cultural Marxism."

It gets worse.

The link then charges: "This conspiracy theory is associated with American religious paleoconservatives such as William S. Lind, Pat Buchanan, and Paul Weyrich; but also holds currency among the alt-right, white nationalist groups, and the neo-reactionary movement."

Yeah? No kidding? The "neo-reactionary movement"? What's that?

For years I've known about cultural Marxism. My first tutorial on it, and the entirety of the Frankfurt School, came from Herb Romerstein, a friend and mentor to whom I dedicated my book *Dupes*. Never did Herb say that the charge of cultural Marxism was a slimy anti-Jewish plot. He walked me through the leading lights in the Frankfurt School, and he didn't single out which ones were Jews.

An "anti-Semitic conspiracy theory"? That sounds like the very conspiracy-mongering that the anonymous writers are charging as conspiracy-mongering.

This flatly isn't right. It's wrong. And it's a shame. It's a nasty charge that's clearly having a pernicious influence. As a case in point, a testimony comes from the UK, where a conservative supporter of Brexit has been accused of peddling the "anti-Semitic trope of 'Cultural Marxism'." That's an actual headline.

The two reporters who wrote that story, slinging that accusation at this unfortunate British conservative, almost certainly Googled a term they knew little to nothing about and landed at the first thing that glared from their screen. The intellectual laziness led to intellectual nastiness — cruelty even, as this is a vicious charge to make against someone, especially if those leveling it really don't have a good idea of the history of the term.

And yet, in fairness to those two reporters, "cultural Marxism" is unquestionably hard to pin down. It would be nice if everyone could be, well, nice, as we all suffer the ideological folly of the men who devised the inane theories and perverse schools of thought which, for better or worse, have come to be known as "cultural Marxism." Take it from someone who reads this poison for living. These ideas are not merely confusing, vague, but often incoherent, incomprehensible, rambling, meandering, and, first and foremost, utterly idiotic and completely destructive to mind and soul. When I slog through it, I think not of "trope" but "tripe." It's awful junk.

Here are some rudimentary facts:

First off, you will not find a foundational book from, say, the 1930s, called *The Cultural Marxism Manifesto*. Maybe the best we can say is that cultural Marxism, for lack of a better term, is essentially, and very simply, Marxism applied to cultural goals. To repeat: *Marxism applied to cultural goals*. This is distinguished from the classical Marxism applied to economics or class goals. It is Marxist theory affixed to culture, and thus referred to commonly and understandably as "cultural Marxism."

Who first coined the term? It's hard to say, just as it's hard to say who first coined the term "communism." Marx and Engels wrote the *Communist Manifesto* in 1848, but they didn't coin the term communism. No one really knows, for sure.

And the fact is, there are many Marxists today working far more aggressively on the cultural front than the economic front. They are, in effect, *cultural Marxists*. And no doubt, 99% of them are not Jews. To criticize them and their *cultural Marxism* would not, by any stretch, be an exercise in anti-Semitism.

Who were some of the early Marxists who applied Marx to culture?

Pivotal was Antonio Gramsci, an Italian, a pioneer of applying Marxist theory to cultural objectives. He was not a Jew, not German, and not a member of the Frankfurt School.

That said, the Frankfurt School was the leading literal "institute" that applied Marxist theory to cultural objectives.

The two leaders of the Frankfurt School were Theodor Adorno and Max Horkheimer, who wrote major works on what they called the "culture industry." This is so well-known that the very same Wikipedia has an entry for "Culture Industry," a term it rightly credits to its founders, "the critical theorists Theodor Adorno and Max Horkheimer," as Wikipedia says in the first line of the entry, and to the wider Frankfurt School, as it lays out. Adorno and Horkheimer had a chapter called "The Culture Industry" in their book, *Dialectic of Enlightenment*. (Sounds a little cultural and a little Marxist, eh?)

Two of the most influential members of the Frankfurt School who applied Marxism to culture (and to other areas) were Herbert Marcuse and Erich Fromm. They were not only *cultural* Marxists but *Freudian* Marxists. One might also call Marcuse a *sexual* Marxist. He was the guru to the 1960s New Left on American college campuses.

An undisputed *sexual* Marxist who applied sex and Freud and Marx to culture was Wilhelm Reich, who coined the term and wrote the book, *The Sexual Revolution*. He's linked to the Frankfurt School, though he was much earlier. He was such a sexual freak, with very disturbing thoughts on the genital stimulation of children (among other things), that the Bolsheviks rejected him.

Georg Lukacs, a Hungarian, a Bolshevik, and a major early influence on the founders of the Frankfurt School, also applied Marxist theory to culture. He was Deputy Commissar for Culture and Education in Bela Kun's Hungarian Soviet Republic. To repeat: *culture and education*. Theodor Adorno adored Georg Lukacs.

Most of the guys in the Frankfurt School were Freudians as well as Marxists. Some, like Fromm especially, sought to devise a field of Freudian-Marxism that was anchored in psychoanalysis.

So, cultural Marxists, sexual Marxists. Yes.

Today, in the 21st century, much of the more culturally inclined Marxism flies under the banner of what is known throughout the academy as "critical theory." There are entire academic departments at universities dedicated to critical theory. Tellingly, most of these academic proponents of Marxism are not econ or Poli Sci professors, or historians, all of which know better, but faculty from English departments.

Today, there are even *gender* Marxists in the academy. There are self-described "queer theorists" and academicians engaged in "intersectionality" who are Marxists focused on cultural work.

This is widely known.

But above all, these Marxists are and were about culture. Culture, culture, culture.

If you Google "critical theory," the first thing that pops up is a boxed definition that states: "**crit-i-cal the-o-ry**, *noun*, a philosophical approach to culture, and especially to literature, that seeks to confront the social, historical, and ideological forces and structures that produce and constrain it. The term is applied particularly to the work of the Frankfurt School."

Precisely. Whoever posted that one nailed it. Hooray for accuracy! Note the words "culture" and "Frankfurt School." Again, *cultural Marxists* — or, if you don't like that, *Marxists in culture*.

As I noted in "Cultural Workers, Unite! Today's Marxist Revolution," *People's World*, the successor to the *Daily Worker*, https://www.peoplesworld.org/about-the-peoples-world/, calls out and rallies what it calls "cultural workers" for the Marxist cause. These are Marxists operating on the cultural front. They are cultural Marxists.

This ain't rocket science, boys and girls. And it ain't anti-Semitism either.

Go back to that original Google box defining cultural Marxism as anti-Semitic conspiracy theory. Ironically, if you click the provided link to the Frankfurt School reference at Wikipedia, it indeed explains: "The works of the Frankfurt School are understood in the context of the intellectual and practical objectives of <u>critical theory</u>…. In the praxis of <u>cultural hegemony</u>, the dominant ideology is a ruling-class narrative story, which explains that what is occurring in society is <u>the norm</u>."

Again, note the words "cultural" and "Frankfurt School."

There, it links (correctly) to Antonio Gramsci, the non-German, non-Jew, Italian. In fact, the Wikipedia page on Gramsci is pretty good, and includes 32 references to "culture" or "cultural." The third paragraph of the Gramsci entry states:

Gramsci is best known for his theory of <u>cultural hegemony</u>, which describes how the state and ruling capitalist class — the <u>bourgeoisie</u> — use cultural institutions to maintain power in capitalist societies. The bourgeoisie, in Gramsci's view, develops a hegemonic culture using <u>ideology</u> rather than violence, economic force, or coercion. Hegemonic culture propagates its own values and norms so that they become the "<u>common sense</u>" values of all and thus maintain the *status quo*. Hegemonic power is therefore used to maintain consent to the capitalist order, rather than coercive power using force to maintain order. This cultural hegemony is produced and reproduced by the dominant class through the institutions that form the <u>superstructure</u>.

That's correct. And there, at the page on Gramsci, are (rightly) no references to "conspiracy." Apparently, that's because certain different anonymous contributors (better informed) contributed to the Gramsci page — obviously not the same ignorant individuals who generated the shameless little box on cultural Marxism; that is, the nasty name-callers alleging anti-Semitism.

For the record, where does the charge of anti-Semitism come from? It, too, comes from laziness, nastiness, or a lack of charity and desire to smear opponents rather than get at the truth. The Wikipedia entry quotes (accurately or inaccurately) one of the individuals it accuses of anti-Semitism stating that all the members of the Frankfurt School were Jews ("to a man, Jewish"). I cannot vouch for that. I've never endeavored to tabulate a scorecard of Jews in the Frankfurt School. I have no desire. I don't do that. Don't ask me. Do your owned damned scorecard.

It's crucial to understand, however, that those who write on the Frankfurt School, including its staunch advocates, always note that many to most of the members were Jewish. You can't read a history that doesn't note this. Why is that? For this reason: Any historian offering even a brief narrative account of the Frankfurt School, including the salient fact of its sudden mass migration to the United States, unavoidably notes that most members were Jews because it's a crucial explanatory factor in their move to America — namely, they relocated because of Hitler's madness. As Jews, they would be targeted by Hitler for genocide. That's why they moved.

Truth be told, the only sympathy I've ever had for the Frankfurt School is that the poor guys could have been murdered by the Nazis. It's my only soft spot for them. Otherwise, their writings are nonsense, useless, fruitless.

But again, historians writing histories of the school can't avoid this fact. To cite just one example of numerous that could be referenced, probably the top academic work on the Frankfurt School (aside from Martin Jay's research) is Rolf Wiggershaus's *The Frankfurt School*, published in 1994 by MIT Press. It's a seminal scholarly work, nearly 800 pages in length, with translations of German writings that no other scholar in English has published. This is a fully sympathetic tome. My sense is that Wiggershaus likely aligns ideologically with — and is at least favorable to — the school. He writes in his opening pages: "The first generation of the Frankfurt School consisted wholly of Jews."

Wiggershaus certainly didn't mean that as a negative. He proceeded to further note how they were persecuted as Jews. Heck, Wiggershaus might even be Jewish himself. (I don't know, I haven't checked.)

Again, it's part of the history.

The first time I wrote about the Frankfurt School in a book, my editor added this query amid the editing process: "Paul, why in the world did they all suddenly leave Germany to come to the United States?"

My editor wanted to know if this was some sort of Comintern-inspired conspiracy or the work of a communist cabal at Columbia University. No, no, I explained. The answer was because they were Jews fleeing Hitler. My editor answered: "Oh! You need to include that!"

Of course. And historians of the Frankfurt School need the freedom to include that key fact without nameless hacks vilifying them online as anti-Semites for doing so.

Even then, assume for a moment, for the sake of argument, that the vast majority of cultural Marxists in the Frankfurt School were Jewish, as its historians have asserted. Well, the vast majority of cultural Marxists today — writing at *People's World*, joining the <u>International Gramsci Society</u>, penning tracts on "queer theory" — are certainly not Jews. Today's cultural Marxism isn't a Jewish thing. That's stupid.

Now, all of that said, could certain agitators on the "alt-right" exploit the fact that so many Frankfurters were Jews to try to create an "anti-Semitic trope" of the Frankfurt School? Of course, they could. That needs to be condemned and countered. But simply noting that many were Jewish, or, more important, simply noting that today there's such a thing as a cultural form of Marxism, should absolutely not be permitted to be labeled an "anti-Semitic trope."

Ironically, these faceless online contributors also threaten leftist academic allies. When I last week checked the website for Occidental College's Department of Critical Theory and Social Justice, which, for years, boasted about instructing its pupils in "Marxism, psychoanalysis, the Frankfurt School," there was no longer any mention of Marxism, nor certainly cultural Marxism. Those leftists at Occidental must have yanked the language, no doubt fearful of being accused of anti-Semitism.

Above all, this is as much a lesson in the power of an enormously influential source like Wikipedia (and the Internet generally) to be abused and to spread bad information that ends up hurting people. Unfortunately, millions if not billions rely on Wikipedia, and what you thus have online is, ironically, the creation of a conspiracy theory about the "conspiracy theory" of cultural Marxism.

Again, if some are guilty of creating a fake conspiracy of a very real ideology or literal theory, then we should condemn that. That does not, however, mean that, say, critical theory, or the application of Marxism to culture, *à la* cultural Marxism, doesn't exist.

Alas, let's also be on guard for those who want to create a conspiracy theory out of term that, properly applied, isn't a conspiracy theory.

PART 2

IDENTIFYING CULTURAL MARXISM IN THE CULTURE

Cultural Marxism has slowly marched into every social institution in America. This part covers topics that are found within the cultural at large, such as our mass media, civil government, business and the church. Part 3, Identifying Cultural Marxism in Education, covers the spectrum of topics within the cultural Marxist worldview which are found primarily in education.

Chapter 8

Marx at 200: Classical Marxism vs. Cultural Marxism

Paul G. Kengor, 2018 [20]

This article first appeared at The American Spectator

This Saturday, May 5, marks the bicentennial of Karl Marx' birth, a cause for literal celebration in certain <u>quarters of the academy</u>.

It's often charged among the political right that America is *going communist*, or at least socialist, or toward some form of Marxism. My concern is less *classical* Marxism than *cultural* Marxism, a strain of communist thought that even most of those engaging in it aren't consciously aware of. If you Google "cultural Marxism," the first thing that pops up is <u>a Wikipedia definition </u>dismissing it as a "conspiracy theory which sees the Frankfurt School as part of an ongoing movement to take over and destroy Western culture."

A *conspiracy theory*? Well, that merely affirms the point. The vast majority of those advancing cultural Marxism aren't even aware they're doing so. Tell them and they'll either blankly stare or mockingly laugh at you as a conspiracy monger.

In truth, cultural Marxism not only exists, but exists as a dominant form of Marxism in America and much of the West today.

Classical Marxism's Decline

Classical Marxism, by contrast, continues to dwindle.

Just this week I caught a rare admission that slipped from the lips of the current chairman of Communist Party USA, John Bachtell: <u>He said that CPUSA has a mere 5,000 members.</u>

---

[20] Kengor, Paul, Dr, "Marx at 200: Classical Marxism Vs cultural Marxism," https://www.faithandfreedom.com/marx-at-200-classical-marxism-vs-cultural-marxism/ (May 4, 2018)

Yes, only 5,000. You could find more members of Unicorn Party USA.

Even more pathetic is that CPUSA has been pounding its chest lately claiming a "surge" in membership under the siege of President Donald J. Trump. Really? Some surge.

Of course, CPUSA never had big numbers. At its heyday in the 1930s, it probably never had more than 100,000 members. That's why communists have always sought out dupes among the broader liberal left. It's why Marxist ringleaders like Angela Davis show up at the Women's March not quoting Lenin but stumping for same-sex marriage and condemning "climate change." Davis didn't dare openly agitate for the KGB at the March; she agitated for LGBT.

The communist movement has always needed liberals as props to enlist at rallies. Rarely could CPUSA ever have filled Central Park with its own members. Bachtell's cohorts today might not fill a sandbox at a Manhattan playground.

The reason for that is good news: The original ambition of an economic/class-based revolution has failed in America. And so, instead, today's Marxists—including those in CPUSA, once the home of classical Marxism—have gone cultural.

It's a form of Marxism so radical in its redefinition of human nature that Marx himself would blush and find it bewildering. As I write, the lead article at CPUSA's website is titled, "The Capitalist Culture of Male Supremacy and Misogyny"—a piece breathtaking in its cultural radicalism. And it personifies the communist movement's thrust today.

Frankfurt School of Freudian-Marxism

So, what is this cultural Marxism, and how did it emerge?

It began not on May 5, 1818, with Marx's birth, but over 100 years later with the birth of what came to be known as the Frankfurt School.

These 1920s and 1930s German Marxists were Freudian-Marxists. For them, orthodox/classical Marxism was too limiting, too narrow, too controlled by the Soviet Comintern that strong-armed national communist parties. This rigidity prevented these more freewheeling neo-Marxists from initiating the cultural transformation they craved, including revolutionary changes in marriage, sexuality, and family. These Frankfurt-based theorists were left-wing intellectuals who looked to the universities as the home base from which their ideas could be launched. They spurned the church and looked to Marx and Freud as the gods they believed would not fail. Rather than organize the workers and factories, the peasants and the fields and the farms, they would organize the students and the academy, the artists and the media and the film industry.

One can look at the Frankfurt school's cultural Marxism not as a replacement for classical Marxism, but as the accelerator pedal that was missing from the wheezing, stalling vehicle. The cultural Marxist agrees with the classical Marxist that history passes through a series of stages on the way to the final Marxist utopia, through slavery and capitalism and socialism and ultimately to the classless society. But the cultural Marxist recognizes that communists will not get there by economics alone. In essence, cultural Marxists shrewdly realized that the classical Marxists would utterly fail to take down the West with an economic revolution; capitalism would always blow away communism, and the masses would choose capitalism. Cultural Marxists understand that the revolution requires a cultural war over an economic war. Whereas the West—certainly America—is not vulnerable to a revolt of the downtrodden trade-union masses, it is eminently vulnerable when it comes to, say, sex or pornography. While a revolution for wealth redistribution would be unappealing to most citizens of the West, a sexual revolution would be irresistible. Put the bourgeoisie in front of a hypnotic movie screen, and it [they] would be putty in your hands.

The key figures of the Frankfurt School included Georg Lukacs, Herbert Marcuse, Wilhelm Reich—who literally wrote the book and coined the term, *The Sexual Revolution*—Max Horkheimer, Theodor Adorno, and others. The formal school began in 1923 as the Institute for Social Research at the University of Frankfurt in Germany. Among its driving forces from within Moscow was Willi Munzenberg, the so-called Red millionaire. "We must organize the intellectuals," exhorted Munzenberg.

And so they would. And how did they slide into America?

The threat of Hitler's Germany drove the Frankfurt School out of Europe and into the welcoming arms of America's left-wing academics. Most to all of the leading practitioners of the Frankfurt School were Jews who needed a safe haven from Hitler's madness. So, they and their Institute came to New York City, specifically to the campus of Columbia University, already a hotbed of communist thought.

Pleading the case for them at Columbia was John Dewey, founding father of American public education and communist sympathizer. (Dewey described himself as a small "c" communist, objecting only to "official Communism, spelt with a capital letter.") Thus, their primary area of operation would be the educational system—the schools, the universities, and particularly the teachers' colleges. It was no coincidence that Columbia housed the nation's top teachers' college—a creation of John Dewey.

From there, the cultural Marxists spread their ideas to campuses nationwide. Their extremist notions would sweep up the '60s New Left, to which the likes of Herbert Marcuse became an ideological guru to the radicals who today are tenured at our universities.

Gramsci's March Through the Institutions

Not to be forgotten in all of this was a critical figure, a non-German. At the age of 35, in 1926, Antonio Gramsci was arrested in his native Italy by Mussolini, and would spend the last 11 years of his life in prison. Samuel Gregg calls Gramsci perhaps "the most dangerous socialist in history."

Whereas Marx and his original followers were all about class economics, seeing wealth redistribution and the seizure of the means of production as the key to their vision, Gramsci looked to culture. If the Left truly wanted to win, it needed to first seize the "cultural means of production:" the culture-forming institutions such as the media and universities and even churches.

Not until leftists came to dominate these institutions would they be able to convince enough people to support their Marxist revolution.

"This part of his thesis was like manna from heaven for many left-wing Western intellectuals," writes Sam Gregg. "Instead of joining a factory collective or making bombs in basements, a leftist professor could help free society from capitalist exploitation by penning essays in his office or teaching students."

And in a really radical stroke—one too radical for its own time, but that would ultimately succeed—Gramsci and his heirs insisted that these leftist intellectuals needed to question everything, including moral absolutes and the Judeo-Christian basis of Western civilization. They needed to frame seemingly benign conventions as systematic injustices that must be exposed. This is where we got professors fulminating against everything from "the patriarchy" to "white imperialism" to "transphobia." By the 21st century, even biological sex was no longer considered a settled issue. As I write, the New York City council offers public employees the option of choosing from 31 different gender identities 31 different gender identities. Of course, that's nothing compared to Facebook, which at various times in the last three years has listed 51 gender options, 53, 56, 58, and 71.

There was no traditional institution off limits to the cultural Left.

In fact, so "critical" was the cultural-Marxist left of anything and everything that it would brand itself as "critical theory." Today, there are entire academic departments and programs dedicated to "critical theory." Barack Obama's alma mater, Occidental College, has a Department of Critical Theory and Social Justice, which at its website promises to instruct wide-eyed students in the principles of "Marxism, psychoanalysis, the Frankfurt School, deconstruction, critical race studies, queer theory, feminist theory, postcolonial theory…." You get the picture.

For the cultural-Marxist left, "critical theory" is the *zeitgeist*, the prevailing spirit of the age. Michael Walsh calls it "the cult of critical theory," the guiding force of what Walsh describes as "The Devil's Pleasure Palace," the instrument for what he rightly calls "the subversion of the West." To quote the '60s radicals, *hey, hey, ho, ho, Western civ has got to go.*

Gramsci himself foresaw societal transformation coming about by a "march through the institutions." In this, he was prophetic.

Sam Gregg puts it well: "The worst part of Gramsci's legacy is that it has effectively transcended its Marxist origins. His outlook is now blankly taken for granted by millions of teachers, writers, even churchmen, who have no idea that they are committed to cultural Marxism." And so, adds Gregg, "the vast structures of cynicism which Gramsci's ideas have built, which honeycomb Western society today, will prove much tougher to dismantle than the crude cement blocks of the old Berlin Wall."

They will indeed. The people of Berlin had no problem recognizing the concrete wrongness of the wall that corralled them. But try to tell those redefining marriage that what they're advocating is concretely wrong.

The Never-Ending Search for the Newest Victim Class

In a crucial respect, classical Marxism and cultural Marxism will always bear an essential, enduring commonality—one that explains a lot about today's modern left.

Both classical Marxists and cultural Marxists see history as a series of struggles that divide the world into hostile/antagonistic groups of oppressors and the oppressed. Both seek out victim groups as the anointed group that will serve as the redeemer group. The victim group becomes the agent for emancipation in ushering in the new and better world. The Marxist must always, then, be on the search for the victim class which, in turn, must always be made aware of its victimization. Its "consciousness" must be raised.

In classical Marxism, this was simple: the victim group was identified by class/economics. It was the Proletariat. It was the factory worker.

In cultural Marxism, this hasn't been so simple, because the culture is always changing: the victim group is constantly being searched for anew by the cultural Marxist. The group one year might be women, the next year a new ethnic minority, the next year another group. Today, there's a hard push by cultural Marxists to tap the "LGBTQIAplus" (*People's World* frequently uses that label) movement as the championed victim group.

Thus, a cultural Marxist like Angela Davis — mentored by Herbert Marcuse — could stand at the Women's March before a sea of young women in pink hats and recite a litany of popular grievances. In her casting about for victim groups, the former Communist Bloc cheerleader hailed Chelsea Manning, "trans women of color," "our flora and fauna," and "intersectional feminism," and denounced "white male hetero-patriarchy," misogyny, Islamophobia, and capitalist exploitation.

This is where today's Marxists in America are toiling hard. They are working diligently on the cultural front. That's where they are confident they can finally take down Western civilization and its Judeo-Christian bedrock.

From Factory Workers to "Cultural Workers"

In closing, consider this striking new term I recently encountered when perusing the latest "About" section of the website of *People's World*, successor to the Soviet-funded *Daily Worker* and the leading mouthpiece of American communism. It singled out a label I hadn't heard before: "cultural workers." It states: "Today, *People's World* offers a daily news platform for the broad labor-led people's movement—a voice for workers, the unemployed, people of color, immigrants, women, youth, seniors, LGBTQ people, cultural workers, students and people with disabilities."

They're looking not for *factory workers* but for *cultural workers*. Forget the factory floor—that project failed long ago. Communists tried to organize the steelworkers, the autoworkers, the teamsters, the coalminers. It didn't work.

Thus, the new recruiting ground is the classroom floor, the campus, the university, the schools. That's where the cultural workers who can usher in the fundamental transformation are being found. These modern cultural revolutionaries are succeeding magnificently in redefining everything from marriage and family to sexuality and gender. And most stunning of all, it's the parents—many of them

67

conservative Christians—who are paying for the grand indoctrination with their lifesavings.

And 200 years henceforth, Karl Marx would be chuckling heartily at that irony.

Note from the Editor –

There are 5 excellent documentaries on cultural Marxism that I recommend if you are motivated to search further. You can share these documentaries with your friends and congregants at church.

1. **IndoctriNation: Public Schools and the Decline of Christianity in America** by Joaquin Fernandez and Colin Gunn
2. **Agenda: Grinding America Down** by Curtis Bowers
3. **Agenda 2: Masters of Deceit** by Curtis Bowers
4. **Cultural Marxism: The Corruption of America** by James Jager
5. **No Safe Spaces: You have the right to remain silent** by Madison McQueen

Chapter 7

SOCIAL ENGINEERING

Verbal Engineering precedes Social Engineering

Dr. Marlene McMillian

Social Engineers are Change Agents are Teachers:

[T]he Chronicle reports that the University of Alabama's College of Education [and all other teachers' colleges] proclaims itself "committed to preparing [teachers] to" – what? "Read, write and reason"? No, "to promote social justice, to be change agents, and to recognize individual and institutionalized racism, sexism, homophobia, and classism...[21]
[inserted by Editor]

What is a Social Engineer? Social Engineering is about using words to move a society towards a pre-designed Revolution. Instead of guns, the weapon of choice is words. The language of culture change is what is commonly called "Political Correctness." The process of getting someone to embrace the new language and thought patterns of postmodernism is called The Dialectic Process. You don't have to understand this process to see its results in the new social order being thrust upon us.

How do you recognize a Social Engineer? They are constantly challenging your language. They make statements against the language of public figures and shame them into public apologies for not speaking correctly. Social Engineers are masters of verbal deception who use Political Correctness for oppression. Their victims are captured not behind the gulag but in an invisible net of fear of offense. Social Engineers constantly talk about offense. Forgiveness is not in their construct.

There is constant talk about what's wrong. Discontent, prejudice,

---

[21] Will, George F, "Ed Schools vs. Education," *Newsweek*, Jan 16, 2006, faculty.tamuc.edu/slstewart/EdSchoolsGeorgeWill.doc

division and hatred have to be fueled. Even the word peace is used as a smokescreen to divide and conquer. Relativism is a creed. Any symbol of absolute truth is an enemy -- especially the father or any authority figure. Destruction is constant. Emotions are habitually heightened. Keeping everyone thinking with their emotions clouds the rational thinking of the masses. They never think to question the kind of life they will have after the revolution. No one stops to ask what, if anything, are we building?

Social Engineers want everyone to speak Politically Correct. In Political Correctness only certain arguments are allowed. Many important topics of discussion are off the table. Whenever a fact that disagrees with their narrative is brought forward, it is ridiculed as being "old fashioned," "something we have moved past," or "no one believes that anymore." They want to remake the world into their own image and are rarely asked, "Who put you in charge?"

There is a law to lawlessness. Right and wrong are passé. Consequences are conveniently ignored. Political Correctness is the only language allowed to be spoken. Deceit is so commonplace it is accepted as normal. Social Engineers hate the facts and prefer opinions. They are worshippers of Relativism so they can believe and promote whatever pleases them at the moment. Social Engineers are message creators. They are storytellers in the worst sense of the word. Their stories have a social agenda and an emotional mark that touches the very soul of their listeners.

A meme is a favorite tool of a Social Engineer. A meme is an unseen but real idea or concept that passes through a culture like a virus. Social Engineers create memes to promote their own ideas. They use symbols as icons and create messages around images like marketers do in advertising. No problem if the facts don't support the meme. One of the skills of a Social Engineer is the ability to create one's own "facts." Like the Ministry of Truth in Orwell's Nineteen Eighty-Four, the "truth" is whatever they say it is.

Social Engineers learn how to seize the moment. They take feelings of discontent and fuel them to new heights. They never let a crisis go to waste. When injustice occurs they use the failings of the system or the misappropriation of good laws to convince people the whole system is broken and needs to be replaced. Again, no one stops to ask, "What will life be like after the Revolution?"

The masses like the deceit and beg for more because it allows them to deny the inevitable consequences of their choices. Words like accountability, responsibility, authority, and truth are either done away with or redefined. If it is inconvenient, uncomfortable, or carries conviction, it is done away with by consensus.

Part of the process of Social Engineering requires that the masses get weaker and more dependent and the leaders become more tyrannical and authoritarian. In the name of "freedom" or "revolution" essential liberties and personal dignity are gradually done away with. At this point the masses have a brief opportunity to awaken but history shows that they usually choose the easier route of continuing the illusion.

The ultimate deceit is when the deceiver deceives the deceivers. At this point, destroyers costumed as builders get the emotionally-charged crowds to repeat the meme as true. The masses are the revolutionaries who supply the labor, tools and money to destroy their own civilization in the name of revolution. After these revolutionaries have outlived their usefulness, the new tyrants turn on their prior supporters, who become the new victims. While they rally for a better future for their children, they are destroying any hope for their children to have a truly better life.

The ultimate tyrant – and that is what Social Engineers really are – gets the masses to beg for their own oppression. The well-conditioned mob instills their own tyrants thinking that because they are "their own" they can be trusted. By the time the masses figure out they have been used as pawns in a very ugly game, it is too late for now they are slaves in their former country. They begged for their slavery and they got what they asked for.

The leader who can take away the wealth of someone else and give it to you can take away your wealth and give it to someone else. Marxism results in chaos which leads to anarchy which results in tyranny. Everyone, rich and poor, will be unhappy with the

71

distribution and eventually the system will run out of money and goods to distribute. When everyone is equally hungry they become equally discontent.

The difference between Traditional Marxists and Transformational Marxist is the choice of weapon. Traditional Marxists use guns and terror to get people to follow them. Transformational Marxists use words to deceive the masses into thinking the new society is good for them. The results are the same: loss of liberty, misery, poverty and despair. The methods are the only difference.

Traditional Marxist dress in military uniforms and gain political and military power. They use power, force, weapons and fear to take control. Bloodshed is necessary to whip the masses into compliance. Transformational Marxists look like everyone else and work through what Lenin called the "commanding heights of culture." They are celebrities, artists, journalists, teachers, attorneys, civic leaders, politicians, clergy, economists, environmentalists, and leaders in every walk of life. A quiet revolution leaves the social structure in tact and allows it to implode out of its own weight.

Social Engineering is not new. It is the tactic of tyrants throughout time. While tyranny has become more sophisticated, a modern tyranny by any other name still results in needless suffering. Social Engineers are change agents. According to Barbara Morris, a change agent is "a person, organization, or institution that changes or helps to change the beliefs, values, attitudes, or behavior of people without their knowledge or consent." The change agent is the facilitator of the thinking of Postmodernism. A change agent uses deceit and manipulation to garner consensus for their vision of how the world ought to be.

Social Engineers really believe that their vision for the future is superior to the uninitiated and uninformed masses. Social Engineers are change agents for Marxism and Revolution. Marxism is the economic system of Communism and is founded on redistribution of wealth. Socialism is a transition word with the purpose of destroying Capitalism so that it can be replaced with Communism. Even people who would never consider themselves Socialists are now promoting the policies of redistribution. While convincing themselves they are acting for the public good they are really furthering the agenda of Marxism.

There are three groups of people in the world. Those who make things happen, those who watch things happen and those who wonder what happened. The intent of the Social Engineers is no secret. For over a hundred years it has been published for the world to see if anyone is paying attention. An easy place to gain a basic understanding of the agenda and game plan of the Social Engineers can be found in the community organizer's handbook *Rules for Radicals* by Saul D. Alinsky.

When the modern Social Engineers started to gain ground some of us issued warnings but the possibility of such radical ideas ever gaining traction and becoming mainstream sounded too wild. At this stage it would have been easy to nip in the bud. But, the idea that anything so sinister could happen here was "unbelievable" and it was ignored.

Now that the Revolution is happening before our eyes many people are asking for an explanation. The problem is they don't like the answer. The truth of how and why this is happening sounds too wild and radical and it is being questioned. There is still time to turn things around but the price will be very high.

Will we have to come to the place where the only question left is, "What happened?" before anyone will listen to those of us who are watchmen on the wall? At that point it will still be the truth, it will still sound radical but it will be too late to do anything about it. All that will be left is mourning. The hopes and dreams of our children will be gone and the suffering of the masses will be severe. Even the masses that begged for their own tyrants will realize that liberty, with all its problems, is far better than the empty promises of tyrants.

The Social Engineers have done an excellent job furthering their agenda. They have operated by being hidden in plain sight. They have made themselves mainstream and worked tirelessly for their cause. They have mobilized almost every cultural structure for their cause. The facilitators of social change are the change agents who have been conditioned to lead the revolution.

Social Engineers are influencers who have learned how to persuade others in the language of the culture war. Once everyone is speaking the same language there is little opposition to total societal restructuring. There must be no "child left behind" or person left out of the net of the process. The change in thinking has to be total and everyone must accept it without question.

Those who know history, logic, or liberty are no longer needed. They are either marginalized or eliminated from places of influence and power. Anyone who challenges the new meme is considered the enemy. Anyone who can't go along to get along, anyone who has convictions or conscience is a problem.

Where did it all start? When we allowed Liberty to be redefined and divided. Since Liberty is Indivisible, the loss of the liberty of one individual or group is the loss of everyone's liberty.

Political Correctness is the voluntary surrender of our right to free speech.

> *"Human liberty can only exist or be restored with an accurate perception of reality. Mind distorting fictions of government must be exposed. To do otherwise is to keep us dependent on an ivory tower mysticism based on lies and the duplicity of politicians and bureaucrats.*
>
> *Government is a parasite cult, organized, and disguised behind a peculiar language of code words and phrases. Without anyone taking notice, change agents distort keywords in our language. This blunts, diminishes and distorts our thinking process to the great advantage of unseen authority. This process is so gradual as to be imperceptible. Out of it evolves very sophisticated control and plunder. When our words are manipulated, our thoughts are manipulated into false realities and illusions. Consequently, our competitiveness and survival instincts are reduced in favor of dependence on government authority."* [22] *[inserted by the Editor]*

---

[22] Livingston, Bob, "Deciphering code words and control phrases," https://boblivingstonletter.com/alerts/deciphering-code-words-and-control-phrases/

Chapter 8

Radical Feminism and Political Correctness

Dr. Gerald L. Atkinson

> *....the messages to women about how to have a happy life – as it relates to love and sex, work and family – have merely served to make women miserable. Not only are they unhappier than their mothers and grandmothers ever were, they're significantly more stressed out; much more so than men. The messages to women about how to have a happy life – as it relates to love and sex, work and family – have merely served to make women miserable. Not only are they unhappier than their mothers and grandmothers ever were, they're significantly more stressed out; much more so than men.* [23]   *[inserted by Editor]*

Perhaps no aspect of Political Correctness is more prominent in American life today than feminist ideology. Is feminism, like the rest of Political Correctness, based on the cultural Marxism imported from Germany in the 1930s? While feminism's history in America certainly extends longer than sixty years, its flowering in recent decades has been interwoven with the unfolding social revolution carried forward by cultural Marxists.

Where do we see radical feminism ascendant? It is on television, where nearly every major offering has a female "power figure" and the plots and characters emphasize inferiority of the male and superiority of the female. It is in the military, where expanding opportunity for women, even in combat positions, has been accompanied by double standards and then lowered standards, as well as by a decline in enlistment of young men, while "warriors" in the services are leaving in droves. It is in government-mandated employment preferences and practices that benefit women and use

---

[23] Venker, Suzanne, "4 Feminist Lies That Are Making Women Miserable" https://thefederalist.com/2019/11/12/4-feminist-lies-that-are-making-women-miserable/, (Nov 12, 2019)

"sexual harassment" charges to keep men in line. It is in colleges where women's gender studies proliferate and "affirmative action" is applied in admissions and employment. It is in other employment, public and private, where in addition to affirmative action, "sensitivity training" is given unprecedented time and attention. It is in public schools, where "self-awareness" and "self-esteem" are increasingly promoted while academic learning declines. And sadly, we see that "a woman's right to choose" leads many fellow Americans, including many with stewardship of public law and culture, to believe it is "the right thing to do" to allow the most helpless to be put to death.

While it is the theme of this essay that the radical feminist movement is embraced by present day Political Correctness ideology, derived from cultural Marxism, feminism as such does have earlier roots. Feminism was conceived and birthed in America in the 1830s, in the generation experiencing the first stage of the industrial revolution. Women, who for centuries had shared the challenges of surviving in an agrarian life, were becoming part of a middle-class gentry with more time and energy to spend writing newspaper articles and novels for their "sisters." The initial stages of the feminization of American culture had started.[24]

These feminists, radical in their time, became a staple of the idealistic Transcendentalists, who included Ralph Waldo Emerson, Henry David Thoreau and many radical Unitarian ministers of the day. They were also abolitionists, bent on destroying slavery and Southern culture as well. Spurred by the rhetoric of Harriet Beecher Stowe (author of *Uncle Tom's Cabin*), Julia Ward Howe (author of the words to "The Battle Hymn of the Republic"), and Margaret Fuller (the first radical feminist newspaper columnist), the men and women of this idealist Transcendentalist generation propelled our nation toward Civil War.

Who were these Transcendentalist idealists, and why should we be reminded of them today? They were the precursors of today's

---

[24] Douglas, Ann, *The Feminization of American Culture*, (Alfred A. Knopf, 1977)

idealistic Boomer generation. While we cannot draw a continuous link between the Transcendentalists and today's Boomers, their characteristics are very similar. We may glimpse where the elite Boomers are leading us by reviewing the history of the Transcendentalists and their causes.

The Transcendentalists supported abolition of slavery, women's rights, temperance, pacifism (but not in the anti-slavery cause), and other causes which we now observe in New Age popular culture. They moved on into spiritualism (talking with the dead), Eastern mysticism and phrenology (discerning personality by the shape of one's skull). They would be right at home in today's New Age milieu. Luther George Williams points out, referring to women's groups and civil rights groups, that:

> Freed slaves secured the vote only after the 13th, 14th and 15th Amendments (ratified in 1870), but women fared worse. They did not receive the vote until the passage of the 19th Amendment in 1920. However, the substantial political victories that these groups achieved (during the Civil War period) guaranteed that they would remain allies. Today, their political organizations dominate every aspect of society, politics and education in America – including the military.[25]

Indeed, the present-day radical feminist assault on VMI and the Citadel has a political parallel to the Transcendentalist activism of the Civil War period. This current assault is in part a continuation of a century-old effort to destroy Southern culture.

In contrast to today's radical feminists, social feminists of the 1890s and early 20th century were of a less totalitarian character. They stood for women's suffrage but also advocated the strengthening of the family.

Today, the feminization of American culture, moving rapidly since the 1960s continues to intensify. Radical feminists demand that

---

[25] Williams, Luther George, *A Place for Theodore: The Murder of Dr. Theodore Parkman.* (Holly Two Leaves, 1977), 161

women be allowed to "choose" entry to the infantry, artillery, special forces and combat engineering positions in the Army and Marine Corps. These demands follow the feminization of combat aviation in the U.S. Navy, Air Force and Army since 1993.

The feminization of American politics was advanced in the 1996 presidential election, when parties produced "feminized" conventions featuring soft, emotional, Oprah Winfrey-type orations and sentimental film clips of the presidential candidates. Both candidates were portrayed as soft, gentle, emotion-driven creatures sufficiently in touch with their feelings that all women across America would feel "comfortable" in their care.[26] With 60 million female votes at stake, both parties pandered to America's "feminine" side.[27]

There is no doubt in the media that the "man of today" is expected to be a touchy-feely subspecies who bows to the radical feminist agenda. He is a staple of Hollywood, the television network sitcoms and movies, and the political pundits of talk shows.[28] The feminization is becoming so noticeable that newspapers and magazines are picking up on it. For example, the *Washington Times* and *National Review* magazine combined to tell us that "behind the breezy celebration of 'guy stuff' in today's men's magazine lurks a crisis of confidence. What does it mean to be masculine in the 90s?" It is revealed that today's men's magazines (*Esquire, GQ, Men's Health, Men's Fitness, Men's Journal, Details, Maxim, Men's Perspective)"*are all geared to a new feminized man...."[29] Some examples? The old masculine attitude toward personal appearance is disappearing. If memory serves, our fathers' acts of personal upkeep were mostly limited to shaving and putting on a tie. According to Lowry:

[26] Kristol, Irving. "The Feminization of the Democrats.", *The Wall Street Journal,* Sept. 9, 1996. Kristol reported that 50% of the Democratic convention delegates were women. Women were described as tending to be more sentimental, more risk-adverse, and less competitive than men, and also more permissive and less judgmental.

[27] Blair, Anita, Independent Women's Forum. *"Mitchells in the Morning,"* NET-TV, (Dec. 5, 1996)

[28] Cladwell, Christopher, "The Feminization of America." *Weekly Standard* , (Dec. 23, 1996)

[29] Culture, et Cetera. "Sissifaction," *The Washington Times*, (Oct. 17, 1997)

78

[I]t's hard to imagine [them] interested in articles on 'A Flat Belly for the Beach' (Verge), or the three new men's fragrances for the fall season (GQ), or even 'The New Fall Suit' (Esquire). But somewhere along the line men became less concerned with being strong and silent, and more worried about making themselves pretty.[30]

Indeed the feminization of American culture is nearly completed. And the last bastion of male domination, the U.S. military, is under assault.

If this "feminization" trend were driven only by radical feminists seeking to pull down a perceived male-dominated hierarchy, there would be more hope that the cycles of history would move America toward a stable accommodation between men and women. But the drive is deeper, and it will not be satisfied by any accommodation. The radical feminists have embraced and been embraced by the wider and deeper movement of cultural Marxism. For dedicated Marxists, the strategy is to attack at every point where an apparent disparity leaves a potential constituency of "oppressed" persons – in this case women, who are the largest of all constituencies. Cultural Marxists, men and women, are making the most of it, and the theory developed by the Frankfurt School provides the ideology.

The Frankfurt School theorized that the authoritarian personality is a product of the patriarchal family. This idea is in turn directly connected to Engels's *The Origins of the Family, Private Property and the State*, which promotes matriarchy. Furthermore, it was Karl Marx who wrote in *The Communist Manifesto* about the radical notion of a "community of women." He also, in 1845, wrote disparagingly in his *The German Ideology* of the idea that the family was the basic unit of society.

The concept of the "authoritarian personality" is not just to be interpreted as a model for the conduct of warfare against prejudice as such. It is a handbook for psychological warfare against the American male, to render him unwilling to defend traditional beliefs and values. In other words, the aim was to emasculate him. Undoubtedly the

---

[30] Lowry, Rich, "Ab Nauseum," *National Review,* (Oct. 13, 1997)

Institute for Social Research at Frankfurt University meant this, as it used the term "psychological techniques for changing personality."

The "authoritarian personality," studied in the 1940s and 1950s by American followers of the Frankfurt School, prepared the way for such psychological warfare against the male gender role. The aim was promoted by Herbert Marcuse and others under the guise of "women's liberation" and in the New Left movement in the 1960s. Evidence that psychological techniques for changing personality are intended to focus in particular on the emasculation of the American male has also been provided by Abraham Maslow, founder of "third force humanist psychology" and promoter of psychotherapeutic techniques in public school classrooms.[31] He wrote that "the next step in personal evolution is a transcendence of both masculinity and femininity to general humanness."[32]

Cultural Marxist stalwarts apparently know exactly what they want to do and how they plan to do it. They have actually already succeeded in accomplishing much of their agenda.

How did this situation come about in American universities? Gertrude Himmelfarb has observed that it slipped past traditional academics almost unobserved until it was too late. It occurred so "quietly" that when they "looked up", postmodernism was upon them with a vengeance. "They were surrounded by such a tidal wave of faddish multicultural subjects such as radical feminism, deconstructed relativism as history and other courses" which undermine the perpetuation of Western civilization.[33] Indeed, this tidal wave slipped by just as Antonio Gramsci and the Frankfurt School had envisioned – a quiet revolution that could not be resisted by force.

---

[31] See *"Hidden Danger in the Classroom"* Pearl Evans, Small Helm Press, 1990. The authors of this classroom approach have since disavowed it, but it continues on in public and other schools.

[32] Raehn, Raymond V. *"The Roots of Affective Education in American Schools."* (March 1995) 17

[33] Himmelfarb, Gertrude. Panel on *"Academic Reform: Internal Sources."* National Association of Scholars, Sixth General Conference, (May 3-5, 1996)

The Frankfurt School had devised the concept of designating the opponents of the Marxist cultural revolution as "authoritarian characters." According to available accounts:

> There was a meeting of American scholars at a conference on religious and racial prejudice in 1944. Over the next five years, a Frankfurt School team under the direction of Max Horkheimer conducted in-depth social and psychological profiles of Americans under a project entitled "Studies of Prejudice." One of the results was a book entitled "The Authoritarian Personality" by Theodor Adorno, et al, that summarized one of the largest public opinion surveys ever undertaken in the United States. It was published in 1950, and conformed to the original Critical Theory in every respect. As a document which testified to the belief system of the Frankfurt School revolutionaries it was essentially anti-God, anti-Christian, anti-family, anti-nationalist, anti-patriot, anti-conservative, antihereditarian, anti-ethnocentric, anti-masculine, anti-tradition, and anti-morality. All of these are elements in critical theory.[34]

"Cultural Marxism," as preached by the Frankfurt School alumni in the U.S., is being implemented by the elite Boomers. This has laid the foundation for and spurred the widely popular and destructive concepts of "affirmative action," "multiculturalism" and "diversity." One can't escape these terms today. They have grown from the study of anti-Semitism and discrimination by the Institute for Social Research during the 1940s and the systematic infusion of the language of "discrimination," "civil rights," 'women's rights," and other "minority rights" into American culture.

According to Raehn:

> Critical Theory as applied mass psychology has led to the deconstruction of gender in the American culture. Following Critical Theory, the distinction between masculinity and femininity will disappear. The traditional

---

[34] Raehn, Raymond V. "Critical Theory: A Special Research Report." (April 1, 1996)

81

roles of the mothers and fathers are to be dissolved so that patriarchy will be ended. Children are not to be raised according to their biological genders and gender roles according to their biological differences. This reflects the Frankfurt School rationale for the disintegration of the traditional family.[35]

Thus, one of the basic tenets of Critical Theory was the necessity to break down the traditional family. The Frankfurt School scholars preached:

> Even a partial breakdown of parental authority in the family might tend to increase the readiness of a coming generation to accept social change.[36]

The transformation of American culture envisioned by the cultural Marxists goes further than pursuing gender equality. Embodied in their agenda is "matriarchal theory," under which they purpose to transform American culture to be female-dominated. This is a direct throwback to Wilhelm Reich, a Frankfurt School member who considered matriarchal theory in psychoanalytic terms. In 1933, he wrote in "The Mass Psychology of Fascism" that matriarchy was the only genuine family type of "natural society."

Erich Fromm, another charter member of the Institute, was one of the most active advocates of matriarchal theory. Fromm was especially taken with the idea that all love and altruistic feelings were ultimately derived from the maternal love necessitated by the extended period of human pregnancy and postnatal care:

> Love thus was not dependent on sexuality, as Freud had supposed. In fact, sex was more often tied to hatred and destruction. Masculinity and femininity were not reflections of "essential" sexual differences, as the romantics had thought. They were derived instead from

---

[35] Ibid.

[36] Jay, Martin. *The Dialectical Imagination: A History of the Frankfurt School and the Institute for Social Research, 1923 – 1950.* (University of California Press, 1973)

differences in life functions, which were in part socially determined.[37]

This dogma was a precedent for today's radical feminist pronouncements appearing in newspapers and in TV programs, including TV newscasts. For its promoters, male and female roles result from cultural indoctrination – an indoctrination carried out by the male patriarchy to the detriment of women.

Indeed, cultural Marxism has, in the 1990s, melded with radical feminism in the elite Boomer generation, that throwback to the dangerous Transcendentalists of the early 19th century. A cauldron of discontent is forming in our nation, a discontent which has the potential to dismantle American civilization.

Destructive criticism of primary elements of American culture inspired the 1960s counter-culture revolution. Idealistic Boomers coming of age strove to transform the prevailing culture into its opposites, in the spirit of social revolution. Now the elite Boomers are in positions of power, and they are working to destroy the nation's historic institutions. They aim to destroy as well the heritage we call "Western Civilization."

Richard Bernstein has written in his book on multiculturalism, "the Marxist revolutionary process for the past several decades in America has centered on race and sex warfare rather than class warfare" as in earlier times.[38] This reflects a scheme more total than economics to restructure American society. As the social revolutionaries readily proclaim, their purpose is to destroy the hegemony of white males. To accomplish this, all barriers to the introduction of more women and minorities throughout the "power structure" are to be brought down by all means available. Laws and lawsuits, intimidation, and demonizing of white males as racists and sexists are pursued through the mass media and the universities. The psycho–dynamic of the revolutionary process aims for psychic disempowerment – decapitation – of those who oppose.

---

[37] Ibid.
[38] Bernstein, Richard. The *Dictatorship of Virtue: Multiculturalism and the Battle for America's Future*. (Knopf, 1994)

Steve Forbes has emphasized:

> This country's founders recognized three primal values in the Declaration of Independence, and they ranked them properly: Life, liberty, and the pursuit of happiness.[39]

Forbes observes that if the order of these fundamental human rights is switched – with happiness before liberty or liberty before life – we come to moral chaos and social anarchy.

This very condition is what Judge Robert Bork describes as "modern liberalism." He defines its characteristics as "'radical egalitarianism' (equality of outcomes rather than of opportunities) and 'radical individualism' (the drastic reduction of limits to personal gratification)."[40]

Judge Bork also identifies radical feminism as "the most destructive and fanatical" element of this modern liberalism. He further describes radical feminism as "totalitarian in spirit."

Most Americans do not realize that they, through their institutions, are being led by social revolutionaries who think in terms of the continuing destruction of the existing social order in order to create a new one. The revolutionaries are New Age Elite Boomers.[41] They now control the public institutions in the United States. Their "quiet" revolution, beginning with the counter-culture revolution of their youth, is nearing completion. A key, or even a dominant element because purportedly it represents that largest political and social constituency among their potential followers, is feminism. The Marxist movement in its "quiet" cultural latter-day phase is seemingly sweeping all before it. With its sway over the media, fully in the grip of feminism, it is hard to discern the stirrings of a counter-culture. Are the elite Boomers, the New Totalitarians, the most dangerous generation in America's history? William Strauss and Neil

---

[39] Snow, Tony. "Moral of the Story: Forbes Virtue Stance." *The Washington Times*, (Oct. 27, 1997) Mr. Snow reports on an article by Forbes in the November 1997 *Policy Review* magazine.

[40] Bork, Robert H. *Slouching Towards Gomorrah: Modern Liberalism and American Decline.* (Harper Collins, 1996)

[41] Atkinson, Gerald L. *The New Totalitarians: Bosnia as a Mirror of America's Future.* (Atkinson Associated Press, 1996)

Howe suggest so, in their book *Generations: The History of America's Future – 1584 – 2069*.[42] James Kurth writes:

> The United States itself has become a great power that opposes much of what was once thought of as Western Civilization, especially its cultural achievements and its social arrangements. The major American elites – those in power in politics, business, the media, and academia – now use American power, especially the "soft power" of information, communications, and popular entertainment, to displace Western Civilization not only in America but also in Europe.[43]

Will American men, of every race, and more traditionalist women of every age and circumstances – who may well be a silent majority of their sex – rise to challenge Political Correctness? Or will American men continue in voluntary submission toward a future of peonage under a new American matriarchy? Would that be a precursor to a condition of anarchy, and an end to America's experiment with democracy? It may well be that the fate of American civilization depends on American men steadfastly resisting Politically Correct feminism. Even more, they must resourcefully oppose the wider grip of Political Correctness, the cultural Marxism for which radical feminism is only one avenue of attack.

[42] Strauss, William and Neil Howe. *Generations: the History of America's Future.* (William Morrow & Co., 1991)
[43] Kurth, James. "NATO Expansion and the ideas of the West." Western Civ in World Politics, *Orbis Magazine*, (Fall 1997)

Chapter 9

A New Front; Environmentalism

Richard W. Hawkins

"In the late 1960s, I traveled to South Africa. I saw children with their legs bound to purposely turn them into cripples for life, presumably so they would make money from donations.

Today, I see children in America and other countries with their minds bound to purposely turn them into mental cripples for life, presumably so they will support votes for a political cause that in the end will destroy their own country. These children have suffered mind-warping child abuse. This abuse has caused them mental and physical harm. " [44]

As the prevailing worldview of the West transforms so also the philosophy and practice of science transforms. Appendix 1 offers a view into this transformation and illustrates the corruption of truth taking place in various scientific fields.

Anthropogenic Global Warming is the spearhead for the United Nation's Agenda21 and companion Agenda2030 collectively referred to as Sustainable Development. This chapter is not about the science of Anthropogenic Global Warming. The 'science' has lost credibility due to fraud, scandals and misrepresentation committed by the politicians, mass media and the scientists involved.[45] [46] [47] [48] [49] More

---

[44] Berry, Dr. Ed, "Stand for climate truth," *Newswithviews*, https://newswithviews.com/stand-for-climate-truth/, (Aug 10, 2019)

[45] Murphy, James, "Climate Alarmists Caught Manipulating Temperature Data Yet Again," *The New American*, https://www.thenewamerican.com/tech/ environment/item/32706-climate-alarmists-caught-manipulating-temperature-data-yet-again, , (26 June, 2019)

[46] Newman, Alex, "UN IPCC Scientist Blows Whistle on Lies About Climate, Sea Level," *The New American,* https://www.thenewamerican.com/tech/ environment/ item/31472-un-ipcc-scientist-blows-whistle-on-un-climate-lies, (12 February 2019)

[47] O'Neil, Tyler, "Libertarian Group Demands NASA Remove False '97 Percent Consensus' Global Warming Claim," *PJ Media*, https://pjmedia.com/trending/libertarian-group-demands-nasa-remove-false-97-percent-consensus-global-warming-claim/, (July 10, 2019)

[48] Durden, Tyler, "Green New Deal Scam Destroyed By New Scientific Study On

time is needed for the science controversies to be settled and truth be told:

> However, the science is not settled. Many renowned climatologists strongly disagree with the IPCC's conclusions about the cause and potential magnitude of Global Warming. More than 20,000 [now 31,487 American scientists including 9049 with PhDs as of 3/25/20] scientists have now signed the Oregon Petition which criticises it as 'flawed' research and states that *"any human contribution to climate change has not yet been demonstrated."* Dr Chris Landsea resigned from the IPCC because he *"personally could not in good faith continue to contribute to a process that I view as both being motivated by pre-conceived agendas and being scientifically unsound."*
>
> The IPCC claims that more than 2,500 respected scientists and policy makers collaborate to write its climate change assessments but less than a tenth of these 'experts' actually hold qualifications in climatology, most were in fact educated in the political and social sciences. The panel that edits and approves the reports are appointed by the United Nations, and more than half are actually UN officials. Dr Richard Lindzen, who is a genuine climate expert, resigned from the IPCC process after his contributions were completely rewritten by the panel. [50]

This chapter is to introduce environmentalism as a new front for Political Correctness. This is another manufactured crisis to create social tension which leads to totalitarian changes. The original faculty of the Frankfurt School are long gone. However, the ideology and its adherents live on and the issues change as the movement advances.

Global Warming," *Technocracy News*, https://www.technocracy.news/green-new-deal-scam-destroyed-by-new-scientific-study-on-global-warming/, (July 12, 2019)
[49] Valle, Joseph, "NOAA scientist turns climate skeptic recounts censorship," *ClimateChangeDispatch*, https://climatechangedispatch.com/noaa-scientist-climate-skeptic/ (Aug 2, 2019)
[50] The Green Agenda, "Global Warming – Settled Science?," http://www.green-agenda.com/science.html

Destruction of capitalism was one of the prime targets identified by the Frankfurt School and the United Nations' environmental agenda is designed to do just that, regardless of the science.

> At a news conference last week in Brussels, Christiana Figueres, executive secretary of U.N.'s Framework Convention on Climate Change, admitted that the goal of environmental activists is not to save the world from ecological calamity but to destroy capitalism.

> "This is the first time in the history of mankind that we are setting ourselves the task of intentionally, within a defined period of time, to change the economic development model that has been reigning for at least 150 years, since the Industrial Revolution," she said. [51]

"Referring to a new international treaty environmentalists hope will be adopted at the Paris climate change conference later that year (2015), she added:

> "This is probably the most difficult task we have ever given ourselves, which is to intentionally transform the economic development model for the first time in human history."" [52]

Former Czech President Klaus, an economist by training and also former prime minister, entered politics in 1989 by helping the overthrow of the Communist government and creation of a new parliamentary republic. He is intimate with Communism and knows the ultimate goal of the United Nations. He has been an outspoken sceptic of Anthropogenic Global Warming with such statements as:

> "It is not fair to refer to the UN panel as a group of scientists. The IPCC is not a scientific institution. It's a political body, a sort of non-government organization of green flavour. It's neither a forum of neutral scientists nor a balanced group of scientists. These people are

---

[51] Editorial, "U.N. Official Reveals Real Reason Behind Warming Scare," *Business Inverstor's Daily,* https://www.investors.com/politics/editorials/climate-change-scare-tool-to-destroy-capitalism/, (Feb 10, 2019)
[52] Ibid

politicized scientists, and UN bureaucrats, who arrive there with a one-sided opinion and a one-sided assignment." [53]

"I'm convinced that after years of studying the phenomenon, global warming is not the real issue of temperature," said Klaus, an economist by training. "That is the issue of a new ideology or a new religion. A religion of climate change or a religion of global warming. This is a religion which tells us that the people are responsible for the current, very small increase in temperatures. And they should be punished." [54]

"We'll be the victims of irrational ideology. They will try to dictate to us how to live, what to do, how to behave," Klaus said. "What to eat, travel, and what my children should have. This is something that we who lived in the communist era for most of our lives — we still feel very strongly about. We are very sensitive in this respect. And we feel various similarities in their way of arguing or not arguing. In the way of pushing ahead ideas regardless of rational counter-arguments." [55]

Environmentalism is the new communism, a system of elite command-and-control that kills prosperity and should similarly be condemned to the ash heap of history….today's global warming activists are the direct descendants of the old Marxists who trampled on individual freedoms and undermined free markets in pursuit of a greater good. [56]

---

[53] The Green Agenda , "Global Warming – Settled Science?"
[54] Koprowski, Gene J, "Czech President Klaus: Global Warming Not Science, but a 'New Religion'," https://www.foxnews.com/science/czech-president-klaus-global-warming-not-science-but-a-new-religion, (June, 22, 2015)
[55] Ibid.
[56] *The Washington Times*, "Climate concern ripped as 'religion'," https://www.washingtontimes.com/news/2008/may/30/climate-concern-ripped-as-religion/, (May 30, 2008)

"On October 14, 2009, Lord Christopher Monckton, former science advisor to British Prime Minister Margaret Thatcher, delivered a scathing refutation of the concept of human-caused global warming at Bethel University in St. Paul, Minnesota. During his presentation, Lord Monckton focused on the UN climate treaty that was being proposed for the United Nations Climate Change Conference in Copenhagen that December. He warned:

> I read that treaty. And what it says is this: that a world government is going to be created. The word "government" actually appears as the first of three purposes of the new entity. The second purpose is the transfer of wealth from the countries of the West to third world countries.... And the third purpose of this new entity, this government, is enforcement.

> Not just any government, mind you. "They are about to impose a communist world government on the world," warned Monckton." [57]

Dr. Edenhofer (was co-chair of a UN Intergovernmental Panel on Climate Change working group) candidly declared:

> "One has to free oneself from the illusion that international climate policy is environmental policy. This has almost nothing to do with the environmental policy anymore, with problems such as deforestation or the ozone hole."

And, he added this shocking admission:

> "We redistribute de facto the world's wealth by climate policy."

> What is the takeaway of this confession? It is nothing less than a shocking admission that man-made global warming is all about politics — Marxist, socialist,

---

[57] Jasper, William F "The United Nations: On the Brink of Becoming a World Government," *The New American,* https://www.thenewamerican.com/world-news/item/13126-the-united-nations-on-the-brink-of-becoming-a-world-government, (11 October 2012)

collectivist politics — masquerading under the false labels of science and environmental concern.

But Dr. Edenhofer is far from being alone in the confessional. The UN's climate czarina, Christiana Figueres, has also been quite vocal in explaining that the UN's imposing climate change agenda extends far beyond mere environmental concerns, such as stopping alleged global warming. She made an especially telling statement at the UN's 2012 Climate Summit in Doha, Qatar, where she said:

"It must be understood that what is occurring here, not just in Doha, but in the whole climate change process is a **complete transformation of the economic structure of the world.**"[58] [Emphasis added]

Truth and liberty are sacrificed for a cultural Marxist's agenda of enslavement predicated on lies:

The main weapon for the Agenda [UN's Agenda 21] was the threat of Environmental Armageddon, particularly manifested through the charge of man-made global warming, later to conveniently become "climate change." It didn't matter if true science refused to cooperate in this scheme as actual global temperatures really are not rising and there continues to be no evidence of any man-made effect on the climate. Truth hasn't been important to the scare mongers. Timothy Wirth, President of the UN Foundation said, "We've got to ride this global warming issue. Even if the theory of global warming is wrong, we will be doing the right thing in terms of economic and environmental policy." To further drive home their complete lack of concern for truth, Paul Watson of Green

---

[58] Gomez, Christian, "What's the Real Agenda Behind Climate-change Alarmism?," *The New American*, https://www.thenewamerican.com/tech/environ-ment/item/22841-what-s-the-real-agenda-behind-climate-change-alarmism, (March 24, 2016)

Peace declared, "It doesn't matter what is true, it only matters what people believe is true." [59]

Bottom Line

Environmental science through the UN's IPCC was, is and will be manipulated as a political, totalitarian tool to enslave us through social engineering. [60] [61]

[59] DeWeese, Tom, "Green New Deal Reveals The Naked Truth Of Agenda 21," *News With Views,* https://newswithviews.com/green-new-deal-reveals-the-naked-truth-of-agenda-21/, (Feb 28, 2019)
[60] Darwal, Rupert, "Environmental Scares: Yesterday and Today," https://www.youtube.com/watch?v=9tLmiJmbZHU
[61] Heartland Institute, The NIPCC Report on Scientific Consensus, "Why Scientists Disagree About Global Warming," https://www.heartland.org/_template-assets/documents/Books/Why%20Scientists%20Disagree%20Second%20Edition%20with%20covers.pdf , 2nd Edition, 2016

Chapter 10

Green New Deal Reveals
The Naked Truth Of Agenda 21

Tom DeWeese, Feb 28, 2019 [62]

Democratic New York Rep. Alexandria Ocasio-Cortez's "Green New Deal" is more about drastically overhauling the American economy than it is about combatting climate change, her top aide admitted. [63]   *[inserted by Editor]*

Sometimes if you fight hard enough and refuse to back down, no matter the odds, your truth is vindicated and prevails!

For twenty years I have been labeled a conspiracy theorist, scaremonger, extremist, dangerous, nut case. I've been denied access to stages, major news programs, and awarded tin foil hats. All because I have worked to expose Agenda 21 and its policy of sustainable development as a danger to our property rights, economic system, and culture of freedom.

From its inception in 1992 at the United Nation's Earth Summit, 50,000 delegates, heads of state, diplomats and Non-governmental organizations (NGOs) hailed Agenda 21 as the "comprehensive blueprint for the reorganization of human society." The 350-page, 40 chapter, Agenda 21 document was quite detailed and explicit in its purpose and goals. They warned us that the reorganization would be dictated through all-encompassing policies affecting every aspect of our lives, using environmental protection simply as the excuse to pull at our emotions and get us to voluntarily surrender our liberties.

Section I details "Social and Economic Dimensions" of the plan, including redistribution of wealth to eradicate poverty, maintain health through vaccinations and modern medicine, and population control.

---

[62] DeWeese, "Green New Deal Reveals The Naked Truth Of Agenda 21,"
[63] Hasson, Peter, "Ocasio-Cortez's Chief Of Staff Admits What The Green New Deal Is Really About — And It's Not The Climate," *Daily Caller*, https://dailycaller.com/2019/07/11/saikat-chakrabarti-green-new-deal/, (July 11, 2019)

To introduce the plan, the Earth Summit Chairman, Maurice Strong boldly proclaimed, "Current lifestyles and consumption patterns of the affluent middle class – involving meat intake, use of fossil fuels, appliances, air-conditioning, and suburban housing – are not sustainable." Of course, according to the plan, if it's not "sustainable" it must be stopped.

In support of the plan, David Brower of the Sierra Club (one of the NGO authors of the agenda) said, "Childbearing should be a punishable crime against society, unless the parents hold a government license." Leading environmental groups advocated that the Earth could only support a maximum of one billion people, leading famed Dr. Jacques Cousteau to declare, "In order to stabilize world populations, we must eliminate 350,000 people per day."

Section II provides the "Conservation and Management of Resources for Development" by outlining how environmental protection was to be the main weapon, including global protection of the atmosphere, land, mountains, oceans, and fresh waters – all under the control of the United Nations.

To achieve such global control to save the planet, it is necessary to eliminate national sovereignty and independent nations. Eliminating national borders quickly led to the excuse for openly allowing the "natural migration" of peoples. The UN Commission on Global Governance clearly outlined the goal for global control stating, "The concept of national sovereignty has been immutable, indeed a sacred principle of international relations. It is a principle which will yield only slowly and reluctantly to the new imperatives of global environmental cooperation." That pretty much explains why the supporters of such a goal go a little off the rails when a presidential candidate makes his campaign slogan "Make America Great Again."

The main weapon for the Agenda was the threat of Environmental Armageddon, particularly manifested through the charge of man-made global warming, later to conveniently become "climate change." It didn't matter if true science refused to cooperate in this scheme as actual global temperatures really are not rising and there continues to be no evidence of any man-made effect on the climate. Truth hasn't been important to the scare mongers. Timothy Wirth, President of the UN Foundation said, "We've got to ride this global warming issue. Even if the theory of global warming is wrong, we will be doing the right thing in terms of economic and environmental policy." To further drive home their complete lack of concern for truth, Paul Watson of Green Peace declared, "It doesn't matter what is true, it only matters what people believe is true."

So in their zealotry to enforce the grand agenda, social justice became the "moral force" over the rule of law as free enterprise, private property, rural communities and individual consumption habits became the targets, labeled as racist and a social injustice. Such established institutions and free market economics were seen as obstructions to the plan, as were traditional family units, religion, and those who were able to live independently in rural areas.

Finally, Agenda 21 was summed up in supporting documents this way: "Effective execution of Agenda 21 will require a profound reorientation of all human society, unlike anything the world has ever experienced. It requires a major shift in the priorities of both governments and individuals, and an unprecedented redeployment of human and financial resources. This shift will demand that a concern for the environmental consequences of every human action be integrated into individual and collective decision-making at every level."

Of course, such harsh terms had to be hidden from the American people if the plan was to be successfully imposed. They called it a "suggestion" for "voluntary" action – just in case a nation or community wanted to do something positive for mankind! However, while using such innocent-sounding language, the Agenda 21 shock troops lost no time pushing it into government policy. In 1992, just after its introduction at the Earth Summit, Nancy Pelosi introduced a resolution of support for the plan into Congress. It's interesting to note that she boldly called it a "comprehensive blueprint for the reorganization of human society." In 1993, new President, Bill Clinton ordered the establishment of the President's Council for Sustainable Development, with the express purpose of enforcing the Agenda 21 blueprint into nearly every agency of the federal government to assure it became the law of the land. Then the American Planning Association issued a newsletter in 1994, supporting Agenda 21's ideas as a "comprehensive blueprint" for local planning. So much for a voluntary idea!

However, as we, the opponents started to gain some ground in exposing its true purpose and citizens began to storm city halls protesting local implementation, suddenly the once proud proponents lost their collective memories about Agenda 21. Never heard of it! "There are no blue-helmeted troops at city hall," said one proponent, meaning policies being used to impose it were not UN driven, but just "local, local, local". "Oh, you mean that innocuous 20 year-old document that has no enforcement capability? This isn't that!" These were the excuses that rained down on us from the planners, NGOs and government agents as they scrambled to hide their true intentions.

I was attacked on the front page of the *New York Times* Sunday paper under the headline, "Activists Fight Green Projects, Seeing U.N. Plot." The Southern Poverty Law Center (SPLC) produced four separate reports on my efforts to stop it, calling our efforts an "Antigovernment Right-Wing Conspiracy Theory." *The Atlantic* magazine ran a story entitled, "Is the UN Using Bike Paths to Achieve World Domination?" Attack articles appeared in the *Washington Post, Esquire* magazine, *Wingnut Watch, Mother Jones*, and *Tree Hugger.com* to name a few. All focused on labeling our opposition as tin-foil-hat-wearing nut jobs. Meanwhile, an alarmed American Planning Association (APA) created an "Agenda 21: Myths and Facts page on its web site to supposedly counter our claims. APA then organized a "Boot Camp" to retrain its planners to deal with us, using a "Glossary for the Public," teaching them new ways to talk about planning. Said the opening line of the Glossary, "Given the heightened scrutiny of planners by some members of the public, what is said – or not said – is especially important in building support for planning." The Glossary went on to list words not to use like "Public Visioning," "Stakeholders," "Density," and "Smart Growth," because such words make the "Critics see red".

Local elected officials, backed by NGO groups and planners, began to deride local activists – sometimes denying them access to speak at public meetings, telling them that Agenda 21 conspiracy theory has "been debunked". Most recently an irate city councilman answered a citizen who claimed local planning was part of Agenda 21 by saying "this is what's "trending." So, of course, if everyone is doing it is must be right!

Such has been our fight to stop this assault on our culture and Constitutional rights.

Over the years, since the introduction of Agenda 21 in 1992, the United Nations has created several companion updates to the original documents. This practice serves two purposes. One is to provide more detail on how the plan is to be implemented. The second is to excite its global activists with a new rallying cry. In 2000, the UN held the Millennium Summit, launching the Millennium Project featuring eight goals for global sustainability to be reached by 2015. Then, when those goals were not achieved, the UN held another summit in New York City in September of 2015, this time outlining 17 goals to be reached by 2030. This document became known as the 2030 Agenda, containing the exact same goals as were first outlined in Agenda 21in 1992, and then again in 2000, only with each new incarnation offering more explicit direction for completion.

Enter the Green New Deal, representing the boldest tactic yet. The origins and the purpose of the Green New Deal couldn't be more transparent. The forces behind Agenda 21 and its goal of reorganizing human society have become both impatient and scared. Impatient that 27 years after Agenda 21 was introduced, and after hundreds of meetings, planning sessions, massive propaganda, and billions of dollars spent, the plan still is not fully in place. Scared because people around the world are starting to learn its true purpose and opposition is beginning to grow.

So the forces behind the Agenda have boldly thrown off their cloaking devices and their innocent sounding arguments that they just want to protect the environment and make a better life for us all. Instead, they are now openly revealing that their goal is socialism and global control, just as I've been warning about for these past twenty years. Now they are determined to take congressional action to finally make it the law of the land.

Take a good look, those of you who have heard my warnings about Agenda 21 over the years. Do you see the plan I have warned about being fully in place in this Green New Deal?

• I warned that Agenda 21 would control every aspect of our lives, including how and w[h]ere (sic) we live, the jobs we have, the mode of transportation available to us, and even what we eat. The Green New Deal is a tax on everything we do, make, wear, eat, drink, drive, import, export and even breathe.

• In opposing Smart Growth plans in your local community, I said the main goal was to eliminate cars, to be replaced with bikes, walking, and light rail trains. The Green New Deal calls for the elimination of the internal combustion engine. Stay alert. The next step will be to put a ban on the sale of new combustion engines by a specific date and then limiting the number of new vehicles to be sold. Bans on commercial truck shipping will follow. Then they will turn to airplanes, reducing their use. Always higher and higher taxes will be used to get the public to "voluntarily" reduce their use of such personal transportation choices. That's how it works, slowly but steadily towards the goal.

• I warned that under Smart Growth programs now taking over every city in the nation that single-family homes are a target for elimination, to be replaced by high-rise stack and pack apartments in the name of reducing energy use. That will include curfews on carbon heating systems, mandating they be turned off during certain hours. Heating oil devises will become illegal. Gradually, energy use of any kind will be continually reduced. The Green New Deal calls for government control of every single home, office and factory to tear down or retrofit them to comply with massive environmental energy regulations.

• I warned that Agenda 21 Sustainable policy sought to drive those in rural areas off the farms and into the cities where they could be better controlled. Those in the cities will be ordered to convert their gardens into food producers. Most recently I warned that the beef industry is a direct target for elimination. It will start with mandatory decreases in meat consumption until it disappears form our daily diet. The consumption of dairy will follow. Since the revelation of the Green New Deal the national debate is now over cattle emissions of methane and the drive to eliminate them from the planet. Controlling what we eat is a major part of the Green New Deal.

• I warned that part of the plan for Agenda 2030 was "Zero Economic Growth." The Green New Deal calls for a massive welfare plan where no one earns more than anyone else. Incentive to get ahead is dead. New inventions would disrupt their plan for a well-organized, controlled society. So, where will jobs come from after we have banned most manufacturing, shut down most stores, stopped single-family home construction, closed the airline industry, and severely regulated farms and the entire food industry? This is their answer to the hated free markets and individual choice.

The Green New Deal will destroy the very concept of our Constitutional Republic, eliminating private property, locally elected representative government, free markets and individual freedom. All decisions in our lives will be made for us by the government – just to protect the environment of course. They haven't forgotten how well that scheme works to keep the masses under control.

Though the label "Green New Deal" has been passing around globalist circles for a while, it's interesting that its leaders have now handed it to a naïve, inexperienced little girl from *New York* who suddenly found herself rise from bartending to a national media sensation, almost over night. That doesn't just happen and there is no miracle here. Alexandria Ocasio-Cortez is a created product. They probably needed her inexperienced enthusiasm to deliver the Green New Deal because no established politician would touch it. Now that it's been introduced and she is set up to take the heat, the gates have swung open allowing forty-five members of Congress to co-sponsor it in the House of Representatives as established Senator Ed. Markey (D-MA) has sponsored it in the Senate. That doesn't just happen either. Nothing has been left to chance.

Behind the sudden excitement and rush to support it are three radical groups each having direct ties to George Soros, including the Sunrise Movement – which markets itself as an "army of young people" seeking to make climate change a major priority. Justice Democrats – which finds and recruits progressive candidates, and New Consensus – organized to change how we think about issues. Leaders of these groups have connections with other Soros-backed movements including Black Lives Matter and Occupy Wall Street. According to *The New Yorker* magazine, the plan was written over a single weekend in December, 2018. Ocasio-Cortez was included in the effort, chosen to introduce it. This may be the single reason why she was able to appear out of nowhere to become the new darling of the radical left.

So there you have it — Agenda 21, the Millennium Project, Agenda 2030, the Green New Deal. Progress in the world of Progressives! They warned us from the beginning that their plan was the "comprehensive blueprint for the reorganization of human society". And so it is to be the total destruction of our way of life.

To all of those elected officials, local, state and federal, who have smirked at we who have tried to sound the alarm, look around you now, hot shots! You have denied, ignored, and yet, helped put these very plans into place. Are you prepared to accept what you have done? Will you allow your own homes and offices to be torn down – or will you be exempt as part of the elite or just useful idiots? Will you have to give up your car and ride your bike to work? Or is that just for we peasants?

Over these years you have listened to the Sierra Club, the Nature Conservancy, the World Wildlife Fund, ICLEI, the American Planning Association, and many more, as they assured you their plans were just environmental protection, just good policy for future generations. They have been lying to you to fulfill their own agenda! Well, now the truth is right in front of you. There is no question of who and what is behind this. And no doubt as to what the final result will be.

Now, our elected leaders have to ask real questions. As the Green New Deal is implemented, and all energy except worthless, unworkable wind and solar are put into place, are you ready for the energy curfews that you will be forced to impose, perhaps each night as the sun fades, forcing factories, restaurants, hospitals, and stores to close at dusk? How about all those folks forced to live in the stack and pack high-rises when the elevators don't operate? What if they have an emergency?

How much energy will it take to rebuild those buildings that must be destroyed or retrofitted to maker (sic) them environmentally correct for your brave new world? Where will it come from after you have banned and destroyed all the workable sources of real energy? What are you counting on to provide you with food, shelter, and the ability to travel so you can continue to push this poison? Because – this is what's trending — now! And how is it going to be financed when the entire economy crashes under its weight? Is it really the future you want for you, your family, and your constituents who elected you?

Every industry under attack by this lunacy should now join our efforts to stop it. Cattlemen, farmers, airlines, the auto industry, realtors, tourist industry, and many more, all will be put out of business – all should now take bold action to immediately kill this plan before it kills your industry. Stomp it so deeply into the ground that no politician will ever dare think about resurrecting it.

For years I've watched politicians smirk, roll their eyes, and sigh whenever the words Agenda 21 were uttered. As George Orwell said, "The further a society drifts from the truth the more it will hate those who speak it". Today I stand vindicated in my warnings of where Agenda 21 was truly headed, because it's not (sic) longer me having to reveal the threat. They are telling you themselves. Here's the naked truth – Socialism is for the stupid. The Green New Deal is pure Socialism. How far its perpetrators get in enforcing it depends entirely on how hard you are willing to fight for freedom. Kill it [Green New Deal] now or watch it [freedom] die.

Author Email: admin@americanpolicy.org or ampolicycenter@hotmail.com
Website: www.americanpolicy.org

Chapter 11

Critical Race Theory, Intersectionality, and the Gospel [64]

By Dr. Tom Ascol, PhD.
Pastor of Grace Baptist Church, Cape Coral, Florida
President of Founders Ministries (www.founders.org)

February 3, 2020

Identity Politics involving race has been a tool used by Progressives and cultural Marxists for over a century.

"In 1909 a group of socialists and socialist sympathizers founded a socialist Negro front organization which they labelled the National Association for the Advancement of Colored People (NAACP). The two prime movers of the organization, Mary White Ovington and William English Walling were prominent white socialists. These two were also key members of the Fabian socialist organization in the United States which went under the name of the Intercollegiate Socialist Society (later called the League for Industrial Democracy).

The NAACP was strictly a Socialist Party front of the white radicals designed to push through measures based on demands for Negro rights which would aid in conditioning the United States for a socialist society.

A few years previously, a parallel organization was organized of Negroes headed by W. E. B. Du Bois, a Harvard educated Negro socialist [who later joined the Communist Party USA]. This movement was termed the Niagara Movement, named after the locale of its organization at Niagara Falls, Canada.

The function of Du Bois and his group was to destroy the effectiveness of the great Negro leader Booker T. Washington. Washington had espoused the philosophy of Negro self-help and

---

[64] Ascol, Tom, "Critical Race Theory, Intersectionality, and the Gospel," https://founders.org/2020/02/03/critical-race-theory-intersectionality-and-the-gospel/, (Feb 3, 2020)

102

self-development in the trades and professions as a means of lifting Negroes into a higher economic and cultural level. The socialist controlled Niagara Movement was quite successful in torpedoing the Booker T Washington program. It was obvious that any successful self-development movement among Negroes would strengthen the present private enterprise system rather than weaken it. The socialist premise has always been to weaken the social order so as to render it easier for the final take-over. This is a fundamental long-range principle of over-all socialistic strategy. Later when the communists split off from the socialist movement they pursued this objective with added vigor."[inserted by Editor] [65]

"In 1912, a man named Israel Cohen....wrote a book on Communist tactics, titled "A Racial Program for the Twentieth Century." An excerpt reads:

"We must realize that our Party's most powerful weapon is **RACIAL TENSION**. *By pounding into the consciousness of the dark races that for centuries they have been oppressed by the Whites, we can mould them to our program. The terms "colonialism" and "imperialism" must be featured in our propaganda. In America we will aim for subtle victory while inflaming the Negro minority against the Whites. We will endeavor to install in the Whites a guilt complex for exploiting the Negroes. We will aid the Negroes to rise to prominence in every walk of life, (Affirmative Action) in the professions and in the world of sport and entertainment. With this prestige, the Negroes will be able to intermarry with the Whites and begin a process which will deliver America to our cause." [inserted by Editor]* [66]

Critical Race Theory, Intersectionality, and the Gospel

Over the last several months evangelical Christians have been forced to think about Marxist concepts that, heretofore, were foreign to them. Due in large part to the infamous "Resolution 9" that was adopted by the 2019 Southern Baptist Convention (SBC), language identifying

---

[65] A Veritas Foundation Staff Study, *The Great Deceit; Social Pseudo Sciences*, (Veritas Foundation, 1964) , 172-174
[66] Freauf, Betty, "Microaggressions And Deconstructing White Privilege," *Newswithviews*, https://newswithviews.com/micro-agressions-and-deconstructing-white-privilege, (Nov 19,2018)

those concepts, if not the proper understanding of them, has become somewhat familiar to evangelicals.

After all, the title of the SBC's Resolution 9 is "On Critical Race Theory and Intersectionality." The Resolutions Committee strongly rejected any critique of their resolution by the messengers present. They also dismissed my attempt to offer an amendment to it that would have made the resolution more explicitly theological and added warnings about the Marxist origins of the ideologies being promoted.

I wrote a brief assessment of that event a few days after the convention that you can read here.[67] For a more in-depth analysis of the resolution itself, see Tom Nettles' three-part evaluation of it (here[68], here[69], and here[70]).

If you want an in-depth, more detailed analysis of the issues involved and why every Bible believing Christian should be concerned, watch the Founders film, _By What Standard? God's World...God's Rules_.[71] We produced it and are distributing it for free in order to help God's people recognize the threats that are confronting us through these subtle, deadly ideologies that have arisen over the last few decades.

As I have repeatedly stated in different forums since last summer, I doubt even 25% of the messengers in the room at the time had even heard of Critical Race Theory (CRT) or Intersectionality (IS) prior to the committee's urging of Southern Baptists to adopt a resolution affirming their use as analytical tools. This is no denigration of the

---

[67] Ascol, Tom, "Resolution 9 and the Southern Baptist Convention 2019," https://founders.org/2019/06/15/resolution-9-and-the-southern-baptist-convention-2019/,(June 15,2019)

[68] Nettles, Tom, "An Anti-Racist Intention | A Critical Analysis of Resolution 9 - Part 1," https://founders.org/2019/12/20/an-anti-racist-intention-a-critical-analysis-of-resolution-9-part-1/, (Dec 20, 2019)

[69] Nettles, Tom, "An Anti-Racist Intention | A Critical Analysis of Resolution 9 - Part 2," https://founders.org/2019/12/21/an-analogy-to-critical-theory-a-critical-analysis-of-resolution-9-part-2/, (Dec 21, 2019)

[70] Nettles, Tom, "An Anti-Racist Intention | A Critical Analysis of Resolution 9 – Part 3," https://founders.org/2019/12/23/the-leaven-of-crt-and-intersectionality-a-critical-analysis-of-resolution-9-part-3/, (Dec 23, 2019)

[71] Founders Ministries, "By What Standard? God's World...God's Rules," https://founders.org/cinedoc/

messengers. Rather, it is a simple recognition of the fact that CRT/IS were not a part of the common parlance of Southern Baptists prior to the 2019 convention.

In order to provide what I hope will be a helpful introduction to the issues involved, consider the following definitions and brief explanations of why these ideologies are incompatible with biblical Christianity.

Critical Race Theory

According to Richard Delgado's & Jean Stefancic's book, *Critical Race Theory: An Introduction,*

> The critical race theory (CRT) movement is a collection of activists and scholars interested in studying **and transforming** the relationship among race, racism, and power... It not only tries to understand our social situation, **but to change it**; it sets out not only to ascertain how society organizes itself along racial lines and hierarchies, but to transform it for the better (pp. 2-3; emphasis added).

Arising from a Marxist (and, therefore, atheistic and materialistic) worldview, CRT assumes that

> "racism is engrained in the fabric and system of the American society." This assumption means that "the individual racist need not exist" in order for "institutional racism [to be] pervasive in the dominant culture." This presupposition, combined with the Marxist view that all relationships are best understood in terms of power dynamics, causes CRT to assert that existing power structures "are based on white privilege and white supremacy, which perpetuates the marginalization of people of color" (from UCLA's School of Public Affairs). [72]

---

[72] UCLA School of Public Affairs/Critical Race Studies, "What is Critical Race Theory?," https://spacrs.wordpress.com/what-is-critical-race-theory/, (June 2009)

So, CRT assumes that "people of color" are inherently oppressed and marginalized by power structures that are rooted in white privilege and white supremacy. Furthermore, CRT does not merely make that observation, it is definitionally committed to transforming the perceived oppressions it identifies.

Why CRT is incompatible with the gospel

CRT (along with every other Marxist ideology) cannot be reconciled with what the Bible teaches about sin and salvation. First, to view all relationships in terms of power dynamics requires that people be seen in terms of the powerful (privileged, oppressors) and the powerless (marginalized, oppressed). Apart from striking out against God-ordained hierarchies and authority structures (by evaluating them as oppressive power structures), this way of viewing the world fails to evaluate people in their primary relationship, which is as creatures made in the image of their Creator.

Mankind's greatest need is met in the gospel.

He who defines the problem gets to define the solution. If the main problem for "people of color" is that they are inevitably oppressed by structures that are inherently oppressive, then the only solution is to tear down those structures in the pursuit of justice. This way of thinking at the very least clouds the fact revealed in the Bible that every person's fundamental problem is that they have sinned against the holy God who created them. This is true for people in any and every category—whether oppressed or oppressor, victim or victimizer, marginalized or privileged.

The fundamental need, therefore, of every person is to be reconciled to God. This is exactly what has been provided through the life, death, and resurrection of Jesus. In other words, mankind's greatest need is met in the gospel.

But what about those orthodox Christians who believe all of this and yet who tell us that CRT can be a useful analytical tool for thinking about race and racism? I'm glad you asked, because the most charitable way to describe such Christians is "naïve." I might even want to add, "dangerously naïve."

106

Why? Because the tool that you choose, matters. Even when a problem is properly diagnosed it can exacerbated rather than solved by addressing it with the wrong tool.

In southwest Florida we are plagued by Ceratopogonidae. These biting insects are popularly known as noseeums because, well, they are hard to see. They are a problem. So much so that when they invade, I don't simply want to be removed from them, I want to smash them. Hammers are good for smashing things. But imagine what would happen if a hammer became my tool of choice to deal with noseeums. Sure, I might kill a few (but not nearly as many as I would like to think) and might even relieve some frustration and feel good about my efforts in the process. but their demise would come at the cost of bruises, broken bones, and structural damage. But what is guaranteed—if I use a hammer the way that it is designed to be used—is that any good that might be accomplished will be far outweighed by damage and harm that are done.

Critical Race Theory comes from a godless, materialistic worldview. It cannot be employed in ways that are true to the ideologies embedded in it without undermining the revelation of God in Jesus Christ.

The same is true of Intersectionality.

Intersectionality

Intersectionality describes the way that different types of discrimination overlap in a marginalized or oppressed person's experience. It is the idea that a person's true identity is measured by how many victim-statuses you can call their own. Like CRT, IS views the world through the lens of power dynamics with a person's social position best understood in terms of discrimination and disadvantage. So, the more disadvantaged groups that you identify with the more oppressed you are.

For example, by current measurements, a black man is more oppressed than a white man. A black woman is more oppressed than a black man. A black lesbian is more oppressed than a black heterosexual woman, and so it goes. As oppressive categories multiply, so do intersectional values. Currently, white, heterosexual, cisgender, able-bodied, Christian males are at the top of the offender list and those who can claim the most opposite categories are the most oppressed.

The more victim-statuses a person has the greater his or her insight into and authority to speak on issues related to justice, oppression, etc. This "standpoint epistemology" claims that a person's lived experience and social location provide an almost gnostic understanding of how the world really works.

Why IS is incompatible with the gospel

Like CRT, the great problem with IS is the worldview that forged it and is necessarily embedded in it. Intersectionality operates on a sub-Christian worldview that makes no account for God's sovereignty over His creation or His prerogative to order it however He chooses. Intersectionality emphasizes the ways that people differ from each other while ignoring, if not rejecting altogether, what the Bible says about the commonality of the human race.

This commonality is seen in three critical ways as taught in Scripture. First, all people are created in God's image. We are all responsible creatures who have come from the same Creator. Second, we have all sinned against our Creator. Paul spends the bulk of the first three chapters of Romans establishing this point. He emphatically declares, "For there is no distinction: for all have sinned and fall short of the glory of God" (3:22b-23). Intersectionality says, "Ah, but there are distinctions—many of them and they are very important if we are going to help people with their real problems in this world."

Our identity is found in our relationship to God. By nature, as His creatures. By sin, as rebels against Him. By grace, as His children.

The third way that IS undermines the Bible's teaching is by downplaying if not rejecting outright the oneness that Christians have with each other because of our union with Christ. To be in Christ is to be spiritually united to all who are in Christ. It is to belong to the family of God. It is to have God as our Father and other Christians as our brothers and sisters. This is precisely the point of Galatians 3:27-28, "For as many of you as were baptized into Christ have put on

Christ. There is neither Jew nor Greek, there is neither slave nor free, there is no male and female, for you are all one in Christ Jesus."

Our identity is found in our relationship to God. By nature, as His creatures. By sin, as rebels against Him. By grace, as His children. Authority comes from Him and belongs to those to whom He vests it in the various spheres of life. Insight into how we are to live in God's world and church comes from Scripture and not from lived experience.

So those who promote the use of Critical Race Theory and Intersectionality are standing against what the Word of God teaches about the nature of humanity, sin, righteousness and grace. These ideologies are incompatible with the authority and sufficiency of God's Word and therefore with the gospel that the Word reveals.

They are not useful analytical tools that Christians can employ as if they are neutral. They have ideas and principles embedded within them that are, at best, antithetical to the way of Christ. Furthermore, they are superfluous to the Christian who reads and understands the Bible and is submissive to its inerrancy, authority, and sufficiency.

For more information on this subject see the Statement on Social Justice and the Gospel and subscribe to the Founders YouTube channel, where additional content is being added regularly. [73], [74]

---

[73] SJ&G, The Statement on Social Justice and the Gospel,
https://statementonsocialjustice.com/#introduction
[74] Founders Ministries, https://www.youtube.com/channel/UC73IkqTseO-dI1qVuqrJ16A

PART 3

IDENTIFYING CULTURAL MARXISM IN EDUCATION

Cultural Marxism was birthed within the institution of education and from there spread through the rest of society. Cultural Marxism itself is a progressive worldview in that it gradually changes into a purer form of Marxism over time. Education is at the forefront of these changes.

Chapter 12

The Elephant in the classroom

Richard W. Hawkins, 2019

Using a century of psychological research, these indoctrination centers are designed to transform children into unthinking cogs in a globalist machine. Many of its architects have boasted of their agenda to weaponize public schools against individualism, Christianity, religion, and more. Now it is under way. – Alex Newman [75]

What is this Elephant?

There's a sinister and obvious problem in our K-12 classrooms that only a few people want to talk about. This metaphorical elephant is cultural Marxism. This elephant has declared war on the family, individuals, Christianity and all other aspects of Western Civilization. The evidence is obvious:

- Over the past couple of decades Barna Research has been showing a steady downward trend of morals, values and beliefs among America's youth.
- Upwards of 58% of recent high school graduates prefer socialism, Communism and Fascism Vs capitalism [76]
- Outspoken, openly socialists politicians get elected into office at both local and national levels.
- Professor Nicholas Giordano said that the National Report Card that studies graduating seniors showed that only 11% of US students are proficient in American history, 23% proficient in government and civics, 22% proficient in math, 34%

[75] Newman, Alex, "Education's Future: Globalization of Indoctrination," *The New American*, https://www.thenewamerican.com/print-magazine/item/31250-education-s-future-globalization-of-indoctrination, (Feb 6, 2019)

[76] Smith, Marion, "Forty-Four Percent of Millennials Prefer Socialism. Do They Know What It Means?" https://www.victimsofcommunism.org/witnessblog/2018/4/19/forty-four-percent-of-millennials-prefer-socialism-do-they-know-what-it-means, (Nov 2, 2017)

proficient in reading, and 24% proficient in writing. Students have been taught how to take a test instead of being given knowledge and how to apply that knowledge in the real world.[77]

- "When contemplating the role of Washington, D.C., in helping them achieve their goals in life, my students, most of whom were educated in America's public schools, wrote that they wanted government to: pay for my tuition, provide me with a job, give me money for a house, make sure I get free health care, pay for my retirement, and raise taxes on rich people so that I can have more money" [78]

- The textbooks are based on the cultural Marxist worldview to complement the Common Core State Standards. Western Civilization topics are demonized or ignored while multicultural diversity, Identity Politics, green agenda issues, and activism are highlighted based on this author's reviews of recent history and ELA textbooks.

- More than 25 percent of children aged 12 to 17 in CA now classify themselves as "gender non-conforming." A separate study found that the number of children identifying as "Lesbian, Gay, Bisexual, or Transgender" surged to about 15% in 2017. [79]

- Some 88% of millennials (a higher percentage than any other age group) believe in the climate change religion and 69% say it will impact them in their lifetimes. [80]

---

[77] https://needtoknow.news/2019/09/professor-nicholas-giordano-exposes-schools-low-standards-that-dumb-down-students-who-have-a-22-proficiency-level-for-education-skills-upon-graduation/

[78] Schoen, Karen, "Social Justice in America," *Newswithviews*, http://newswithviews.com/Schoen/karen114.htm, (Oct 4, 2015)

[79] Newman, Alex, "Government Schools Are Sexualizing, Perverting, and Confusing Children," *The New American*, https://www.thenewamerican.com/print https://needtoknow.news/2019/09/professor-nicholas-giordano-exposes-schools-low-standards-that-dumb-down-students-who-have-a-22-proficiency-level-for-education-skills-upon-graduation/

[80] Slavo, Mac, "Young People Blaming Climate Change For Not Saving For Retirement," http://www.prophecynewswatch.com/article.cfm?recent_news_id=3222, (May 26, 2019)

- The PEERS Test of Nehemiah Institute has been tracking a similar downward trend of Christian youth for their politics, economics, education, religion and sociological beliefs and values; the trend is from moderate Christian values in 1988 to those of Secular Humanism and Marxism today [81]

70-100: Biblical Theism
30-69: Moderate Christian
0-29: Humanism
<0: Socialism

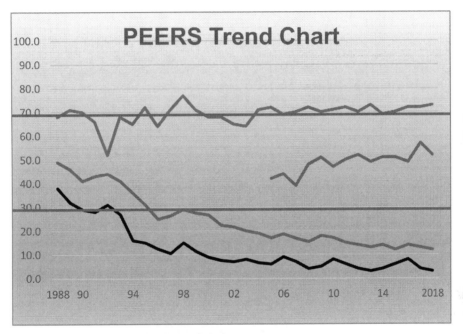

Top line-Biblical Worldview School (Christian schools which emphasize Biblical worldview understanding in:
        1) Curriculum selections,
        2) Faculty training and
        3) training for parents
2nd line-Homeschool Groups
3rd line-Traditional Christian Schools (approximately 95% of the 8,000 Christian K-12 schools in U.S.)
Bottom line-Public Schools (testing of Youth Groups in churches where majority of youth, if not all, attend public schools)

These worldview results show that over 90% of youth from Christian homes are in agreement with basic principles of Secular Humanism.

---

[81] Nehemiah Institute, http://nehemiahinstitute.com/

- **Many, if not most, teachers are heavily biased and motivated to indoctrinate their students into cultural Marxism by direction of their unions; the NEA or the AFT.** [82, 83]

The government controlled K-12 classroom is the indoctrinating middle man for the cultural Marxist agenda. The agenda is driven by an extensive network of like-minded individuals and organizations that I bundle together and refer to them collectively as the Education Establishment. Previous chapters have described the actions of John Dewey placing the Communist focused Frankfurt School faculty into our university system. The Teachers Colleges were influenced by such cultural Marxist luminaries and devotees as Theodor Adorno, Abraham Maslow, Erich Fromm, Betty Friedan, Georg Lukacs, Wilhelm Reich, Herbert Marcuse, and Benjamin Bloom.

The Myth

> ....The function of education is thus to school persons in the ultimate values of a culture. This is inescapably a religious task. Education has always been a religious function of society and closely linked to its religion [a.k.a. worldview – editor]. When a state takes over the responsibilities for education from the church or from Christian parents, the state has not thereby disowned all religions [worldviews] but simply disestablished Christianity in favor of its own statist religion, usually a form of humanism.-- Rousas John Rushdoony [84]

There is a common myth that both teachers and parents hold regarding their public school. **The myth is that public education is**

---

[82] Brown, Michael, "A Generation of School Teachers Who See Their Jobs as Political Advocacy," http://www.prophecynewswatch.com/article.cfm?recent_news_id =3372, (July 31, 2019)

[83] Jasper, William F, "Union to Teachers: Inject Race and Racism Into Every Subject and Every Conversation," *The New American,* https://www.thenewamerican.com/ culture/edu-cation/item/33677-union-to-teachers-inject-race-and-racism-into- every-subject-and-every-conversation. (Oct 15, 2019)

[84] Rushdoony, Rousas John, *The Philosophy of the Christian Curriculum* (Ross House Books, 2001), 3

values neutral; being neutral is impossible! Every human based institution is founded on a worldview, especially educational institutions. Unfortunately, the public schools are not founded on either the Christian Worldview or the more secular based Western Civilization worldview of our founding era.

Cultural Marxism is THE predominant worldview inculcated into all students in the government controlled K-12 school houses. The individual worldview of any particular teacher has little impact in the classroom if that worldview is different than cultural Marxism.

War on the student and his family

> *"Once the earthly family is discovered to be the secret of the heavenly family, the former must be destroyed in theory and in practice."-- Karl Marx* [85]

Dr. Chester Pierce, Harvard professor and psychiatrist who pioneered the Politically Correct concept of microaggression, stated at a teachers' conference in 1973:

> "Every child in America entering school at the age of
> five is insane because he comes to school with certain
> allegiances toward our founding fathers, toward his
> parents, toward a belief in a supernatural being. It's up
> to you, teachers, to make all of these sick children well
> by creating the international child of the future."[86]

When I first read this quote about 20 years ago I thought, "How outlandish!" But reflecting on it I find his charge to the teachers and Education Establishment was taken seriously. The schools are psychometrically analyzing children and there is a national call for mental health testing of all school children. There is a very strong anti-American bias built into the curriculum and the founding fathers are now considered "white supremacists" as their statues are torn down. No one should be surprised that there is a pervasive anti-Christian bias built into the government controlled schools and most

---

[85] Gotcher, Dean, "Benjamin Bloom and his Taxonomies ("modernized" by Marzano and Webb) compared to Karl Marx," https://www.authorityresearch.com/ Articles/Blooms%20Taxonomies%20and%20Karl%20Marx.html
[86] http://www.gospelweb.net/CultureWar/childrenmentallyill.htm

teachers today are teaching their students to be global citizens as opposed to being Americans. Few are aware of the anti-parent bias built into the "higher order thinking skill" methods of educating.

What educators call **critical thinking** or **higher order thinking skills** is actually application of the cultural Marxist **Critical Theory**, a form of **deconstruction used to criticize the traditional social order.** The Hegelian Dialectic (a.k.a. Delphi Technique) consensus building process shuns absolute truth and relies on feelings, opinions and compromise. This inculcates moral relativism that also builds collectivist habits by destroying individualism and personal responsibility. Another outcome is to foster the democratic process applicable for all situations that end up deconstructing the parents' and supervisor's superior-subordinate authority by changing the relationship to an equalized democracy between superior and subordinate.

The highly influential education theorist, psychologist and cultural Marxist Benjamin Bloom wrote:

> ...a student attains 'higher order thinking' when he no longer believes in right or wrong. A large part of what we call good teaching is a teacher´s ability to obtain affective objectives by challenging the student's fixed beliefs. ...a large part of what we call teaching is that the teacher should be able to use education to reorganize a child's thoughts, attitudes, and feelings. [87]

Likewise, in 1968 Warren Bennis and Philip Slater wrote in <u>The Temporary Society:</u>

> One cannot permit submission to parental authority if one wishes to bring about profound social change....In order to effect rapid changes, any such centralized regime must mount a vigorous attack on the family lest the traditions of present generations be preserved. It is necessary, in other words, artificially to create an

---

[87] Gotcher, "Benjamin Bloom and his Taxonomies ("modernized" by Marzano and Webb) compared to Karl Marx"

experiential chasm between parents and children to insulate the latter in order that they can more easily be indoctrinated with new ideas. The desire may be to cause an even more total submission to the state, but if one wishes to mold children in order to achieve some future goal, one must begin to view them as superior, inasmuch as they are closer to this future goal. One must also study their needs with care in order to achieve this difficult preparation for the future. One must teach them not to respect their tradition-bound elders, who are tied to the past and know only what is irrelevant. [88]

Brock Chisholm (1959 Humanist of the Year) was at one time head of the World Health Organization, and in the February 1946 issue of PSYCHIATRY he wrote,

To achieve world government, it is necessary to remove from the minds of men their individualism, loyalty to family tradition national patriotism, and religious dogmas....We have swallowed all manner of poisonous certainties fed us by our parents, our Sunday and day school teachers, our politicians, our priests....The reinterpretation and eventual eradication of the concept of right and wrong which has been the basis of child training, the substitution of intelligent and rational thinking for faith in the certainties of old people, these are the belated objectives...for charting the changes in human behavior. [89]

Anita Hoge, a powerful watchman-on-the-wall who monitors the Education Establishments' numerous attempts over the past 30 years to conduct psychological testing and conditioning of students without parental consent, states:

Schools in the United States have been used in experimental research in the area of the affective domain

---

[88] https://sagaciousnewsnetwork.com/humanity-under-attack-the-tactics-of-social-engineering/
[89] Ibid

including the spiritual aspect of a child's being, the heart. The teaching method is called the "**whole child**." This has been the area where values, attitudes, beliefs, and dispositions have been the focus for behavioral conditioning and value change. United States citizens must have their individualist qualities, their freedom loving values, and their individualistic competitive personalities changed. Change in America is a must to conform the U.S. into a socialistic country including global compromise. Americans must become global citizens. [90]

It is the conscience that is the target for this indoctrination. That area of conscience is known as the affective domain. That is the domain Chisholm, Bloom, Bennis and Slater are aiming at with their higher order thinking skills. Teachers are trained change agents to influence the affective domain and alter a student's conscience. But the goal is to inculcate the cultural Marxist worldview. David French discusses academic bias by illustrating from the University of Alabama College of Education's "Conceptual Framework":

The College of Education conceptualizes the **promotion of social justice** in an education setting as an issue…..

The College of Education is committed to preparing individuals to promote social justice, **to be change agents**, and to recognize individual and institutionalized **racism, sexism, homophobia, and classism** (Abelove, 1993; Fine, 1993; Fordham, 1996; Post, 1998). It includes educating individuals to break silences about these issues, propose solutions, provide leadership, and develop **anti-racist, anti-homophobic, anti-sexist community and alliances**. [91] [emphasis added]

---

90 Hoge, Anita, "A Wake-Up Call For Every Family and Church In The United States," *Newswithviews,* http://newswithviews.com/a-wake-up-call-for-every-family-and-church-in-the-united-stares/, (May 28, 2019)
91 French, David, "Re: Where Academic Bias Really Is," *National Review*, May 4, 2006 https://www.nationalreview.com/phi-beta-cons/re-where-academic-bias-really-david-french/

Another method of changing a student's conscience without him or his parents being made aware is through BF Skinner's Operant Conditioning process designed into computer based instruction known as Integrated Learning System. This is a one-on-one system between the student and an Education Establishment corporation using a tablet and the Internet. In certain instances, neither the parent nor the teacher has access to the student's material.

One of the most insidious aspects of our government controlled education system with credentialed teachers as change agents is the war on the individual's conscience, a stealth invasion of our inalienable rights of property. Founding Father James Madison summed this up best in his "Memorial and Remonstrance Against Religious Assessments (1785):"

> The religion then of every man must be left to the conviction and conscience of every man; and it is the right of every man to exercise it as these may dictate. This right is in its nature an unalienable right. It is unalienable; because the opinions of men, depending only on the evidence contemplated by their own minds, cannot follow the dictates of other men: It is unalienable also; because what is here a right towards men, is a duty towards the Creator. [92]

And Gerald R. Thompson states:

> We must take care not to force an interpretation which puts anyone in the position of violating either their own conscience, or the conscience of another. If the conscience is truly sacred, then the last thing God would ever call anyone to do is to violate anyone's conscience, including their own. [93]

---

[92] https://www.revolutionary-war-and-beyond.com/memorial-and-remonstrance-against-religious-assessments.html
[93] Thompson, Gerald R., "Self-Government, Conscience & True Liberty: The Law of Conscience," https://lonang.com/commentaries/foundation/self-government-law-of-conscience/

119

Recall the goal of the Hegelian Dialectic is to abandon absolute truth, adopt moral relativism and reach consensus by compromise. Does this not require each participant to compromise their incoming conscience of values, beliefs and attitudes to play by the dialectic rules for consensus?

The battle is over which sovereign, social sphere is responsible for the child? Is it the family and parents' sphere or the state's sphere? From a Western Civilization worldview the parents are responsible. From the cultural Marxist worldview the state demands the responsibility, by force if necessary.

Do you recall Hillary Clinton's book *It Takes a Village* to raise a child? Dr. Melissa Harris-Perry, a professor of political science at Tulane University and host of the Melissa Harris-Perry show on Saturday and Sunday mornings on MSNBC summed it up recently:

> "We have never invested as much in public education as we should have because we've always had kind of a private notion of children: your kid is yours and totally your responsibility. We haven't had a very collective notion of these are our children....So part of it is we have to break through our kind of private idea that kids belong to their parents or kids belong to their families, and recognize that kids belong to whole communities" [94]

And as the state takes responsibility away from the parents the parents are forced to relinquish their authority to the brainwashing efforts by the state. California is only one example, but not unique. Most teachers believe they are doing the right thing because this is part of their worldview:

> Normally, parents are not notified that their children are going to be subjected to propaganda on homosexuality or transgenderism. But increasingly, governments are outright prohibiting parents from opting their children

---

[94] James, Michael, "MSNBC: We Have to Break Through This Idea 'That Kids Belong to Their Parents'," https://www.cnsnews.com/news/article/msnbc-we-have-break-through-idea-kids-belong-their-parents April 8, 2013

out. Even in California's Orange County, once a conservative bastion, school officials declared that all children must be exposed to material that "discusses gender, gender identity, gender expressions, sexual orientation," and more. Parents who disagree "may not excuse their children from this instruction," the school board said in a legal memo, adding that parents were still allowed to "advise their children that they disagree with some or all of the information……..

The madness is now worldwide, too. In early 2018, the UN Educational, Scientific, and Cultural Organization (UNESCO) released its Comprehensive Sexuality Education standards for use in every school in every country on Earth, beginning in kindergarten at age five. Among other controversies, the UN's planetary sex-ed scheme advocates masturbation, abortion, gender confusion, homosexuality, homosexual parenting, contraception, fornication, and much more. The full-blown assault on parental rights and traditional morality could devastate a generation of young people, critics said. [95]

The Education Establishment classifies all students as 'human capital.' Over the years we have abdicated our roles as sovereign individuals to be controlled cogs strictly for the purposes of the state. Government controlled schools are assuring this movement to total control without parental consent or the student's knowledge:

[T]he "social and emotional learning" schemes under ESSA will not just gather information on children's attitudes and beliefs, but systematically work to change them, too. As reported by Benjamin Herold in *Education Week*, under the guise of providing "personalized learning experiences," new technology is targeting students' "individual emotions, cognitive processes,

---

[95] Newman, "Government Schools Are Sexualizing, Perverting, and Confusing Children"

'mindsets,' and character and personality traits." These schemes include "new efforts to dramatically expand the types of data collected in the classroom and to focus more attention on responding to individual students' 'mindsets,' non-cognitive skills, and emotional states." [96]

The War on Western Civilization

…multiculturalism involves the systematic restructuring of the curriculum so as to hinder students from learning about the Western tradition.–T. Kenneth Cribb, Jr., from a previous chapter titled 'Political Correctness in Higher Education'

Allen Quist, farmer, professor, former Minnesota House of Representatives member, and editor of CurriculumModules.org, also authored *FedEd: The New Federal Curriculum and How It is Enforced*. He summarized the themes of Goals 2000 that the Clinton administration produced that also carried over to No Child Left Behind of the Bush II administration and Common Core of the Obama administration. The 7 themes are: [97]

1. undermine national sovereignty [for a New World Order}
2. redefine natural rights [w/ positive rights & social justice]
3. minimize natural law [w/ positive law]
4. promote global environmentalism [undo capitalism]
5. emphasize global economy/global citizenship [undo nationalism & patriotism]
6. enforce multiculturalism [undo E Pluribus Unum]
7. emphasize job skills over knowledge [dumb down & collectivize]

Journalist Alex Newman noted the methods for scaring school children to accept the UN's agenda towards globalism:

---

[96] Newman, Alex and Pesta, Duke, "Insanity In the Classroom: Government Schools Today," *The New American,* https://www.thenewamerican.com/print-magazine/item/31227-insanity-in-the-classroom-government-schools-today (February 4, 2019)

[97] Quist, Allen, *FedEd:The New Federal Curriculum and How It's Enforced*, St Paul, MN, Maple River Education Coalition, 2002)

At school, children are already being indoctrinated and terrorized. In an interview with Fox host John Stossel, terrified little children admit they are worried Global Warming will kill them and flood their town. "What are you most worried will happen?" Stossel asks a classroom full of children who appear to be between six and eight. One little boy quickly responds, "We'll all die!" The children then admit they are being taught this by their teachers. Similar brainwashing is taking place at every government school in America and around the world. In some U.S. schools children are given letters to send their local elected officials urging them to take climate action.[98]

"In the summer of 2016, a UN summit in Korea came up with a planetary "Action Plan" outlining how to use "education" to transform children into "global citizens." …The document reveals that the spirituality the would-be global educators envision has nothing in common with Christianity or Western civilization. Schooling must, for instance, inculcate "a sense of care for the earth" and "reverence for the interdependent kinship of all life." … The document goes on to "commit" the signatories to an educational regime that promotes "a deep appreciation for diversity," "gender equality" (read: radical feminism), "interdependence," "multicultural competence, "social justice, "sustainable development," and more. [99]

Dr. Mary Graber, PhD, addresses the conscience bending Social and Emotional Learning (SEL) initiatives that began during the Obama era of education reform and continues today. From her report "Changing Consciousness: Conflict Resolution, Emotional Intelligence, and Peace Studies for a One-World Government A report from the Third

[98] Newman, Alex, "Rescuing Our Children," *The New American,* https://www.thenewamerican.com/print-magazine/item/31225-rescuing-our-children, (February 4, 2019)
[99] Newman, "Education's Future: Globalization of Indoctrination,"

International Conference on Conflict Resolution Education" we find the goal of global citizenship and global governance:

> The fact that an anti-American and anti-Western bias provides the impetus for this movement can be seen by an objective look at the history of Western civilization. A study of our history, politics, and philosophy reveals a progression of means to resolve conflicts nonviolently whenever possible. Traditional notions like free speech, reasoned debate, nondiscriminatory laws, freedom, and citizen rights all reveal a march toward a progressively less violent society. In the classroom, students were once taught such values through didactic and imaginative literature of the Western cultural tradition. They were taught the skills of debating both orally and in written form using logic and evidence. A common goal of truth informed the process. These lessons were reinforced by a classroom atmosphere of discipline and order in small neighborhood schools less subject to the educational bureaucracies and legal requirements of today. (Now, a few specially designated traditional schools, designed to meet the demand for parents who want that kind of atmosphere for their students, have appeared.)

> *But safety and civility are redefined in the brave new schools envisioned by Kevin Jennings and his boss, Education Secretary Arne Duncan. A new kind of citizen will be molded in Jennings' "safe schools," which through his re-definition means no student will be subject to "social rejection, uncivil behavior, verbal threats, and hate language." Draconian methods are needed to dictate to children even their social choices.*

> The methods are scary, and involve such group activities as "truth sessions" and "trust exercises." As I describe in my report [100] such exercises invade students' privacy and further

---

[100] Grabar, Mary, "Indoctrination without Apology: Social Studies Teachers Share Strategies on How to Mold Students", https://marygrabar.com/images/sample-data/pdfs/Indoctrinationwithoutapology.pdf

subject them to emotional manipulations. Citizens, parents, and elected officials should be concerned.

The larger goal is to train the student in peace-building skills that he can carry over into adulthood as a "global citizen" and perhaps a global leader. In the attempt to achieve this goal American and Western values of justice, fairness, and lawfulness are shunned in favor of international law, cooperation, and global social justice.

....This new approach fits with the goals of educators who see their roles as agents of social change and their students as subjects to carry it out. While it makes sense that individuals who are stymied by emotionally upsetting home lives or poor coping skills would be helped by learning new strategies aimed at addressing these problems, the way such therapy is used—on an indiscriminate group scale—and the ideological goals it is mixed up with—reveal that it is not the individual student and her academic success that is the prime concern of such educators. [101]

Refer to the chapters *A New Front: Environmentalism* and *Green New Deal Reveals the Naked Truth of Agenda 21* (chapters 9 & 10) in this book for additional details of the environmentalism agenda and its drive for global citizenship, global governance.

Across the nation, in the government controlled K-12 institutions, teachers have been organizing their students into cultural Marxist political props to protest against Western Civilization values. This is straight out of Saul Alinsky's *Rules for Radicals*. The Common Core compliant textbooks emphasize activism as the way to control society. The irony is these students have intentionally been severely short-changed on a decent American history and civics education but heavily brainwashed to be 'cultural workers' to destroy liberty.

---

[101] Grabar, Mary, "Changing Consciousness: Conflict Resolution, Emotional Intelligence, and Peace Studies for a One-World Government," https://marygrabar.com/images/sampledata/pdfs/grabar_reprt_kevinjennings.pdf

Why do despots and big government left-wing authoritarians focus on the indoctrination and deployment of the youth? It is because they are the most vulnerable to propaganda. They lack the critical intellectual skills to weigh values – especially when alternative opinion is abolished.

This is why the American left attempts to control the education of the next generation. It is why they proffer only one view to the exclusion of free speech and civil debate.

The left is using the children of America to advance their narrow agenda. To see hundreds of thousands of school children being organized to skip school, and to take up partisan issues, should shock and scare every freedom loving American. [102]

What can be done?

Cultural Marxism is so deeply embedded in the K-12 government controlled education system that there is very little room for honest reform. The Education Establishment is too powerful to overcome at every level of government control. Charter schools can offer some relief from total indoctrination into cultural Marxism, if the curriculum is an actual classical liberal arts program based solely on Western Civilization. The charter schools, however, are missing the most important reason for educating children....to know and understand Jesus Christ as Lord and Savior and the center of Truth.

A Christian family is left with two choices that conform to scripture: homeschool or enroll in a Christian Worldview school. This is not only biblical for raising Godly children, but necessary to restore America back from its current death spiral.

---

[102] Horist, Larry, "HORIST: Stop misusing school kids as political props and puppets," http://punchingbagpost.com/2019/05/09/horist-stop-misusing-school-kids-as-political-props-and-puppets/?listab_list=listab_list, (May 9, 2019)

Chapter 13

Political Correctness in Higher Education

T. Kenneth Cribb, Jr.

The University of Florida defines social justice by invoking identity-group politics and oppression. The social justice the University teaches is the social justice of the radical activists.

Radical social justice theory – which we'll just call "social justice" from now on, since the radicals dominate higher education – draws heavily on scholarly schools that have grown up around the work of a few notable intellectuals. Key words in social justice vocabulary make this debt clear. **Power** *invokes the writings of Michel Foucault and Saul Alinsky.* **Gender identity and expression** *draws upon Judith Butler.* **Critical race theory** *cites Derrick Bell.* **Privilege** *depends upon the work of Peggy McIntosh. Virtually every abstract concept in the University of Florida's definition of social justice –* **access, allyship, inequality, needs, social responsibility** *– draws upon social justice's theoretical framework instead of the common-sense definitions of the dictionary. -- David Randall, director of research at the National Association of Scholars* [103] [inserted by Editor]

On a growing number of university campuses the freedom to articulate and discuss ideas – a principle that has been the cornerstone of higher education since the time of Socrates – is eroding at an alarming rate. Consider just one increasing trend: hundreds (sometimes thousands) of copies of conservative student newspapers have been either stolen or publicly burned by student radicals. In many cases these acts have taken place with the tacit support of faculty and administrators. The perpetrators are rarely disciplined.

---

[103] Randall, David, "Social Justice Education in America," National Association of Scholars, https://www.nas.org/reports/social-justice-education-in-america/full-report , Dec 2019, 41-42

While it would be easy to dismiss such demonstrations of tolerance as student pranks, these incidents are the surface manifestations of a more pervasive and insidious trend – a trend that has as its goal the destruction of the liberal arts tradition that has helped create and sustain Western civilization.

Though some pundits have claimed that the prevalence of the ideological intolerance known as political correctness has been exaggerated, the opposite is closer to the truth. Political correctness has become so deeply ingrained in American higher education that many campuses are now dominated by an atmosphere of uncertainty and apprehension. An increasing number of dedicated students and faculty members now live in fear that their intellectual pursuit of truth will offend the Grand Inquisitors of political correctness.

The techniques of political correctness are now well known: attacks on the curriculum in the name of "multiculturalism," the imposition of restrictive and vaguely-worded "speech codes," and mandatory "sensitivity training" courses for freshman that are little more than systematic efforts at ideological indoctrination. But the influence of political correctness has spread in other disturbing ways. Consider a few recent incidents from the university battlefield.

- At Amherst College in Massachusetts, a homosexual student group covered the university's sidewalks with graffiti, including the slogan "Queer by Divine Right," which was scrawled in front of the campus chapel on Good Friday. When the *Amherst Spectator*, a conservative student newspaper, criticized these chalkings as promoting "hatred and division," student protestors publicly burned copies of the paper.

- When the *Cornell Review*, another conservative student newspaper, published a parody of the course descriptions from Cornell's heavily-politicized Africana Department, campus militants blocked traffic at the center of the campus for several hours and burned stolen copies of the *Review* in a metal trash can. The militants went on to demand that the university provide "racial sensitivity" classes for incoming freshman, a campus speech code, and more money for segregated minority programs such as a blacks-only dormitory.

- Students who participate in ROTC programs have told friends and family that they are afraid to show up for class wearing their uniform because their grades have been arbitrarily marked down by faculty members who are hostile to the military.

- In the wake of a rash of sexual harassment charges that have been filed by extreme feminists against their alleged enemies, some professors have begun to take out insurance policies to protect themselves from the crushing financial burden of malicious and frivolous lawsuits.

- A faculty questionnaire at the University of Massachusetts asks professors what "contribution to multi-culturalism" they have made. The questionnaire is then used in making decisions about tenure and promotion.

It is worth remembering that for every dramatic and well-publicized example of political correctness, there are innumerable instances where it is more subtle, but just as real.

The Origins of Political Correctness in Higher Education

While the ideology of political correctness is hardly restricted to our campuses, there is no doubt it originated there. The intellectual roots of this phenomenon stretch back over centuries. Ultimately, the origins of PC can be traced to the rise of modern ideology and its quest for power. In contrast to the classical and Judeo-Christian traditions, which stressed man's need to understand the moral order and conform himself to it, modern ideologies have sought to dominate and control the world. In the twentieth century these ideologies gained political power in Communist states.

But in the West, ideology has not been able to make such a direct assault on our traditions of ordered liberty. Rather, radical intellectuals have sought to undermine the foundations of knowledge itself, concentrating their efforts on the transformation of the university.

The turning point in the academy came in the 1960s, when militant students launched a guerilla attack on the traditions of Western culture and the liberal arts. Seeing that they could not gain lasting power through demonstrations alone, many of these militants opted to remain "in the system," going on to become professors themselves. This generation of "tenured radicals" (to use Roger Kimball's phrase) has now become the establishment in the vast majority of our institutions of higher learning. As university presidents, deans, and department chairmen, they have set about hiring other ideologues in their own image and have instigated the repressive policies we know as political correctness. These politicized academics will be extremely difficult to dislodge from their current positions of power.

Ideology vs. Liberal Education

The stakes in this war of ideas are high, for they include the very concept of freedom itself. Americans have always understood the intimate and vital connection between liberal education and political liberty. That is why political correctness is nothing less than a death blow aimed at the heart of our republic.

In his seminal book *The Idea of a University*, Cardinal John Henry Newman defined the "liberal arts" as a pursuit of knowledge for its own sake. By way of contrast, he defined the "servile arts" as those modes of study that serve only specific, immediate ends. The liberal arts are liberating, Newman argued, because they enable men to discover the underlying principles that guide us toward wisdom and virtue.

Were he alive today, Newman would view political correctness as "servile" because its purpose is to advance a political agenda to a position of national power. Militant professors in increasing numbers are shamelessly turning their podiums into pulpits, abandoning the search for objective truth and setting about the task of indoctrinating their students.

The Devastated Curriculum

The proponents of political correctness have concentrated their efforts on the core of a liberal education, the curriculum. Their efforts will radically alter what new generations of Americans will learn. In this battle the handmaiden of political correctness has been the "multicultural" movement. A number of critics have rightly pointed out that multiculturalism is more than an argument for courses that concentrate on groups that at one time were disadvantaged or oppressed. Rather, multiculturalism involves the systematic restructuring of the curriculum so as to hinder students from learning about the Western tradition. Since the ulterior motive behind political correctness is an attempt to restructure American society along egalitarian lines, it is imperative for its proponents to instill in the minds of students a thoroughgoing cultural relativism.

Perhaps the most disturbing aspect of the politically correct assault on the curriculum is that it has occurred at many of America's elite universities. Take, for example, the case of Stanford University, an institution that has long played a leadership role in American higher education. Stanford eliminated its long-standing Western civilization requirement in 1988 and replaced it with a multicultural program known as "Cultures, Ideas, and Values." Under this new program freshmen at Stanford can just as easily study Marxist revolutionaries in Central America as they can Plato, Shakespeare, or Newton.

Stanford has also led the movement away from serious study of history. Students at Stanford, like students at all but one of the other top 50 universities in the United States, are not required to take a single course in history. Instead, they are offered a choice of courses under the heading of "American Cultures." According to one recent graduate at Stanford, it is impossible to fulfill the "American Cultures" requirement by studying Protestantism, Irish Americans, or the American West, while courses that do fulfill the requirement include "Film and Literature: US-Mexico Border Representations" and "Contemporary Ethnic Drama." Stanford students must also take courses in "World Cultures" and "Gender Studies" that include

"Chicana Expressive Culture" and "Misogyny and Feminism in the Renaissance."

Because elite institutions such as Stanford set an example for the rest of American higher education, other universities eagerly adopt these devastating assaults on the curriculum. This "trickle-down" effect will have a long-lasting impact on the way future generations of Americans will be educated.

Intolerance and the Assault on Freedom

The two pillars that have traditionally sustained the liberal arts are academic freedom and freedom of speech. Without the freedom to pursue the truth and to write and speak freely, authentic scholarship is impossible. But both of these fundamental freedoms have been routinely abrogated by the establishment of speech codes, "sensitivity" classes, and a general atmosphere of fear and intimidation on campus.

For example, younger professors who have not received tenure must not only be careful of what they say, but of what they publish. Ideological university administrators in the 1990s have created an environment dominated by suspicion that is far more intense than anything spawned by anti-Communist Senator Joseph McCarthy in the 1950s.

The most tragic victims of this age of political correctness are the students. The traditional goal of a liberal arts education – acculturation, whereby students absorb the inherited wisdom of the past – has been set aside. Increasingly, a university education today seems to involve rote learning of political opinions. When all is said and done, political correctness substitutes smug feelings of righteousness for the traditional habits of critical thinking. One distinguished scholar recently lamented that "higher education is increasingly about acquiring attitudes and opinions that one puts on like a uniform."

Because the academy is a relatively isolated world, it can allow politicized administrators to turn the campus into a laboratory for experiments in social transformation. When critics of political correctness have compared the atmosphere on campus to that of a totalitarian state, liberal pundits have been quick to denounce them as hysterical. Few of these pundits have any first-hand experience of daily life on campus.

The Movement for Academic Reform

Despite the institutional power of the campus radicals, forces are at work seeking to spur authentic academic reform. The academic reform movement relies on the principles of accountability, communication, and a commitment to authentic scholarship. One force of academic reform is a growing demand among parents for greater accountability from colleges and universities. At a time when studies show that students are paying more and learning less than ever before, parents in increasing numbers are becoming discriminating consumers.

Another force is independent student newspapers whose journalists publicize the antics of political correctness on campus. In the past, campus radicals thrived unchallenged in the enclosed world of the university, but their actions are no longer going undetected. The advent of conservative student newspapers on dozens of campuses has forced campus militants into the open where they are most vulnerable to the scrutiny of an exasperated public.

Two years ago, those who fund the Collegiate Network asked the Intercollegiate Studies Institute to take over the administration of their program to support and enhance responsible student journalism. The Collegiate Network contributes seed money, practical help, and intellectual guidance to the 60 conservative student newspapers which provide alternative forums of discussion at many of the nation's most elite (and closed-minded) universities.

These alternative papers have identified abuses at all levels of academic life and engaged in investigative journalism that has been remarkably fair and accurate. Perhaps the most well-known "scoop" came from Yale University's alternative paper, *Light & Truth*, a publication supported by the Collegiate Network. The editors of *Light & Truth* discovered that the $20 million gift of alumnus Lee Bass was not being used for its intended purpose of supporting an integrated course in Western civilization. Their report broke open the scandal, which ended when Yale returned Mr. Bass's money. The subsequent furor cost Yale a great deal more than Mr. Bass's $20 million – both in monetary terms and in the loss of confidence of many Yale donors that the current administration can be trusted.

Not all the scandals uncovered by alternative campus papers are of this magnitude, but there are innumerable abuses that can be exposed by investigative student journalism. The law school at the University of North Carolina, Chapel Hill, banned representatives of the U.S. military from setting up recruiting tables there, despite receiving federal tax dollars from the Defense Department. An article about this outrageous assault on freedom that ran in both the student-run *Carolina Review* and in the national student newspaper published by ISI, *CAMPUS*, raised a hue and cry on and off campus. North Carolina legislators took immediate action and passed a bill prohibiting taxpayer-supported schools from discriminating against the military when prospective employers come to the university.

At the University of Wisconsin, Madison, the *UWM Times*, a conservative student newspaper, revealed that a university administrator had been soliciting signatures for local Democrat candidates for public office, in direct violation of a state law forbidding university employees from engaging in political campaigning. The university refused to reprimand the administrator in question – perhaps because the chancellor himself violated both the state law and his own directive by signing one of the petitions while at work. The story was picked up by the *Milwaukee Journal-Sentinel* and the abuse was brought to an end.

Now that alternative newspapers and organizations dedicated to academic reform are spreading the word, the larger communities that surround our institutions of higher education are getting more involved in serious academic reform. For example, the National Association of Scholars is encouraging university trustees to take a more active and vocal role in opposing the excesses of political correctness. Efforts of this type must be expanded and intensified.

In the long run, the most direct method of defeating the inquisitors of political correctness is simply to stand up to them. Individual acts of defiance often entail serious risks: students can face star-chamber proceedings that are humiliating and demoralizing while faculty can lose their bids to receive tenure. But every act of resistance causes a ripple, encouraging others to stand up to ideological intimidation. With the support of a significant number of parents, donors, and alumni, these Davids may yet slay the Goliaths who tower over them.

The Fire of True-Learning

Perhaps the strongest force for true academic reform is that which seeks to defeat the ideological depredations of political correctness by winning the war of ideas. The best students have a questioning intelligence that cannot be satisfied with political slogans. When such students have access to serious scholarship they respond with enthusiasm. Even today acculturation still takes place under the mentorship of outstanding scholars at various institutions around the country. Moreover, some colleges and universities continue to swim against the ideological tides of our time.

The Intercollegiate Studies Institute (ISI), in conjunction with the Templeton Foundation, has identified the best professors, departments, colleges, and textbooks in American higher education today. This program, the Templeton Honor Rolls for Education in a Free Society, celebrates excellence and serves as a guide for parents and students contemplating the daunting choice of which college or university to attend. By singling out the best in higher education, the Templeton Honor Rolls also encourage donors to reward universities that preserve the traditions of the free society.

Prospective college students, their parents, and donors can also benefit from a comprehensive guide to 100 of the top institutions of higher learning in America published by the ISI. The guide contains substantial, essay-length treatments of all 100 institutions, including 80 elite schools that were selected on the basis of competitive admissions standards and 20 schools that ISI particularly recommends for their commitment to a liberal arts education. The ISI college guide warns students about the ideological dangers on the campuses and steers them in the direction of the best professors and departments. As best-selling author William J. Bennett wrote of this project, "All too often, Americans treat colleges and universities with a deference that prevents them from asking hard questions and demanding real results. But if there was ever to be a genuine, long-lasting education reform, parents and students will have to become shrewder and better-informed consumers of education. The ISI guide is a powerful tool in this effort."

One of Edmund Burke's most famous sayings is that "the only thing necessary for the triumph of evil is for good men to do nothing." For generations, Americans have treated higher education with awe – a token of their faith in the liberating power of the liberal arts. But in the face of political correctness, it is time for the American public to temper its respect with a critical sensibility, and to undertake a more direct effort to call academia to account. It is time for good men and women to demand that American higher education live up to its best traditions and eschew the tyranny of political correctness.

Chapter 14

Social Justice Education in America[104]

Executive Summary
December 2019
by Dr. David Randall, Ph.D.

Chapter 13, Political Correctness in Higher Education by T. Kenneth Cribb, Jr., was penned during the early stages of the transition takeover in higher education. This chapter discusses the more recent progression of cultural Marxism in higher education. Not too surprising, this progression has also taken hold in government K-12 education, the mass media, industry, government institutions and political parties.

Cultural Marxism is a transitional worldview designed to fundamentally transform America into a Marxist nation under global governance. This process requires constant, incremental changes to our culture through its institutions which also includes changes of meaning for terms and labels. Over the past 60 years cultural Marxism has been called the New Left, Progressivism, radical social justice, Post Modernism, Political Correctness, Socialism, etc. You will encounter such terms in this chapter. Editor

American universities have drifted from the political center for fifty years and more. By now scarcely any conservatives or moderates remain, and most of them are approaching retirement. The radical establishment triumphed on campus a generation ago. What they have created since is an even more disturbing successor to the progressive academy of the 1990s. In the last twenty years, a generation of academics and administrators has emerged that is no longer satisfied with

---

[104] Randall, "Social Justice Education in America, " National Association of Scholars, https://www.nas.org/reports/social-justice-education-in-america/full-report, (Dec 4, 2019)

using the forms of traditional scholarship to teach progressive thought. This new generation seeks to transform higher education itself into an engine of progressive political advocacy, subjecting students to courses that are nothing more than practical training in progressive activism. This new generation bases its teaching and research on the ideology of *social justice*.

The concept of *social justice* originated in nineteenth-century Catholic thought, but it has become secular and progressive in twenty-first-century America. Justice traditionally judges freely chosen individual acts, but social justice judges how far the distribution of economic and social benefits among social groups departs from how they "ought" to be distributed. Practically, social justice also justifies the exercise of the state's coercive power to distribute "fairly" goods that include education, employment, housing, income, health care, leisure, a pleasant environment, political power, property, social recognition, and wealth.

What we may call *radical social justice theory*, which dominates higher education, adds to broader social justice theory the belief that society is divided into social identity groups defined by categories such as class, race, and gender; that any "unfair distribution" of goods among these groups is *oppression*; and that oppression can only— and *must*—be removed by a coalition of "marginalized" identity groups working to radically transform politics, society, and culture to eliminate *privilege*.

A rough, incomplete catalogue of the social justice movement's political goals includes increased federal and state taxation; increased minimum wage; increased environmental regulation; increased government health care spending and regulation; restrictions on free speech; restrictions on due process protections; maximizing the number of legislative districts that will elect racial minorities; support for the Black Lives Matter movement; mass release of criminals from prison;

decriminalizing drugs; ending enforcement of our immigration laws; amnesty for illegal aliens; open borders; race and sex preferences in education and employment; persecution of conscientious objectors to homosexuality; advocacy for "transgender rights"; support for the anti- Israeli Boycott, Divest, and Sanction movement; avowal of a right to abortion; and mob violence to enforce the social justice policy agenda.

Social justice advocates' emphasis on words such as *justice, equity, rights,* and *impact* all register social justice's fundamental goal of acquiring governmental power. Social justice advocates tend to dedicate any activity in which they engage to the effort to achieve the political ends of social justice. Activism is the exemplary means to forward social justice. This word signifies the collective exertion of influence via social justice nonprofit organizations. *Activism* may take the form of organization-building (staff work, fundraising, membership recruitment), publicity, lobbying, and actions by responsible officials in pursuit of social justice. It may also take the form of "protest" — assembling large numbers of people on the streets to "persuade" responsible officials into executing the preferred policies of social justice advocates. Social justice activism formally eschews violence, but far too many social justice advocates are willing to engage in all "necessary" violence.

Social justice activists in the university are subordinating higher education toward the goal of achieving social justice. Social justice education takes the entire set of social justice beliefs as the predicate for education, in every discipline from accounting to zoology. Social justice education rejects the idea that classes should aim at teaching a subject matter for its own sake, or seek to foster students' ability to think, judge, and write as independent goods. Social justice education instead aims directly at creating effective social justice activists, ideally engaged during class in such activism. Social justice education transforms the very definitions of academic disciplines — first

139

to permit the substitution of social justice activism for intellectual endeavor, and then to require it.

Social justice educators define education as *the practice of social justice activism. Experiential learning,* which is vocational training in social justice activism, is the heart of social justice education. Other prominent elements include *action learning, action research, action science, advocacy-oriented research, classroom action research, collaborative inquiry, community research, critical action research, emancipatory research, participatory action research,* and *social justice research.*

Most colleges and universities today operate under tight fiscal constraints, which lead to dwindling numbers of tenure-track faculty jobs and allow expanding numbers of administrative jobs. These constraints shape the means by which social justice educators extend their influence. They focus on four broad strategic initiatives: 1) the alteration of university and department mission statements; 2) the seizure of internal graduation requirements; 3) the capture of disciplines or creation of pseudo- disciplines; and 4) the capture of the university administration.

The first strategic initiative, alteration of mission statements, provides a wedge by which to pursue the latter three. Social justice educators pursue these other three initiatives with the practical goal to reserve as many jobs as possible for social justice advocates, particularly in higher education, K–12 education, and social work. The capture of the university administration, above all, gives social justice advocates a career track and the expectation of lifetime employment. Social justice advocates want to reserve for themselves *all* of the ca. 1.5 million American jobs for postsecondary teachers and administrators.

Social justice advocates' first goal is to incorporate *social justice,* or related words, into college and university mission statements. This social justice vocabulary sometimes serves as hollow words to fob off social justice advocates. Yet it also works as a promissory note for more detailed changes to impose social justice education. A social justice mission statement generally indicates that a higher education institute no longer really aims to educate students. It really aims at social justice activism, and it will only provide education that doesn't conflict with social justice ideology. The ideal of social justice does not complement the ideal of education. **The ideal of social justice *replaces* the ideal of education.**

Social justice advocates' most important curricular tactic within higher education is to insert one or more social justice requirements into the general education requirements. They give these requirements different names, including Diversity, Experiential Learning, Sustainability, Global Studies, and, forthrightly, Social Justice. This tactic forces all college students to take at least one social justice course, and thereby maximizes the effect of social justice propaganda. The common practice of double counting a social justice requirement so that it also satisfies another requirement powerfully reinforces the effect of social justice requirements. These requirements also effectively reserve a large number of teaching jobs and tenure-track lines for social justice educators. No one but a social justice advocate, after all, is really qualified to teach a course in social justice advocacy. **The direct financial burden of social justice general education requirements is at least $10 billion a year nationwide, and rising fast.**

Social justice advocates also have taken over or created a substantial portion of the academic departments in our universities. The departments most likely to advertise their commitment to social justice are those most central to the social justice educators' ideological vision, political goals, and ambition for employment. The heaviest concentrations of social justice departments are the Identity Group Studies, Gender Studies, Peace Studies, and Sustainability Studies pseudo-disciplines; the career track departments of

141

Education, Social Work, and Criminology; and the departments dedicated to activism such as Civic Engagement, Leadership, and Social Justice. Social justice takes over departments by incorporating social justice into their mission statements, inserting departmental requirements for social justice education, and dedicating as many elective courses as possible to social justice education. When social justice educators control departments entirely, they rapidly shift the definition of that discipline so that it requires social justice education. These changes make it practically impossible to study that discipline without embracing social justice.

Social justice departments denominate their vocational training in activism as *experiential learning* — or related terms such as *civic engagement, community engagement, fieldwork, internships, practica*, and *service-learning*. *Service-learning* usually refers to relatively unpoliticized experiential learning, which habituates students to the basic forms and techniques of activism, while *civic engagement* usually refers to more avowedly political social justice activism. The term *experiential learning* disguises what is essentially vocational training in progressive activism by pretending that it is no different from an internship with an engineering firm. Many supposedly academic social justice courses also focus on readying students for experiential learning courses — and for a further career in social justice activism. Experiential learning courses are what particularly distinguishes social justice education from its progressive forebears. Experiential learning courses, dedicated outright to progressive activism, drop all pretense that teachers and students are engaged in the search for knowledge. *Experiential learning* is both a camouflaging euphemism and a marker of social justice education.

While social justice education has made great strides among university professors, its dizziest success has been its takeover of the university administration. Higher education administration is now even more liberal than the professoriate. The training of higher education administrators, especially within the labyrinth of "co-curricular" bureaucracies, increasingly makes commitment to social justice an explicit or an implicit requirement. These administrators insert themselves into all aspects of student life, both outside and inside the classroom. Overwhelmingly, they exercise their power to promote social justice. Social justice administrators catechize students in social justice propaganda; select social justice advocates as outside speakers; funnel students to off-campus social justice organizations that benefit from free student labor; and provide jobs and money for social justice cadres among the student body. The formation of social justice bureaucracies also serves as an administrative stepping stone to the creation of social justice departments. Perhaps most importantly, university administration provides a career for students specializing in social justice advocacy.

Higher education's administrative bloat has facilitated the growth of social justice bureaucracies — among them, Offices of Diversity and Multicultural Affairs; Title IX coordinators; Offices of First-Year Experience and Community Engagement; Offices of Student Life and Residential Life; Offices of Service-Learning and Civic Engagement; Offices of Equity and Inclusion; Offices of Sustainability and Social Justice; and miscellaneous institutes and centers. These bureaucracies focus on *co-curricular activities*, which consist largely of social justice activities such as Intersectionality Workshops and Social Justice Weekend Retreats. Social justice administrators aim to subordinate the curriculum to the co-curriculum, as the practical way to subordinate the pursuit of truth to social justice advocacy.

Social justice administrators have set up institutions that make social justice advocacy inescapable. Offices of Residential Life have turned large amounts of housing into venues for social justice advocacy. The most intensive advocacy proceeds through *Living Learning Communities*—

143

housing units dedicated to themes such as Global Citizenship, Gender and Social Justice, and Social Justice Action. Bias Incident Response Teams, which rely on voluntary informers ("active bystanders") throughout campus, dedicate themselves to gathering reports of "bias incidents"—which, practically speaking, can include any word or action that offends social justice advocates. Bias Incident Response Teams act as enforcers of social justice orthodoxy on campus. Break and Study Abroad programs have also been largely taken over by social justice advocates, and are now frequently exercises in service-learning and social justice advocacy. Offices of Residential Life subject students to social justice education even while they are eating and sleeping, Bias Incident Response Teams monitor every private social interaction, and Study Abroad and Break programs subject students to social justice education even while they are away from campus.

The social justice bureaucracies sponsor a large number of social justice events on campus. These events are the actual substance of social justice education on campus. The varieties of social justice events include activism programs, commencements, community mobilizations, conferences, dialogues, festivities, films, fine arts performances, hunger banquets,[105] lectures, projects, residence hall programs, resource fairs, retreats, roundtables, student education, student training, workshops, and youth activities. The subjects of these events have included activism, ally education, Black Lives Matter, civic engagement, community organizing, diversity, food, gender identity, health care, illegal aliens,

---

[105] "During a Hunger Banquet, each group experiences the wealth or poverty of their representative group. The very rich dine on a meal that most North Americans would consider standard: meat, vegetables, side dishes and clean water. The middle class receives a small bowl of rice and beans, typical of the meal that middle-class households often consume around the world. The poorest group sits on the floor, receiving only a communal pot of rice that leaves them all hungry." Host a Hunger Banquet, Food for the Hungry, https:// www.fh.org/2014/03/06/host-a-hunger-banquet/.

implicit bias, leadership, LGBTQ, mental illness, policing, power, prisons, racial identity, social justice, and sustainability.

The social justice bureaucracies also engage in large amounts of student training. This student training identifies, catechizes, and provides work experience for the next generation of social justice advocates. This student training is especially useful for training the next generation of social justice educators. By scholarships, the provision of student jobs, and linking social justice cadres to careers, social justice educators ensure that social justice education is linked to social justice jobs for graduates. **The Diversity Peer Educator of today is the Dean of Diversity of tomorrow. Today's Social Justice Scholar will become tomorrow's Dean of Student Affairs.** Student training provides the cadres for social justice activism.

Social justice education, in addition, prepares students for positions in private industry (human resources, diversity associates), progressive nonprofit organizations, progressive political campaigns, progressive officials' offices, government bureaucracies, K-12 education, social work, court personnel, and the professoriate. University administration and faculty directly provide a massive source of employment for social justice advocates: the total number of social justice advocates employed in higher education must be well above 100,000. [106] Soon *all* of higher education may be reserved for social justice advocates, since university job advertisements have begun explicitly to require affirmations of diversity and social justice. These ideological loyalty oaths will effectively reserve higher education employment to the 8% of Americans who are progressive activists.[107]

---

[106] This is an informal estimate. No detailed study exists; one is sorely needed.
[107] Stephen Hawkins, et al., *Hidden Tribes: A Study of America's Polarized Landscape* (More in Common, 2018),
https://static1.squarespace.com/static/5a70a7c3010027736a22740f/t/5bbcea 6b7817f7bf7342b718/1539107467397/hidden_tribes_report-2.pdf., 6

Since social justice educators have to publish a minimum amount of peer-reviewed academic research to receive tenure, they have also created an apparatus of journal and book publication as *cargo-cult scholarship*—an imitation of the form of academic research, largely consisting of after-action reports on social justice activism on campus. The core of this cargo-cult apparatus is a network of hundreds of academic journals dedicated to social justice scholarship, whose editors and peer reviewers are also social justice educators. Their specializations mirror the range of social justice education—ethnic studies and gender studies, education journals and sustainability journals, journals devoted to critical studies, dialogue, diversity, equity, experiential education, inclusive education, intercultural communication, multicultural education, peace, service-learning, social inclusion—and, of course, social justice.

The bureaucracy of accreditation plays an important role in forwarding social justice advocacy at America's colleges and universities. Some accreditation bureaucracies require *diversity*, or other keywords that can be used to justify the creation of social justice requirements, programs, or assessments. Where accreditation bureaucracies do not explicitly require social justice advocacy, college bureaucrats often justify social justice advocacy as a way to fulfill other accreditation requirements. In both cases, social justice advocates within colleges and universities twist accreditation to advance their own agenda.

Education reformers must disrupt higher education's ability to provide stable careers for social justice advocates. These reforms cannot be aimed piecemeal at individual campuses. Social justice education is a national initiative, which has taken over entire disciplines and professions. Social justice's capture of higher education must be opposed on a similarly national scale. Above all, the opposition must aim at cutting off the national sources of funding for social justice education. A priority should be to deny public tax dollars for social justice education.

Nine general reforms would severely disrupt social justice education:

1. eliminate experiential learning courses;

2. remove social justice education from undergraduate general education requirements;

3. remove social justice education from introductory college courses;

4. remove social justice requirements from departments that provide employment credentials;

5. remove social justice positions from higher education administration;

6. restrict the power of social justice advocates in higher education administration;

7. eliminate the "co-curriculum";

8. remove social justice requirements from higher education job advertisements; and

9. remove social justice criteria from accreditation.

Most importantly of all, college students must cease cooperating with social justice requirements. **A mass, coordinated campaign of civil disobedience, in which students simply stop taking social justice classes, attending social justice events, or obeying social justice administrators, would deal a body-blow to social justice education.**

The New Civics Movement

New Civics has appropriated the name of an older subject, but not the content of that subject or its basic orientation to the world. Instead of trying to prepare students for adult participation in the self-governance of the nation, the New Civics tries to prepare students to become social and political activists who are grounded in broad antagonism towards America's founding principles and its republican ethos.[108]

"What is most new about the New Civics is that while it claims the name of civics, it is really a form of anti-civics. Civics in the traditional American sense meant learning about how our republic governs itself. The topics ranged from mastering simple facts, such as the branches of the federal government and the obligations of citizenship, to reflecting on the nature of Constitutional rights and the system of checks and balances that divide the states from the national government and the divisions of the national government from one another. A student who learns civics learns about voting, serving on juries, running for office, serving in the military, and all of the other key ways in which citizens take responsibility for their own government.

The New Civics has very little to say about most of these matters. It focuses overwhelmingly on turning students into "activists." Its largest preoccupation is getting students to engage in coordinated social action. Sometimes this involves political protest, but most commonly it involves volunteering for projects that promote progressive causes. At the University of Colorado at Boulder, for example, the New Civics includes such things as promoting dialogue between immigrants and native-born residents of Boulder County; marching in support of the United Farm Workers; and breaking down "gender binary" spaces in education.

Whatever one might think of these activities in their own right, they are a considerable distance away from what Americans used to mean by the word "civics." These sorts of activities are not something *added* to traditional civics instruction. They are presented as a complete and sufficient *substitute* for the traditional civics education." [109]

---

[108] Wood, Peter, preface to "Making Citizens: How American Universities Teach Civics," by David Randall, https://www.nas.org/reports/making-citizens-how-american-universities-teach-civics/full-report, (National Association of Scholars, Jan 24, 2017), 13
[109] Ibid. 11

"What we call the "New Civics" redefines civics as progressive political activism. Rooted in the radical program of the 1960s' New Left, the New Civics presents itself as an up-to-date version of volunteerism and good works. Though camouflaged with soft rhetoric, the New Civics, properly understood, is an effort to repurpose higher education.

The New Civics seeks above all to make students into enthusiastic supporters of the New Left's dream of "fundamentally transforming" America. The transformation includes:

- de-carbonizing the economy [Green New Deal legislation, Anthropogenic Global Warming alarmism, carbon taxes, legal prohibitions and restrictions of carbon based products],

- massively redistributing wealth [universal health care, free college tuition, universal basic income, reparations for grievances, growing list of entitlements],

- intensifying identity group grievance [dividing by Identity Politics, institutional oppression, LGBTQ+ agenda, Black Lives Matter protests, amnesty and resettlement for the Illegal Alien invasion, anti-Christian rhetoric, white privilege condemnations, anti-conservative protests, speech control],

- curtailing the free market [divesting from politically incorrect enterprises, excessive regulations, punitive taxation, lawfare and protests against politically incorrect enterprises],

- expanding government bureaucracy [surveillance of citizens, environmental controls, education controls, energy production and distribution controls, forced 'health' care, continual warfare],

- elevating international "norms" over American Constitutional law [educating for global citizenry, trade agreements towards a global economy and global governance], and

- disparaging our common history and ideals.

New Civics advocates argue among themselves which of these transformations should take precedence, but they agree that America must be transformed by "systemic change" from an unjust, oppressive society to a society that embodies social justice.

The New Civics hopes to accomplish this by teaching students that a good citizen is a radical activist, and it puts political activism at the center of everything that students do in college, including academic study, extra-curricular pursuits, and off-campus ventures.

New Civics builds on "service-learning," which is an effort to divert students from the classroom to vocational training as community activists [via Alinskyite community organizing methods]. By rebranding itself as "civic engagement," service-learning succeeded in capturing nearly all the funding that formerly supported the old civics. In practice this means that instead of teaching college students the foundations of law, liberty, and self-government, colleges teach students how to organize protests, occupy buildings, and stage demonstrations. These are indeed forms of "civic engagement," but they are far from being a genuine substitute for learning how to be a full participant in our republic.

New Civics has still further ambitions. Its proponents want to build it into every college class regardless of subject. The effort continues without so far drawing much critical attention from the public. This report aims to change that."[110]

---

[110] Randall, David, National Association of Scholars, "Making Citizens: How American Universities Teach Civics," https://www.nas.org/reports/making-citizens-how-american-universities-teach-civics/full-report, Jan 24, 2017, 14

Chapter 15

Political Correctness: Deconstruction and Literature

Jamie McDonald

Literature is, if not the most important cultural indicator, at least a significant benchmark of a society's level of civilization. Our nature and environment combine to form each individual mind, which in turn expresses itself into words. Literature, as the words society collectively holds up as exemplary, is then a starting point of sorts – a window into the culture.

Today's literary field is therefore worth examining for the insights it provides into our current cultural milieu. The contemporary American literary field is awash in "isms:" Marxism, Freudianism, feminism, and so on. Most of these are the academic cousins of what is called in the common culture "political correctness." Literary theorists take their particular brand of criticism and apply it to literature in an effort to find self-affirmation in a "discovered" meaning of the text. For a feminist critic, for example, no longer does Andrew Marvel's "Upon Appleton House" have the beauty of the grounds as its theme; it speaks instead of the evils of a patriarchal line of inheritance. These "cultural critics," so named because they critique literature based on the point of view of a particular culture, arose in the 60's, but their schools of criticism only truly began to pick up steam with the arrival of the schools of deconstruction in the 70's.

The works of the father of deconstruction, Jacques Derrida, began to be translated from the French by American professor Gayatri Spivak in the mid-1970s, a time when the U.S. literary scene was ripe for its influence. The economic Marxists were alive and well on American campuses, and the cultural critics were still being fed by the radical ism of the times. Feminists, "queer theorists," and "literature-by-people of color" critics had gained a foothold in the earlier decade, but they had in their meager arsenals only a vague feeling of repression. What they lacked was philosophical backing – the courage prompted by having their own *logos*. The arrival of deconstruction from France provided that philosophy.

At that time, that generation of academics was doing what all academics do, telling the previous generation that it had it all wrong. In this case the rebellion was against the New Critics – so-called even now, decades after their prime. The New Critics specialized in finding the meaning of texts without regard to background information such as authorial intent, a process that had "the text is everything" as its guiding principle.

The new generation of critics set out to turn that principle on its head. Instead of "the text is everything," the new generation claimed that "everything is text" and turned to analyzing anything and everything in relation to the literary work. If a poet wrote a poem that included a female character, the critics would look into the poet's relationship with his mother, his wife, his sister, and so on in an effort to offer up an interpretation of the work. This could have (and often did have) the positive effect of using biographic information to gain new understanding of the work; however, these new interpretations were not attempts to discern the true meaning of the work (as the New Critics had done) or even to discover the author's intended meaning (as traditional readings attempted). This new generation of critics instead became prime practitioners of what is known in literary circles as "cultural criticism." They strained to view literature from the "woman's point of view" or the "gay point of view" or the "radical minority point of view." Their attempts were not to find meaning – they were influenced too greatly by relativists for that – but to find sexism, racism, or "homophobia" in the works of male, European, or heterosexual authors.

Chapter 16

Critical masses

Education has become an exercise in tearing down without rebuilding [111]

Janie B. Cheaney (jcheaney@winsdtream.net)

*What educators call **critical thinking** or **higher order thinking skills** is actually the cultural Marxists' **Critical Theory**, a form of **deconstruction by criticizing the traditional social** order. The Hegelian Dialectic, consensus building process shuns absolute truth and relies on feelings, opinions and compromise. This inculcates moral relativism that also builds collectivist habits by destroying individualism and personal responsibility. – [inserted by Editor]*

Last month, in the journal *First Things*, senior editor R.R. Reno confessed his participation in "An Error Worse Than Error," namely the purported goal of higher education to question everything. "Students are trained — I was trained — to believe as little as possible so that the mind can be spared the ignominy of error. The consequences: an impoverished intellectual life."

Reno must know he's late to the party. The premise of Alan Bloom's *The Closing of the American Mind* (1987) is that "almost every student entering the university believes, or says he believes, that truth is relative." In *The Abolition of Man* (1947), C.S. Lewis described how the exchange of skepticism for truth created Men without Chests. In Chesterton's parable of the lamppost, widespread zeal to tear down a public source of light (because it's out of fashion and inconvenient) leads to men arguing forever after in the dark. All three authors were contemplating the effect of dismissing foundational principles as an aim of education. John Dewey already occupied that dark public

---

[111] Cheaney, Janie, "Critical masses: Education has become an exercise in tearing down without rebuilding," *WORLD Magazine*,
https://world.wng.org/2010/08/critical_masses, (Aug 27, 2010)

square, passionately arguing that "education as such has no aims" beyond equipping workers to work.

So the idea has been around for a while, but in order to seem fresh and relevant, it's tricked out in a new name: "critical thinking."

To think critically is a useful, often necessary tool; "critical thinking" is a noble concept that's lost its dignity after a mauling by ed-school theorizers. Like a gullible servant thrust onto the emperor's throne by manipulative handlers, it's become a figurehead: a catchphrase for deconstructing old received truths in order to replace them with new received truths. No child is to be left behind: Roger Kimball recalls a parent orientation meeting at his 5-year-old's school, where the virtues of critical thinking were eagerly promoted for the crayon set.

If old standards are overthrown, what will take their place? The recommended substitute is "creativity"—no one noticing, apparently, that "creative critical thinking" is an oxymoron. Critical thinking is essentially destructive; it's all about tearing down. To tear down false presuppositions is good and necessary but not complete; in education, the only valid purpose for destruction is to rebuild. That's where creativity is supposed to come in. But creativity doesn't exist in a vacuum—like skepticism, it's a means, not an end. It cries out for a theme. To treat creativity as an end in itself is to assume godlike character for humans, as though they could somehow create *ex nihilo*.

Of the many consequences of the critical-thinking fad, two stand out. One, if the destruction is allowed to stand, educated humans will be in the same situation as the man from whom one demon was cast out only to have seven others take its place. Declaring the great truths to be purely subjective (and therefore, ultimately, untrue) is not progress. Instead, it returns us to paganism, where moral authority belongs to the elites and the masses fall prey to superstition. As the saying goes, "He who stands for nothing will fall for anything."

Two, skepticism about major premises leads to over-reliance on minor ones. When the international website Wikileaks posted thousands of classified documents regarding the war in Afghanistan, it did so with the purpose of exposing American malfeasance. Wikileaks had the facts—lots of them. But focusing on isolated incidents obscures the

154

larger issue of what we're fighting about. Is the aim of one side — to destroy or neutralize an enemy that threatens world order — superior to the aim of the other side, which is to impose its radical agenda on an ever-larger slice of the globe? Facts can be marshaled or manipulated to support any contention, but without a common commitment to such basic ideas as freedom, order, and individual responsibility, they won't prove anything.

Foundational principles can't be proved; they must simply be believed. Critical thinking can be useful in helping a student determine the truth. But it [the critical thinking fad] isn't truth, and it won't give him any place to stand.

PART 4

ENGAGING IN THE WORLDVIEW BATTLES

The first three parts of this book have taken you through a journey exposing the workings of cultural Marxism. This should provide sufficient insight to recognize it quickly, understand what the end goal is, and begin to contend for the truth in a winsome and competent manner. This is spiritual warfare and winning a battle for truth here and there will not stop the onslaught of this satanic worldview. The war entails winning the hearts and minds of the nation, one person at a time.

This final part addresses paths for affecting the hearts and minds of those close to us to have a chance for offering salvation for those lost souls and turning the tide of a self-destructing culture. Focusing on formal and informal education, discerning the proper use of mass and social media and encouraging biblical veracity in the church are the key points to consider. It is essential that you engage with family and friends on this life and death issue and let God change hearts.

Chapter 17

The Worldview Battle

Richard W. Hawkins

"The only foundation for a useful education in a republic is to be laid in religion. Without this there can be no virtue, and without virtue there can be no liberty, and liberty is the object and life of all republican governments." – Founding Father Dr. Benjamin Rush [112]

"Almost no one believes that our public schools are doing a passable job of teaching American and Western civilization." Textbooks and class lectures in our education system today often start with the assumption that America and Western ideals are bad for civilization. He concludes that: *"Many American children have never heard a good word for the United States, the West, Judaism or Christianity their whole lives." David Galernter* [113]

And what are they teaching in public schools?

"I dislike the United States and American culture. American society treats people unfairly. American culture elevates the wealthy and the privileged over everybody else. It is oppressive. I'm oppressed. I want to change everything. I especially want to change things in the direction of redistributing wealth and privilege. Those should be taken away from the people I don't like and given to me and the people I do like. The key to making this happen is to raise awareness among those who are oppressed and who don't necessarily know they are oppressed. Calling for social justice is a way of bringing people together to overthrow the systemic injustices all around us." – Peter Wood, President of the National Association of Scholars [114]

---

[112] Benjamin Rush, *Essays, Literary, Moral and Philosophical* (Philadelphia: Thomas and William Bradford, 1806), 8, https://www.strategypage.com/military-forums/89-81686-page1.aspx#startofcomments,

[113] Gelernter, David, "David Gelenter: What Is the American Creed," http://latinosreadytovote.com/david-gelernter-what-is-the-american-creed/ (Jul 2, 2012)

[114] Wood, preface to " Social Justice Education in America," 12

157

WORLDVIEWS

If you were asked, "What is the philosophy of our government K-12 education system?" I trust, at this point in the book, you'll have the answer. Could you describe the traits of today's ideal human capital (high school) graduate as designed by the Education Establishment? This is a skill that you can develop if you engage in discussions on the topic.

If you were asked what education philosophy is necessary to pass on traditional American values would you know for certain what your response would be? Could you describe what Western Civilization is? Can you describe the difference between a Classical Liberal Arts education Vs a servile arts, skill based education? Answers to these questions are essential and this chapter will begin to answer these questions.

So far, this book has focused exclusively on cultural Marxism. These next three chapters and the Appendices will point the way out of the quandary that cultural Marxism has driven us into. Ultimately, however, the culture is dependent upon the worldview of the individual citizens and the health and strength of the social spheres of marriage and family, the church, the local community, commerce and civil government. We the People occupy these various spheres and have opportunities to affect their cultures. A personal worldview is established through formal and informal education and experiences with family and friends, the church, schools, community and neighbors, and the media which includes the arts, literature, entertainment, news, talk shows, etc. The parents and grandparents, formal schooling and the media are usually the most influential sources to forming a person's worldview depending on how much time and energy is devoted from or to each.

A worldview is a comprehensive system of values and beliefs that every individual develops through his life whether or not the individual is aware of that development. Most people are totally unaware of the worldview they are developing due to their parents not being aware of their own worldviews. Most, if not all, teachers in the government controlled K-12 schools are unaware of the cultural

Marxist worldview they are inculcating into their young charges and virtually no popular media sources divulge the worldview they are espousing.

A worldview answers life's ultimate questions such as:

1. Where did we come from?
2. What is the meaning and purpose of life?
3. How do I distinguish good and evil?
4. What has gone wrong with the world and what is the fix?
5. What happens when I die?

Each worldview has established truth-claims based on presuppositions that cannot be empirically proven. These truth-claims provide answers to life's questions and may be true, partially true or false (i.e., the truth-claim doesn't match reality). If a truth-claim turns out to be not true then it is considered a lie. The law of non-contradiction disallows two competing truth-claims to both be true. For instance, based on the following Worldview Comparison Chart, the competing truth-claims for theology are between a supernatural God and no supernatural god. One of these two positions has to be a lie. The Worldview Comparison Chart provides an apples-to-apples comparison for ten subjects as these truth-claims can't be empirically proven but are accepted as "truth" by faith. This helps to bring focus to any discussions regarding these two worldviews by dealing with a level playing field.

A worldview can be considered the "software" of a person's mind and conscience that is constantly applied for making decisions and controlling behavior. A worldview is a person's identity that establishes his nature and character based on beliefs he has developed either consciously or unconsciously. Formal education is based on a worldview and that worldview is inculcated into the students and those students and their parents are generally unaware what worldview is involved.

Education philosophy

Education philosophy within America has changed significantly over the past 400 years since our European settlement. It started out based on sustaining Western Civilization with the Bible as the primary textbook and conducted by the family as the parents have the God given responsibility for their children's education. By the mid-1800s

WORLDVIEW COMPARISON CHART

Sources ⇒ Subjects ⇓	WESTERN CIVILIZATION (Judeo/Christian)	POLITICAL CORRECTNESS (a.k.a. cultural Marxism)
	Greek philosophy, Roman government, Bible, Reformation, Enlightenment	Frankfurt School, Marx, Freud, Nietzsche, Rorty, Foucault, Derrida
THEOLOGY	Theism (Trinitarian)	Atheism
PHILOSOPHY (truth)	Corresponds to reality; Faith, Reason & Logic; Exegesis	Pluralism; no absolute truth; Anti-Rationalism; Eisegesis
ETHICS	Moral Absolutes per God's nature and character	Moral Relativism (victimhood & anarchy)
ORIGINS SCIENCE	Creationism (Intelligence, Time, Matter, Energy)	Materialistic Naturalism (Time, Matter, Energy)
PSYCHOLOGY	Mind/Body Dualism (fallen)	Monism (no soul); Socially constructed self (tabula rasa)
SOCIOLOGY	Traditional Family, Church & State	Destroy Patriarchal Family, Church and Constitution Emancipatory Sociology
CULTURE	Theonomous (self-governed via Laws of Nature and Nature's God)	Autonomous (law unto self)
LAW	Divine & natural law (negative rights)	Critical legal studies (positive rights)
POLITICS	Legal Justice, liberty, order Sovereign Spheres	Social Democracy, Social Justice & Technocracy
ECONOMICS	Stewardship of private property	Social Democracy Socialism/Fascism
HISTORY	God's Plan of Redemption	Critical Theory

Worldview chart comparing only two of the most predominant worldviews found in America today. Based on David Noebel's original chart from his book Understanding the Times.

the states began to assume responsibility for education and downplayed the role of the Bible and purpose for education. By the early 1900s Secular Humanism was beginning to displace Western Civilization as the educational worldview which itself began to give way to cultural Marxism in the 1970s. Education methodology changed from the classical liberal arts to a servile arts, skill based (Progressive) program.

John Dewey, the father of progressive education, was heavily funded and supported by the Rockefeller Foundation with establishment of Teachers College at Columbia University and a $1 million donation to the congressionally approved General Education Board. The Board's purpose was to establish an educational laboratory to experiment with early innovations in education. *Occasional Letter No 1* expressed the Board's aims:

> In our dreams, we have limitless resources and the people yield themselves with perfect docility to our molding hands. The present education conventions fade from their minds, and unhampered by tradition, we work our own good will upon a grateful and responsive rural folk. We shall not try to make these people or any of their children into philosophers or men of learning, or men of science. We have not to raise up from among them authors, editors, poets or men of letters. We shall not search for embryo great artists, painters, musicians nor lawyers, doctors, preachers, politicians, statesmen, of whom we have an ample supply. The task we set before ourselves is very simple as well as a very beautiful one, to train these people as we find them to a perfectly ideal life just where they are. So we will organize our children and teach them to do in a perfect way the things their fathers and mothers are doing in an imperfect way, in the homes, in the shops and on the farm. [115]

---

[115] Chapman, Ron, "Dumbing Down US Education: Part II – Wundtian Psychology & Rockefeller Finance," http://abundanthope.net/pages/Ron_71/Dumbing_

The implications of this shift in worldviews is tremendously destructive. The truth-claims changed from:

- God is to God is not
- Truth is absolute to truth is not absolute
- Interpreting literature from the author's intent to how the reader desires the literature to be interpreted
- Morals are objective to morals are relative; goals justify the means
- We are created in the image of God to we are an accident of blind chance and a plague on the environment
- We are born with a sin nature to we are born tabula rasa (born good on a clean slate)
- We have a soul and conscience as the basis of freewill to there is no soul or freewill and our conscience is a result of chemical synapses in the brain; therefore, we are easily reprogrammable
- God designed a harmonious social order based on traditional, sovereign spheres of family, church and state to destruction of this social order to 'prevent another Hitler' by forming a socialist, global government.
- Self-government based on virtue and morality as the center piece of government that offered maximum liberty and a civil society to everyone is right in their own eyes that leads to anarchy and chaos.
- An era of negative rights the individual owns without outside interference to positive rights where civil government bestows benefits and entitlements to the few at someone else's expense in the name of social justice.
- An era of private property and private enterprise to one of a mixture of socialism, fascism and interventionism.
- Individualism and free associations to collectivism into tribal groups fostering identity politics and social justice animosities.

- Nationalism and national sovereignty to global citizenship and globalism [116]

T Kenneth Cribb, Jr. pointed out in Chapter 13, Political Correctness and Higher Education:

> The stakes in this war of ideas [worldviews] are high, for they include the very concept of freedom itself. Americans have always understood the intimate and vital connection between liberal education and political liberty. That is why political correctness is nothing less than a death blow aimed at the heart of our republic.

The classical liberal arts education is the pursuit of knowledge (implied in this is the pursuit of truth) for its own sake. The root meaning of "liberal" is freedom of liberty, not today's twisted definition for more civil government interventions. Cardinal Newman argued that the liberal arts are liberating because they "enable men to discover (and understand) the underlying principles (a.k.a. worldview) that guide us toward wisdom and virtue" that is found comprehensively only in the Western Civilization worldview. A classical liberal arts program is designed to pass on the traditions of a culture from one generation to the next to sustain that nation's culture.

Put another way, this pursuit of knowledge guides the students to test the truth-claims of competing worldviews using knowledge, classical laws of logic and reasoning. The students explore the pros and cons of ideas following the evidence wherever it leads and come to an understanding of the consequences of those ideas.

Cardinal Newman had defined a servile arts program, on the other hand, as one that 'serves only specific, immediate ends' such as 'college and career readiness.' As T K Cribb had noted, Cardinal Newman would view the cultural Marxist worldview as servile because its purpose is to advance an agenda to a position of national power. Common Core, along with No Child Left Behind and Goals

---

[116] Fonte, John, "Who Makes the Rules in a 'Rules-Based' Liberal Global Order?" https://www.amgreatness.com/2019/08/12/who-makes-the-rules-in-a-rules-based-liberal-global-order/, (Aug 12, 2019)

2000 of the past, is a servile arts, skill based (Progressive) program without educating the students to truly think critically. They are steered to a predetermined outcome. The primary goal of the servile arts program used in America's public schools is to destroy the traditions of the nation for, one might say, "fundamentally transforming the United States of America." [117]

Os Guinness in *A Free People's Suicide: Sustainable Freedom and the American Future* stated:

> It could be argued that the very fact of the American culture wars is an expression of a deepening corruption of American customs. Many notions that were once self-evident in America and could be taken for granted across a wide spectrum of differences have been blighted beyond recognition. What is life? What is marriage? What is a family? Does character matter in a leader? Is there such a thing as truth? Does any society, does Western civilization and in particular does the American republic need any compelling truths and objective standards? In each case, changes in thinking and living in the past fifty years have reduced these notions to fictions and in the process have changed American customs beyond recognition. [118]

USE AND ABUSE OF LANGUAGE

One of the features of a totalitarian worldview such as cultural Marxism is control of words and language. George Orwell's *1984* described this beautifully. New words are created, old words are redefined or eliminated in order to minimize the effect of all other competing worldviews and narrow the focus of acceptable thought. The cultural Marxists have grabbed control of our language and it's high time we push back by reintroducing and using the following

---

[117] https://www.breitbart.com/politics/2015/11/16/obamas-fundamental-transformation-began-at-mizzou/
[118] Os Guinness. A Free People's Suicide: Sustainable Freedom and the American Future (Kindle Locations 1507-1511). (Kindle Edition, 2012)

words properly in the court of public opinion and denouncing those dangerous words used by the cultural Marxists.

Words To Be Restored To The Lexicon

American Dream -- The American Dream is the belief that anyone, regardless of where they were born or what class they were born into, can attain their own version of success in a society where upward mobility is possible for everyone. The American Dream is achieved through sacrifice, risk-taking, and hard work, rather than by chance. Its tenets can be found in the Declaration of Independence, which states: "We hold these truths to be self-evident, that all men are created equal, that they are endowed by their Creator with certain unalienable Rights, that among these are Life, Liberty, and the pursuit of Happiness." In a society based on these principles, an individual can live life to its fullest as he or she defines it.

America is a melting pot – Assimilation by new, legal immigrants into America and become part of American Exceptionalism is essential for sustaining our unique Western Civilization culture that is based on liberty and self-government. The cultural Marxist forces are destroying this with their multiculturalism and open borders.

Conscience – "The religion then of every man must be left to the conviction and conscience of every man; and it is the right of every man to exercise it as these may dictate. This right is in its nature an unalienable right. It is unalienable; because the opinions of men, depending only on the evidence contemplated by their own minds, cannot follow the dictates of other men: It is unalienable also; because what is here a right towards men, is a duty towards the Creator." -- James Madison [119]

"We must take care not to force an interpretation which puts anyone in the position of violating either their own conscience, or the conscience of another. If the conscience is truly sacred, then the last

---

[119] Madison, "Memorial and Remonstrance against Religious Assessments"

165

thing God would ever call anyone to do is to violate anyone's conscience, including their own." – Gerald R Thompson [120]

Constitutional Republic – A state where the officials are elected as representatives of the people, and must govern according to existing constitutional law that limits the government's power over citizens. The founding fathers did not intend the United States to be a democracy [mob rule]. However, in recent years, many people have criticized the federal government for moving away from a Constitutional Republic, as defined by the Constitution, and towards a pure democracy [and socialism]. [121]

Critical thinking – The only true thinking is using knowledge, laws of logic and reasoning (not feelings, emotions and opinions as used for higher order thinking skills) to test truth-claims between competing worldviews to discern truth from lies.

E Pluribus Unum – "out of many, one." meaning the federation of 13 states into one nation and other founding documents expressed the uniting of peoples from many European nations into one nation.

Freedom – this term is not the ultimate goal as many express today. Today's use leads to anarchy and chaos when used without constraint. As used in the definition for liberty, freedom is thus constrained to prevent anarchy.

Government – We have allowed the word government to mean almost exclusively that which is found in Washington DC which has caused us to minimize or ignore the design for the governing of the sovereign spheres. Each sovereign sphere has its own government; the individual is self-governed, marriage is based on the government by the spouses, family is based on the government led by the father, church government led by the pastor and elders or deacons, commerce's governments are the business owners, etc.

Human Dignity – Man is God's special creation and blessed with certain human rights. The Declaration of Independence established

---

[120]Thompson, Gerald R., "Self-Government, Conscience & True Liberty: The Law of Conscience"
[121] Constitutional Republic defined,
https://www.conservapedia.com/index.php?title=Constitutional_Republic

the purpose for the United States that all men are created equal and endowed by their Creator with certain unalienable rights and it is up to government to protect those rights. These correspond well with scripture. Man is created in the image of God and thus has a certain dignity. Murder, including abortion and euthanasia, are heinous crimes and the murderer must be put to death as commanded by God for violating another's dignity in God's image.

Inalienable Rights Vs state given rights – Inalienable rights are negative rights each individual possesses at the time of conception without outside benefits or interference or requiring impositions on others. Positive rights, on the other hand, occur when civil government bestows benefits and entitlements to some at someone else's expense by violating his negative rights in the name of social justice.

Individualism – The most basic unit of society is the individual. Each individual person is a creation of God, and is something he is born into. Self-government is also the most basic unit of government. That the individual is also a unit of government should be obvious, when you consider that each person is a moral being, made in the image of God, such that each person is ultimately responsible for his own individual behavior... all natural rights, and all natural freedoms, are bestowed exclusively on individuals. There are no group rights or corporate freedoms, and no collective salvation. We each stand alone before God as a moral agent... Each person is morally aware of certain fundamental principles of right and wrong as evident in our consciences, which awareness guides us in our behavioral decisions. **I daresay that without self-government, none of the other social institutions would be sustainable.** [emphasis added by Editor] [122]

Justice – The virtue which consists in giving to everyone what is his due; practical conformity to the laws and to principles of rectitude in the dealings of men with each other; honesty; integrity in commerce or mutual intercourse. *Justice* is *distributive* or *commutative*. *Distributive justice* belongs to magistrates or rulers, and consists in distributing to

---

[122] Thompson, Gerald R., "Self-Government, Conscience & True Liberty: The Basis of Self-Government"

every man that right or equity which the laws and the principles of equity require; or in deciding controversies according to the laws and to principles of equity. *Commutative justice* consists in fair dealing in trade and mutual intercourse between man and man.[123]

Liberty – The freedom to make a choice, to assume responsibility, and accept the Consequences thereof. Liberty is the ultimate goal behind the founding of our nation.

Marriage – The act of uniting a man and woman for life; wedlock; the legal union of a man and woman for life. Marriage is a contract both civil and religious, by which the parties engage to live together in mutual affection and fidelity, till death shall separate them. Marriage was instituted by God himself for the purpose of preventing the promiscuous intercourse of the sexes, for promoting domestic felicity, and for securing the maintenance and education of children. [124]

Morality – The quality of an action which renders it good; the conformity of an act to the divine law, or to the principles of rectitude. This conformity implies that the act must be performed by a free agent, and from a motive of obedience to the divine will. [125]

Nationalism – loyalty and devotion to a nation; a sense of national consciousness exalting one nation above all others and placing primary emphasis on promotion of its culture and interests as opposed to those of other nations or supranational groups. [126] Nationalism unifies diverse groups to prevent tribalism and Identity Politics. Nationalism is interfering with the cultural Marxists goal of global governance – editor Nationalism unifies diverse groups to prevent tribalism and Identity Politics. Nationalism is interfering with the cultural Marxists goal of global governance.

Patriarchy – The father is ruler and spiritual head of the family; one who governs by paternal right.

---

[123] Webster, N. (2006). *Noah Webster's first edition of An American dictionary of the English language.* Anaheim, CA: Foundation for American Christian Education.
[124] Ibid.
[125] Ibid.
[126] Nationalism defined, https://www.merriam-ebster.com/dictionary/nationalism

Religion – "Congress shall make no law respecting an establishment of religion, nor prohibiting the free exercise thereof;..." "The free exercise thereof" has been under attack by the enemy of liberty since the last half of the last century. Lately, the enemy consistently misquotes this phrase by stating, "the right to worship," in an attempt to confine specifically Christian activity to just within the four walls of the church and kept out of the public square of ideas. To carry out the Great Commission and be the salt and light to the world as Christ's ambassadors we are bound to uphold the phrase "the free exercise thereof."

Sovereign – God is the *sovereign* ruler of the universe. A supreme lord or ruler; one who possesses the highest authority without control. Some earthly princes, kings and emperors are *sovereigns* in their dominions. Each social sphere as designed by God is governed by sovereigns; the individual over self, husband in a marriage, husband and wife in a family, etc. We the People are designed to be the sovereigns of America with elected officials and bureaucrats our servants [127]

Sovereign Spheres – God has given us a design for social order with sovereign spheres of the Individual, Marriage and Family, church, state, commerce and community. Each of these spheres is sovereign meaning they govern themselves without the interference of the other spheres. Each sphere has been designated by God with its particular set of roles and responsibilities which harmonize with the other spheres and human nature.

Totalitarian – Herbert Schlossberg insightfully diagnosed the essential nature of totalitarianism as aggressive and intrusive civil authority which attempts "to control every aspect of communal life, and to bring as much of private life as possible into the sphere of the communal." .... "the scope of its purview," or its unlimited jurisdiction, constitutes a truly authoritarian and therefore tyrannical rule. Such absolute and sovereign civil authority, of necessity,

---

[127] Webster, *Noah Webster's first edition of An American dictionary of the English language*

169

encroaches upon personal self-governance and individuality to sustain itself and its objectives.[128]

Virtue – Bravery; valor. Moral goodness; the practice of moral duties and the abstaining from vice, or a conformity of life and conversation to the moral law. [129]

Words and Concepts Used to Kill Liberty:

Collective – "Collectivism is the idea that the individual's life belongs to the group or society of which he is merely a part, that he has no rights other than those the group or society gives him, and that he must sacrifice his values and goals for the group's "greater good." The individual is of value only insofar as he serves the group."[130] **Collectivism destroys individualism resulting in the total destruction of God's design of social order and the sovereign spheres.**

Democracy – The majority rule which always devolves into mob rule. Students are indoctrinated into thinking America is a democracy in government controlled K-12 schools rather than being taught the United States of America is a constitutional republic.

Equality – Used by the cultural Marxists believing everyone must be equal in outcome Vs equal before the law. Equal in outcome is impossible to achieve. The user of this term has to be challenged to define what he means and this will usually result in some form of positive rights.

Global Citizen – Changes the focus from patriot or nationalist or American while believing America as a racist, sexist, bigoted and oppressive nation needing to be destroyed for a New World Order. This is an important mindset necessary to carry out the Sustainable Development program of the UN's Agendas 21 and 2030. K-12 students are now taught they are global citizens.

---

[128] Ferdon, G. M. (2007). *A Republic If You Can Keep It* (p. 98). San Francisco: Foundation for American Christian Education.
[129] Ibid
[130]Biddle, Craig, "Individualism vs. Collectivism: Our Future, Our Choice," https://www.theobjectivestandard.com/issues/2012-spring/individualism-collectivism/ , (Spring 2012)

170

Intersectionality – A hierarchy established among the victim groups to imply one higher up the hierarchy is more "oppressed" than another. For example, a black LGBTQ female is at a higher level of "oppression" than a white LGBTQ female. A hilarious example is a transgender male allowed to compete in women's athletics. I suppose that this establishes different degrees of sympathy for each victim class.

Living, Breathing Constitution – Used to increase totalitarianism while those in power use eisegesis to interpret the constitution to make it say what they want it to say.

Opinion polls – Truth doesn't need a majority or agreement to be true.

Social justice – "Social justice" is a noun referring to justice in terms of the redistribution of wealth, opportunities, and privileges within a society. The term is thrown around as if it is obviously a noble and good thing to work towards as it is designed to take from the imagined oppressor groups (whites, Jews, males) and give to the imagined oppressed groups based on race, gender and/or sexual abnormalities. [akin to **Identity Politics**] [131]

Social Democrat – A combination of socialism and fascism with state ownership of certain programs and state intervention and heavy regulation of industry. The Social Democrat advocates for government totalitarianism in the name of social justice.

Toleration – Cultural Marxists have twisted the meaning from not only allowing all persons to express differing opinions but use its twisted yet formidable power to silence and destroy publicly by shaming those who deviate from the accepted narrative when speaking about protected identity groups. This is speech control via ad hominin attacks with such name calling as homophobe, Islamophobe, transphobe, misogynist, racist, Nazi, Facist, White Supremacist, white nationalist, science denier, deplorable, etc.

---

[131] Paulson, Terry, "Social Justice Is No Justice at All,"
https://www.freerepublic.com/focus/f-news/3738571/posts, (Mar 30, 2019)

Chapter 18

What can be done?

Richard W. Hawkins, 2019

EDUCATION, n. [L. educatio.] The bringing up, as of a child; instruction; formation of manners. Education comprehends all that series of instruction and discipline which is intended to enlighten the understanding, correct the temper, and form the manners and habits of youth, and fit them for usefulness in their future stations. To give children a good education in manners, arts and science, is important; to give them a religious education is indispensable; and an immense responsibility rests on parents and guardians who neglect these duties. [132]

There are four dimensions [to the NCSS C3 Framework] which are intended to make the children question all things their grandparents might have been taught so as to loosen their hold on the ideas of America's Constitutional Republic and individual rights. Dimension 4 is called "Taking Informed Action" which is designed so that the children physically act out their newly adopted Globalist ideas to build commitment to the new concept their teacher just indoctrinated them with. It's a form of psychological conditioning practice that is explained by a well respected ASU Marketing Professor Richard Cialdini in his book The Power of Persuasion. *The technique is extremely effective in building commitment to a (Social Justice/Socialism) cause. – Kristen Williamson, activist*

What can be done? I haven't beaten around the bush so far, and I won't start now. So I'm going to come right out and say it: Parents who really care about what happens to their children will take them out of government schools as quickly as possible. I realize that's easier said than done, but it must be done and it can be done if parents make up their minds to do it. [133]

Up until now this book has been presenting the deceitfulness and false truth-claims of the cultural Marxist worldview. In the last chapter I provided an apples-to-apples comparison between the

---

[132] Webster, *Noah Webster's first edition of An American dictionary of the English language*

[133] Morris, Barbara M., *Change Agents In The Schools; Destroy Your Children, Betray Your Country*, (The Barbara M. Morris Report, 1979), 249

Western Civilization worldview and that of cultural Marxism. Assuming the reader is on the more mature end of Christianity he should be adequately equipped to defend the faith and be the salt and light in the culture around him as Christ's ambassador. He should also be an encourager for his fellow brothers and sisters and, especially, for his pastor and elders.

Much of the church had turned a blind eye to this spiritual warfare which is ravaging the church and our culture. 10% of conservative evangelical pastors are true shepherds looking after their flock by aggressively speaking out against Christians attending public schools. Another 20-25% of conservative evangelical pastors are generally supportive of Christians exiting public schools but are not aggressive about it. 28% of supposed conservative evangelical pastors are in opposition to Christians leaving the public schools. The rest of the conservative evangelical pastors remain silent. We are looking at 65-70% of conservative evangelical pastors who are unfortunately hirelings and looking out after their flock. In addition, many of the active Christian public school teachers remain silent among the church congregants and/or fight against efforts for fellow Christians to exit public schools. Needless to say, most Christian parents will not receive support or encouragement from their church to withdraw their child from the government controlled school system.

The two primary sources for indoctrination into cultural Marxism are the media and government controlled K-12 schools. Individuals and parents have immediate control of the media they and their children read, listen to, attend, or watch. It is up to their conscience to take control of the access to these mediums. Formal education, however, is another animal.

Prayer and coming to the full realization of the parents' responsibility to raise up their children the way they should go is the first order of business. Taking up the cause with other Christian parents is always wise for encouraging each other and sharing wise counsel. Visiting with homeschool groups in your community is a must to hopefully find out it is not as difficult as first imagined. The biggest challenge maybe the sacrifices of comfort the family will have to make or overcoming the discouraging words from friends and family for the hard work of helping the salvation and proper raising of their child.

Ideally, the pastors would coordinate among different congregations to form a classical Christian Worldview K-12 education program. The congregants would be encouraged to contribute towards scholarship funding to this program. But this would be a long term goal knowing that 65-70% of conservative evangelical pastors are AWOL. It may be time for these parents to seek a congregation where they will receive the help they need in this arena.

One resource I find greatly underutilized are the retired congregants. What a wonderful ministry that is available to help educate, both formally and informally, the young especially with the many families displaced from their extended family members. Talk about the building up the body of Christ....what an opportunity! Imagine Ephesians 4:11-16 playing out as God has designed this.

The Education Establishment has floated many myths regarding homeschooling. This is propaganda to try and stem the fallout from public schools which impacts their budgets and union membership. Quite amazingly, I've had pastors warn against homeschooling as they are concerned that parents aren't up to the task. But realize that both professional teachers and pastors are products of highly specialized training and are led to believe that education of children requires a highly trained specialist; this is one of those myths. Homeschooled children, on average, are socialized and educated by parents to a much higher level than can be achieved in a government controlled school environment. Parents need to spend the time and energy to seek the truth about proper education for their children. It is the most rewarding task a parent is commanded to take.

Each family will have to deal with their own unique situation. But I will suggest this is the priority for educational choices:

1. Homeschool with a classical Christian worldview curriculum
2. Church lead classical Christian worldview school

3. Charter school with a Western Civilization based classical liberal arts program

The traditional public school is not a choice because it is compulsory unless you act on one of the three choices above. These traditional schools are immersed in cultural Marxist indoctrination and the regressive Progressive model of educating. Christian students will only receive a smattering of Christian truth due to the limited time at home and church and be miseducated for a great part of their development. In addition, many public education teachers are trained change agents and inculcate into their young charges with values contrary to parents, church and nation.

> When educators attempt "...to bring about desired values" they consider "crucially important", what happens if those "desired values" are in conflict with what is taught at home and church? Well, that's easy to deal with. They simply teach children to "respect" the "speech" of their parents. For instance:

> "It is vital that the curriculum not be used to turn the children against their parents and the community, even if the parents and community stand against reason, freedom and equality...We are teaching children to respect the speech of their parents and to understand that those speech patterns are results of their parents' past."

> What the above really says is that while educators [who consider themselves the epitome of reason freedom and equality] alienate children from the values of their parents, they salve their consciences by saying they teach children to "respect the speech of their parents."[134]

> "It is necessary, in other words, artificially to create an experiential chasm between parents and children to insulate

---

[134] Morris, *Change Agents In The Schools; Destroy Your Children, Betray Your Country,* 10

the latter in order that they can more easily be indoctrinated with new ideas." [135]

Students are being encouraged to oppose the government rather than to engage in the established political process. The preference for protests and civil disobedience, driven by bitterness and resentment, reflects their ignorance about how our democratic republic operates. The leaders of the "progressive left" hide behind a facade of love for the poor, the stranger, and their neighbor, while endeavoring to replace our Constitution with utopian ideas that have failed horribly. [136]

There are numerous philosophies (or styles) of K-12 education. The government controlled schools are based primarily on the cultural Marxist worldview implemented into a servile arts education format. The primary purpose is to develop human capital with work force training for a socialist, global economy/global citizenship as well as social justice activism. What I'm going to address now are two alternatives to this Marxist based, servile arts format.

The two alternatives are either the classical Christian liberal arts program or a classical liberal arts program based on Western Civilization. The first is based on a pure Christian worldview format where God and the Bible are foundational for all subjects. The latter is based on the Western Civilization worldview and Judeo/Christian values but set on a secular foundation. The former are found either in homeschools or church schools and the latter is appropriate for taxpayer funded charter schools. The former has no civil government strings attached for curriculum content and the latter are controlled by those strings and other government entanglements.

Refer to both Appendix-2 and Appendix-3 for additional discussions to better understand and compare the Progressive,

---

[135] https://sagaciousnewsnetwork.com/humanity-under-attack-the-tactics-of-social-engineering/

[136] Takacs, Bailey, "Our Way of Life is Wortht Preserving," https://www.discovery.org/education/2020/03/11/our-way-of-life-is-worth-maintaining/ (Mar 11, 2020)

Marxist based model of education versus the classical liberal arts model.

A classical Christian education is centered on Jesus Christ and a classical liberal arts education is centered on Western Civilization with its Judeo/Christian morality and virtues. Assure they are built upon Dorothy Sayers' Trivium and Quadrivium concepts that are geared on the child's natural stages of development. The Socratic Method of instruction is essential and the individual is taught to think independently and not collectively via the dialectic process. The Great Classics are a must Vs the modern 'range of authors' literature emphasizing multiculturalism in the traditional schools. The ACCS and ACSI websites listed below provide sufficient information for you to be able to make a wise decision.

What is the approach to a classical Christian education that makes it different from any other form of education? True education is teaching and learning embedded in and flowing from the knowledge and truths of God through His Word—as opposed to education based in man's subjective and limited achievements. By asserting God's sovereignty in all of life, and acknowledging His Hand in historical and present human history, students reason by principles and leading ideas to develop and internalize a true and comprehensive Biblical worldview. Teaching and learning are formative for Biblical reasoning. The formation of wisdom is the fruit of the knowledge of truth. This classical Christian approach provides the structure of truth that frames true education. Wisdom is the key and this method forms wisdom as children learn how to think and reason from a Biblical perspective in order to redirect their humanness towards God. No other form of education comes close to this. [137]

RESOURCES

General Information
  1. Christian Education Initiative https://christedu.org/
  2. Exodus mandate https://exodusmandate.org/

---

[137] Concept borrowed from the Principle Approach published by Foundation for American Christian Education, https://face.net/

3. Nehemiah Institute http://nehemiahinstitute.com/
4. Society for Classical Learning
    https://societyforclassicallearning.org/
5. Association of Classical Christian Schools (ACCS)
    https://classicalchristian.org/
6. Association of Christian Schools International (ACSI)
    https://www.acsi.org/membership/acsi-overview

Homeschooling:
1. Homeschool Legal Defense Association
    https://hslda.org/content/
2. Doug Wilson's Logosonline
    https://logosonlineschool.com/pages/curriculum
3. Foundation for American Christian Education
    https://face.net/
4. Abeka https://www.abeka.com/HomeSchool/
5. Freedom Project Academy
    https://www.fpeusa.org/commoncore
6. Liberty University Online Homeschool
    https://www.liberty.edu/online-academy/academics-
    curriculum/
7. Bob Jones Online
    https://www.bjupresshomeschool.com/content/about-
    distance-learning-online
8. Apologia https://www.apologia.com/
9. Robinson Curriculum
    https://www.robinsoncurriculum.com/rc/homeschool-
    curriculum-excellence/
10. Classical Conversations
    https://www.classicalconversations.com/

Christian Worldview School Associations
1. Association of Classical Christian Schools
    https://classicalchristian.org/
2. Foundation of American Christian Education
    https://face.net/

Western Civilization based Charter Schools
1. Barney Charter School Initiative from Hillsdale College https://www.hillsdale.edu/educational-outreach/barney-charter-school-initiative/

Christian Worldview Retreats for youth
1. Summit Ministries https://www.summit.org/
2. Worldview Academy Camps https://worldview.org/camps/
3. Impact 360 Institute https://www.impact360institute.org/
4. rethink Apologetics http://rethinkapologetics.com/

Other Christian Worldview Education Resources
1. Christian Bookstore https://www.christianbook.com/page/homeschool/homeschool-curriculum-index
2. Summit Ministries https://www.summit.org/
3. Answers In Genesis https://answersingenesis.org/store/
4. Institute for Creation Research https://store.icr.org/tags/student/
5. Theology Degrees https://www.theologydegrees.org/best-christian-homeschool-curriculum/
6. The Truth Project https://www.focusonthefamily.com/promos/the-truth-project

God Bless and may you experience unlimited blessings in your journey of raising up Godly children to carry the torch of Truth into the next generation.

Chapter 19

WHY THE CHURCHES ARE EMPTY

William S. Lind, 2019

Romans 12:2 (ESV)
Do not be conformed to this world, but be transformed by the renewal of your mind, that by testing you may discern what is the will of God, what is good and acceptable and perfect.

Matthew 7:15-16 (ESV)
"Beware of false prophets, who come to you in sheep's clothing but inwardly are ravenous wolves. You will recognize them by their fruits.

Since World War II, most mainline Protestant denominations have suffered heavy losses of membership. There is more than one reason for those denominations' empty churches. But one cause of their shrinkages has been the displacement of the Holy Trinity as an object of worship with an unholy trinity of "racism, sexism and homophobia," sins detested not by God but by an ideology. That ideology, known most commonly as "political correctness" or "multiculturalism," is in fact cultural Marxism – Marxism translated from economic into cultural terms in an effort that goes back not to the 1960s but to 1919. All ideologies are counterfeit religions, and the adoption by many churches of this particular ideology is nothing less than idolatry. People have left those churches in droves because they are no longer churches but temples to a strange god.

The history of cultural Marxism is important if Christians are to know this particular enemy. Marxist theory had predicted that if another great European war broke out, the proletariat across Europe would rise up as one man to overthrow bourgeois liberalism and establish communism. But when war came in 1914, that [overthrow] didn't happen. In 1919, two Marxist theorists, working independently, Antonio Gramsci in Italy and Georg Lukacs in Hungary, explained why. They said that Western culture and the Christian religion so blinded the working class in Western Europe to its true class interests that communism was impossible until both could be destroyed. Gramsci called for a "long march through the institutions," while Lukacs, as deputy commissar for culture in the short-lived Bolshevik Bela Kun government in Hungary, asked, "Who will save us from Western civilization?" and proclaimed a program of "cultural terrorism" that included introducing sex education into Hungarian schools. He knew that if he could destroy a country's sexual morals, he would take a large step toward destroying its culture as a whole.

Mussolini threw Gramsci in jail and let him rot. But Lukacs went on to have profound influence on a think-tank established at Frankfurt University in Germany in 1923. Originally to be called the Institute for Marxism, its founders decided they could have more influence if they gave it a neutral-sounding name, the Institute for Social Research. This set the Institute, which soon became known as the Frankfurt School, on a course of hiding its real nature and intentions which its heirs still follow.

At first, the Institute focused on orthodox Marxist topics such as the labor movement. But in 1930 when a new director took over, a brilliant young thinker named Max Horkheimer, its work shifted radically. Horkheimer disagreed with Marx that culture was merely "superstructure," determined by ownership of the means of production. He argued that it was an independent and highly important variable. He also said, heretically, that the working class would not be the agent of revolution because it was becoming part of the middle class. Horkheimer began the difficult intellectual task of translating Marx from economic into cultural terms, work that was quickly condemned by Moscow.

To assist in this vast task, Horkheimer brought in additional intellectuals who thought as he did. The most important was Theodor Adorno, who argued that because life under capitalism was by definition alienating, music, art, architecture, etc. must also be alienating in order to be "true." As what we see and hear around us today testifies, Adorno's influence was immense. Two other recruits, Wilhelm Reich and Eric Fromm, helped the Institute cross Marx with

Freud to argue that in Western culture everyone lived in a constant state of repression, from which they must be "liberated." The results of that began to become apparent in the 1960s.

In 1933, when Hitler came to power in Germany, the Institute fled to New York where it soon reestablished itself. There it began a series of "studies of prejudice" which argued that every aspect of bourgeois society, including Christian morals, was based on "prejudice" that had to be criticized relentlessly ("critical theory"). These studies provided the intellectual basis for the various "studies" departments that now litter the campuses of what were once serious universities. They culminated in Adorno's vastly influential book *The Authoritarian Personality* (1950), the research behind which has been shown to be bogus but whose conclusion that any and all traditional ways of believing or behaving are "fascist" is now dogma in most intellectual circles. Adorno's work came to have a great deal of influence over educational theory in this country, in which learning has been replaced with psychological conditioning. The Frankfurt School said explicitly that it does not matter whether children in school learn any skills or any facts. All that matters is that they leave with certain "attitudes." [138]

Shortly before the Institute left Germany (to which it returned after the war), it picked up a new member, a young graduate student named Herbert Marcuse. In the 1950s and 1960s Marcuse, who

---

[138] *Taxonomy of Educational Objectives Book 1 Cognitive Domain* and *Taxonomy of Educational Objectives Book 2 Affective Domain* are more commonly referred to as Bloom's Taxonomies, despite David R. Krathwohl being the leading editor of Book 2. Despite the rot that John Dewey and his progressive religion has brought to education these books have had more to do with the erosion of morals and ethics in America than any other books...Every teacher (certified) has to study and apply Bloom's Taxonomies in the classroom...Couched in the language of "academia" they are actually the work of Transformational [cultural] Marxists, using the language of social-psychology, i.e. *psychotherapy* (Marx and Freud, both dialectic in mind) to communicate to their agents an agenda to destroy the sovereignty of this nation for a dream of a one world order.... Bloom admitted that his *worldview* was that of two Transformational [cultural] Marxist, i.e., Erich Fromm and Theodor Adorno, who were dedicated to 'liberating' children, and therefore society, from parental authority. –
Gotcher, Dean, "Benjamin Bloom and his Taxonomies," [footnote by the Editor]

remained in the United States, translated the highly abstruse work of Horkheimer and Adorno into books college students could easily read and understand. His book *Eros and Civilization* (1955), which became the bible of the New Left in the 1960s, argued that by replacing repression with "non-procreative eros" and dumping the "reality principle" for the "pleasure principle," we could create a society of no work and all play. Horkheimer had left open the question of who would be the agent of revolution, since the working class would not. Marcuse filled that void by saying that revolution would come from a coalition of young people, blacks, feminist women, gays, etc., the sacred "victim groups" of political correctness. In a famous essay written in the 1960s, Marcuse argued for what he called "liberating tolerance," which he defined as tolerance for all ideas and movements coming from the left and *in*tolerance for all ideas and movements coming from the right. When the left todays calls for "tolerance," that is what it means.

Marcuse injected the cultural Marxism of the Frankfurt School into the baby boom generation during and after the 1960s, and it remains the ideology of much of that generation today, including much of the clergy in many mainline churches. You cannot defy it and be a member of the elite. Cultural Marxism's death-grip on education, in the public schools, universities, and many seminaries, ensures it has been pumped into succeeding generations as well. Because it relies not on logical argument but on psychological conditioning, to which the video screen media lend themselves well, it is difficult to fight. Anyone who rejects it has been conditioned to look into the mirror and see "another Hitler."

For people who want to rescue their denominations or individual churches from cultural Marxism, the tool cannot be another ideology. That would simply replace one idol with another. A starting point in Jesus Christ's own answer to those who demand he lead a fight for "social justice" as Jews defined it: "My kingdom is not of this world." (John 18:36) But just as cultural Marxism has infected not only many churches but most of America's institutions, so a broader answer to cultural Marxism may offer a way forward for empty churches. That way is Retroculture.

Retroculture is simply living in the old ways, the ways in which most Americans lived up through the 1950s. From lifetime marriage and family meals to regularly taking children to the art museum and symphony, Retroculture is the opposite of ideology. It is concrete, not abstract. It deals with cultural Marxism not by confronting it but by ignoring it. It says to all ideologies, "We're not listening to you anymore. We're just going to live in the old ways again, because we know those ways worked. The new ways, those developed from the 1960s onward, have not worked. Goodbye." Click.

Thomas Hobbes has recently published a new book, a novel titled *Victoria*. It is *Leviathan* (1651) for our time that cannot read a book as serious as *Leviathan* and that insists everything be presented as entertainment. Set 50 years in the future, *Victoria: A Novel of Fourth Generation War* (2014) offers a future history where a culturally Marxist federal government eventually loses all legitimacy and the American state fragments, much as we are seeing states in the Middle East fragment. The old American northeast forms a new state where the people, not the government, adopt Retroculture. One of *Victoria's* central characters, Bill Kraft, explains how it works:

> You cannot create, or more precisely re-create, the world
> we want simply through words, least of all through
> words of politicians. You have to do it by how you live.
> The Retroculture Movement is people – individuals,
> families, sometimes whole neighborhoods – striving to
> live again in the old ways, following the old rules. [139]

---

[139] Another perspective to look at Retroculture is the turning away from the current collectivized movement of cultural Marxism and back to individualism and self-government. Self-government's counterfeit governing approach is centralized state power. The state's totalitarian nature absorbs decision-making authority relegated to the intermediate layers of families, churches and the other sovereign, local spheres. Robert Nisbet in his *The Quest for Community* (1953, 1990) states:
"Totalitarianism is thus made possible only through the obliteration of all the intermediate layers of value and association that commonly nourish personality and serve to protect it from external power and caprice. Totalitarianism has been well described as the ultimate invasion of human privacy. But this invasion of privacy is possible only after the social contexts of privacy—family, church, association—have been atomized. The political *enslavement* of man requires the *emancipation* of man

184

Here Kraft expounds one of *Victoria*'s main themes that is also a theme of Christianity: the highest power is the power of example. Lives lived well, following the old rules, will draw more people into doing the same. This is how Christianity spread in the ancient world when it was powerless and persecuted, as traditional Christians have been powerless and persecuted for decades in some mainline churches.

Those who want to live Retro lives will of course work to remove cultural Marxism's conditioning mechanisms from their homes. This means getting rid of most if not all video-screen devices. Not only are they mechanisms for psychological conditioning, they raise what ought to be profound theological questions which most churches fail to address. All virtual realities come from Hell, for the obvious reason that if there can be more than one reality there can also be more than one god; so falls monotheism. On video screens, the image is much more powerful than the word. So the Word loses a three-thousand-year struggle it has until recently largely won and paganism rises reborn. We already have at least one generation that cannot read a book, including the Bible, because it does not have the attention span. How long will it be before they can read only the hieroglyphics we call emoji? It should not surprise us that if you turn a computer over, on the bottom you find inscribed a small pitchfork.

As *Victoria* makes clear, Retroculture people will still go to the doctor and the hospital when they need to, shop at grocery stores if they live in the city and drive if they live in the country. Most of these things are incidentals: they do not strike at the ways of believing, thinking, and living that made past societies work.

We already have a large and growing group of Retro fellow-Americans and fellow Christians who do not drive: the Amish. I have Amish friends, and they live lives that are both comfortable and good. Their basic rule is a simple one: in every situation, they try to do what they think Jesus would do. They drive buggies instead of cars

---

from all the [intermediate layers of] authorities and memberships ... that serve, in one degree or another, to insulate the individual from external political power."
Nisbet, Robert, *The Quest for Community*, (Intercollegiate Studies Institute, Kindle Edition, 1970) 3490-3498 [Footnote insertion by the Editor]

because they want their lives to be local; local is real. If they could put bumper stickers on them (they can't), theirs would read, "We know what Jesus would drive."

A spreading Retroculture movement might offer those mainline churches that have lost so many members an opportunity to refill their empty pews. Retroculture people will want to attend church regularly, because that is what people used to do [for both worship and fellowship]. But they will be looking for Retro churches. They will want churches that worship God, not the idol of ideology. They will also want the old services again, which for mainline churches will mean that most of them offered up through the 1950s: a certain formality, proper decorum, and, in liturgical churches, the old liturgies.

Churches that have replaced God with ideology may not want to do this. Some would rather have empty church buildings than fill those buildings with congregations of traditionalists. Others may at least be willing to offer two services on Sunday: a modern, informal service for those who want such, and the old, formal service for people who are going Retro, or are old enough to remember when things were better done.

But in those cases where cultural Marxism has such a grip on the national church that it effectively forbids any return to traditional Christian worship, new denominations will have to be formed. This has already occurred in some cases, e.g., the Continuing Anglican churches. As Retroculture succeeds and grows, though the power of example, those continuing or restored churches will grow with it, and the official churches will shrink until they vanish. As the 20th century convincingly showed, no ideology has a long life.

Defeating cultural Marxism within and beyond the church will require the Christian virtue of patience. Haste could result in replacing it with another ideology, which would lead to another round of idolatry. In the end, we would find ourselves no better off. The enemy is ideology itself. Ideology is literally "anti-Christ," because it is counterfeit religion: religion without God, without promise of eternal salvation, without the beauty of Holiness. In "political correctness," it has become the worst of all Puritanisms, Puritanism without virtue.

Our Victorian forefathers got it right. As 21st century Americans tire of the downward slide that began in the 1960s, we can turn again to what they knew and did. What worked then can work again. In God's favorite language, Latin, *Victoria* does, after all, mean victory.

Appendix 1

The Transformations of Science
From Western Civilization to Cultural Marxism

By Richard W. Hawkins

True science arose in the West due to the unique worldview of Christianity and Western Civilization. It was based on knowing that a rational God of order is the Creator and, being created in His image, we could discover His eternal power and divine nature in His creation. Science at that time was impartial and considered as one of many paths to truth. Technologies, the arts of science, were revolutionary and allowed the West to become far superior above any other civilization at the time.[140]

With the transformation of the nation's worldview from Christian/Western Civilization through Secular Humanism and now into Cultural Marxism the nature of science has transformed to conform to each of these worldview paradigms. With the transformation to Secular Humanism scientism became an easy belief system that corrupted the search for truth. With the transformation into cultural Marxism truth has become relative and science is now politically driven and even more corrupt.

The nature of Science under each of the three worldviews follows:

Under Western Civilization science was based upon the general and special revelations of God. Theology was considered the "queen of the sciences." Science was open to the study of all subjects per the following definition: [141]

SCI'ENCE, *n.* [Fr. from L. *scientia,* from *scio,* to know; Sp. *ciencia;* It. *scienza. Scio* is probably a contracted word.]

---

[140] Stark, Rodney, *The Victory of Reason: How Christianity Led to Freedom, Capitalism, and Western Success,* (Random House Trade Paperbacks, 2005)
[141] *Webster, Noah Webster's first edition of An American dictionary of the English language*

1. In *a general sense*, knowledge, or certain knowledge; the comprehension or understanding of truth or facts by the mind. The *science* of God must be perfect.

2. In *philosophy*, a collection of the general principles or leading truths relating to any subject. *Pure* science, as the mathematics, is built on self-evident truths; but the term science is also applied to other subjects founded on generally acknowledged truths, as *metaphysics;* or on experiment and observation, as *chimistry* and *natural philosophy;* or even to an assemblage of the general principles of an art, as the science of *agriculture;* the science of *navigation. Arts* relate to practice, as painting and sculpture.

A principle in *science* is a rule in art.   *Playfair.*

5. One of the seven liberal branches of knowledge, viz. grammar, logic, rhetoric, arithmetic, geometry, astronomy and music. *Bailey. Johnson.*[142]

This allows scientists to follow the evidence wherever it leads. The shortcoming of this Christian based science is that the truths of the Bible have to be accepted by scientists and society at large as the final arbiter for verifying the interpretations of the scientific observations and experimentations. Where Christianity is marginalized it follows that its Christian based Creation Science is marginalized.

As the Christian influence in the West began to wane in the 1800s the influence of Secular Humanism grew, especially since the publication of Darwin's *Origin of Species* in 1859 and importation of German higher education philosophy into our universities. The whole of Secular Humanism is based on its science of origins without God. The nature of this 'modern' science likewise transformed into what is called hard science and soft science:

The <u>Science Council</u> gives this definition of science:

"Science is the pursuit and application of knowledge and understanding of the natural and social world following a systematic methodology based on evidence."

---

[142] Ibid.

The council goes on to describe the scientific method as being comprised of the following components:

- Objective observation
- Evidence
- Experiment
- Induction
- Repetition
- Critical analysis
- Verification and testing

Sciences that explore the workings of the natural world are usually called hard sciences, or natural sciences. They include:

- Physics
- Chemistry
- Biology
- Astronomy
- Geology
- Meteorology

Studies in these hard sciences involve experiments that are relatively easy to set up with controlled variables and in which it is easier to make objective measurements. Results of hard science experiments can be represented mathematically, and the same mathematical tools can be used consistently to measure and calculate outcomes.

In general, the soft sciences deal with intangibles and relate to the study of human and animal behaviors, interactions, thoughts, and feelings. Soft sciences apply the scientific method to such intangibles, but because of the nature of living beings, it is almost impossible to recreate a soft science experiment with exactitude. Some examples of the soft sciences, sometimes referred to as the social sciences, are:

- Psychology
- <u>Sociology</u>
- Anthropology
- Archaeology (some aspects)

Particularly in sciences dealing with people, it may be difficult to isolate all the variables that can influence an outcome. In some cases, controlling the variable may even alter the results![143]

The shortcomings of the Secular Humanist 'modern' version of science is only the natural world (time, matter and energy) can be considered in the research and results. This leaves God, and intelligence, deliberately excluded. Another major shortcoming for many scientists and the society at large is that the scientific method cannot be applied for past, singular events such as the origins of the universe and origins of life. What is passed off as "fact" (i.e. the singularity of the Big Bang and neo-Darwinian evolution) is no more than conjecture lacking empirical evidence. **Due to this second shortcoming and reliance on the ethical standard of the 'goals justify the means' logical fallacies have to be used to preserve the worldview by trying to silence the opposition:**

- **The overwhelming consensus of scientists is....**
- **Appeals to authority**
- **Ad hominem attacks**
- **Refusing to rebut or debate skeptics**

The controversies facing neo-Darwinian evolution provide excellent examples of the use of these fallacies to prevent the truths of both Intelligent Design concepts and Christian based Creation Science from the public square. Unfortunately, preservation of a faulty worldview trumps truth!

A final shortcoming of this 'modern' science is the formation of scientism within the minds of many people. They believe that only

---

[143] Helmenstine, Anne Marie, PhD, "What is the difference between hard and soft science?" https://www.thoughtco.com/hard-vs-soft-science-3975989 Nov 29, 2019

science can find truth and truth is nowhere else to be found. The obvious conclusion for scientism is God doesn't exist and the Bible is rendered "just another book of stories." You often hear the ignorant refrain "science says...." from those that hold to scientism.

As cultural Marxism has become the prevailing worldview **certain controversial aspects of science have taken on a new paradigm to conform to the Politically Correct narrative and agenda while a more militant form of the logical fallacies cited above and scientism continue on**. Such controversial topics for today include Anthropogenic Global Warming, Sustainable Development, normalizing LGBTQ+ perversions[144], [145] and cultural pressures for coerced vaccinations.[146], [147] By applying Critical Theory, deconstruction and social constructs the concept of post-normal (i.e. cultural Marxist or post-modern) science has transformed as follows:

> The concept of post-normal science goes beyond the traditional assumptions that science is both certain and value-free. Post-normal situations have in common that facts are uncertain, values in dispute, stakes high and decisions urgent, unlike normal science situations where these elements are small. ... judgement becomes necessary as well as involvement of extended peer communities. This new social organization of science is also named post-academic science ... **The exercise of scholarly activities is defined by the dominance of goal orientation where scientific goals are controlled by political or societal actors.** Science

---

[144] Miller, Dave, "This is the Way God Made Me," http://www.apologeticspress.org/apcontent.aspx?category=7&article=1388, 2004
[145] Wanta, JW, et al, "Mental Health Diagnoses Among Transgender Patients in the Clinical Setting: An All-Payer Electronic Health Record Study," https://www.ncbi.nlm.nih.gov/pubmed/31701012?inf_contact_key=ea93e771fad84 faf74fbac1121dda82eb7af0999dac2af6212784c39e05d2aef
[146] Blaxill, Mark, "First-Ever Peer-Reviewed Study of Vaccinated vs Unvaccinated Children Shows Vaccinated Kids Have a Higher Rate of Sickness, 470% Increase in Autism," https://needtoknow.news/2017/05/first-ever-peer-reviewed-study-vaccinated-vs-unvaccinated-children-shows-vaccinated-kids-higher-rate-sickness-470-increase-autism/, (May 7, 2017)
[147] Livingston, Bob, "More on the myth of vaccinated health," https://boblivingstonletter.com/alerts/more-on-the-myth-of-vaccinated-health/

operates in a strong two-way dialogue [the Hegelian dialectic] with society.

Facts are still necessary, but no longer sufficient. The guiding principle of normal science - the goal of achievement of factual knowledge - must be modified to fit the post-normal principle **to achieve the goal of quality** [as practiced, quality is measured by the goals and agenda of cultural Marxism]. For this purpose, post-normal scientists should be capable of establishing extended peer communities and allow for **'extended facts'** from non-scientific experts.....In post-normal science, the **maintenance and enhancement of quality**, rather than the establishment of factual knowledge, is the key task of scientists. [148]

The UN's IPCC Anthropogenic Global Warming alarmism is a good cultural Marxist example of the use and abuse of science. Key findings from the NIPCC report *Why Scientists Disagree About Global Warming*[149] illustrates in great detail **"The exercise of scholarly activities is defined by the dominance of goal orientation where scientific goals are controlled by political or societal actors"** and the **"maintenance and enhancement of quality**, rather than the establishment of factual knowledge, is the key task of scientists." When tied with Sustainability the UN goals for global governance, global citizenship, global economy, continued breakup of the family and marriage, marginalization of Christianity, destruction of constitutional republicanism and reduction of private property/private enterprise becomes paramount.

KEY FINDINGS

No Consensus

- "Scientific consensus" in favor of the catastrophic man-made global warming hypothesis are without exception

---

[148] Kunseler, Eva, "Towards a New Paradigm of Science," http://www.nusap.net/downloads/KunselerEssay2007.pdf, 2007

[149] Idso, Craig, et al, "Why Scientists Disagree about Global Warming," NIPCC, https://www.heartland.org/publications-resources/publications/why-scientists-disagree-about-global-warming, (Nov 23, 2015)

methodologically flawed and often deliberately misleading.

Why Scientists Disagree

- Climate is an interdisciplinary subject requiring insights from many fields of study. Very few scholars have mastery of more than one or two of these disciplines.
- Fundamental uncertainties arise from insufficient observational evidence, disagreements over how to interpret data, and how to set the parameters of models.
- IPCC, created to find and disseminate research finding a human impact on global climate, is not a credible source. It is agenda-driven, a political rather than scientific body, and some allege it is corrupt.

Scientific Method vs. Political Science

- The hypothesis implicit in all IPCC writings, though rarely explicitly stated, is that dangerous global warming is resulting, or will result, from human-related greenhouse gas emissions.
- In contradiction of the scientific method, IPCC assumes its implicit hypothesis is correct and that its only duty is to collect evidence and make plausible arguments in the hypothesis's favor.

Flawed Projections

- GCMs [climate models] systematically over-estimate the sensitivity of climate to carbon dioxide (CO2), many known forcings and feedbacks are poorly modeled, and modelers exclude forcings and feedbacks that run counter to their mission to find a human influence on climate.
- Four specific forecasts made by GCMs have been falsified by real-world data from a wide variety of sources. In particular, there has been no global warming for some 18 years.

False Postulates

- Neither the rate nor the magnitude of the reported late twentieth century surface warming (1979–2000) lay outside normal natural variability.
- The late twentieth century warm peak was of no greater magnitude than previous peaks caused entirely by natural forcings and feedbacks.
- Historically, increases in atmospheric CO_2 followed increases in temperature, they did not precede them. Therefore, CO_2 levels could not have forced temperatures to rise.
- Solar forcings are not too small to explain twentieth century warming. In fact, their effect could be equal to or greater than the effect of CO_2 in the atmosphere.
- A warming of 2°C or more during the twenty-first century would probably not be harmful, on balance, because many areas of the world would benefit from or adjust to climate change.

Unreliable Circumstantial Evidence

- Melting of Arctic sea ice and polar icecaps is not occurring at "unnatural" rates and does not constitute evidence of a human impact on the climate.
- Best available data show sea-level rise is not accelerating. Local and regional sea levels continue to exhibit typical natural variability – in some places rising and in others falling.
- The link between warming and drought is weak, and by some measures drought decreased over the twentieth century. Changes in the hydrosphere of this type are regionally highly variable and show a
- closer correlation with multidecadal climate rhythmicity than they do with global temperature.
- No convincing relationship has been established between warming over the past 100 years and increases in extreme weather events. Meteorological science

195

suggests just the opposite: A warmer world will see milder weather patterns.

- No evidence exists that current changes in Arctic permafrost are other than natural or are likely to cause a climate catastrophe by releasing methane into the atmosphere.

Policy Implications

- Rather than rely exclusively on IPCC for scientific advice, policymakers should seek out advice from independent, nongovernment organizations and scientists who are free of financial and political conflicts of interest
- Individual nations should take charge of setting their own climate policies based upon the hazards that apply to their particular geography, geology, weather, and culture
- Rather than invest scarce world resources in a quixotic campaign based on politicized and unreliable science, world leaders would do well to turn their attention to real problems their people and their planet face.

Appendix 2

Common Core Common Sense: Why It's Illiberal and Unconstitutional [150]

Dr. Daniel B. Coupland, Associate Professor of Education, Hillsdale College

On May 29th, 2009, Arne Duncan, the new Secretary of Education for the Obama Administration, gave a speech at the National Press Club in Washington, D.C. In the speech, he said,

> "We want to raise the bar dramatically in terms of high standards. What we have had as a country, I'm convinced, is what we call a race to the bottom. We have 50 different standards, 50 different goal posts. And due to political pressure, those have been dumbed down. We want to fundamentally reverse that. We want common, career-- ready internationally benchmarked standards." [151]

In this short paragraph, the Secretary of Education identified the problems of the past and set a new vision for education in this country. He correctly assessed the damage created by the Bush Administration's Education policy from 2002 known as No Child Left Behind (or NCLB). While supporters of NCLB can point to limited success in a few areas, the Bush Administration's education policy left the nation's schools in a bureaucratic mess. In the National Press Club speech, the new Secretary of Education was arguing that the mess was created by — what he and others have called — a "patchwork of state standards" that left states to compete in a fundamentally flawed and unfair process for limited federal funds. Secretary Duncan's argument — presented at the National Press Club and elsewhere — was

---

[150] Coupland, Daniel B, "Common Core Common Sense: Why It's Illiberal and Unconstitutional," https://www.hillsdale.edu/wp-content/uploads/2016/02/Charter-School-2016-Common-Core-Common-Sense.pdf, (Jun 4,2013)
[151] US Dept of Education, "NPC" Speech," https://www2.ed.gov/news/newsletters/edreview/2009/0605.html, (Jun 5, 2009)

very persuasive to those in the education community who had suffered under the separate and very unequal policies of the era know as No Child Left Behind. Four years after Arne Duncan's 2009 speech, all but a handful of states have signed on to a common set of curricular standards known as Common Core.

Common Core will now provide the framework for what students learn in math and English language arts, but it will also establish two federally funded and approved tests that will replace what states currently use to measure students' academic success. Afraid to be left out of the new national education marketplace, private companies are quickly trying to align themselves with the Common Core standards. In order to survive in the Common Core era, textbook publishers and other education--related industries must show how their materials meet these national standards. SAT and ACT are now aligned to Common Core. Those who think they can avoid the Common Core by sending their children to private schools or by homeschooling should think again. The Iowa Test of Basic Skills and the Stanford 10—two popular tests of private schools and homeschool parents—will also be aligned to Common Core.

Within a few short years, Common Core has gone from virtual unknown to national educational powerhouse that may influence the formal education of some 50 million K--12 students in America. In the next few minutes, I'll try to give you some insight on what Common Core is, what the major arguments are both for and against Common Core, and I will also try to show how these arguments are missing the most important ideas about education altogether. But first, I will start with a brief history.

A Brief History of Educational Standards in America

The idea of a rich educational experience finds its roots deep in American history. The Founders of this country believed an "informed citizenry" was necessary for good government. In the early 1800s, Horace Mann continued this legacy by arguing for widespread public education. Today, Horace Mann is known as the "Father of the *Common* School Movement." In the late 1800s, politicians and social leaders looked to the schools to solve pressing social needs brought on by industrialization, urbanization, and immigration. Many leading education theorists of the late nineteenth and early twentieth century —including John Dewey, William H. Kilpatrick, G. Stanley Hall, and others—developed or promoted progressive solutions to these pressing social needs. For the first half of the 20thCentury, progressive theories—such as child--centered pedagogy and practical/work--related curricula—dominated much of the education landscape.

In October of 1957, the United States was awakened from its educational malaise when the Soviet Union successfully launched Sputnik, the first space satellite, in to orbit. This one event signaled America's educational decline and brought attention to the need for a return to rich content—at least in the fields of math, science, and foreign languages. But these reforms were quickly lost in the cultural turmoil of the 1960s and early 1970s, and schools once again offered a smorgasbord of academically weak classes. Students were earning academic credit in courses titled "personal relationships," "what's happening," and "girl talk," and they were receiving academic credit for extra--curricular activities such as "student government," "mass media," and "cheerleading."

In 1983, the National Commission on Excellence in Education published a landmark study on American education titled *A Nation at Risk*, which warned that the country's economic, political, and cultural future was threatened by our weak education system. The report stated the now famous lines,

> Our nation is at risk, the educational foundations of our society are presently being eroded by a rising tide of mediocrity that threatens our very future as a Nation and a people...If an unfriendly foreign power had attempted to impose on America the mediocre educational performance that exists today, we might well have viewed it as an act of war. [152]

---

[152] "A Nation At Risk," https://www2.ed.gov/pubs/NatAtRisk/risk.html, Apr 1983

A Nation at Risk signaled a turning point in American Education and brought about a renewed focus on what Americans should know and be able to do. E.D. Hirsch's 1987 book, *Cultural Literacy*, argued that schools should focus on the basics and pass along "core knowledge" that every educated American should know. But many in the education establishment resisted these content--based reforms and continued to push a progressive agenda for America's schools.

With the collapse of the Soviet Union in the late 1980s and the end of the Cold War, international trade boomed, and many countries had greater opportunities to participate in the global marketplace. Globalization led to international comparisons across a variety of social indicators—including education. Many of the Asian countries—with whom we were now competing—seemed to move further and further ahead of the United States. One of the obvious features of the education in these countries was the existence of clear national education standards. Many reformers pushed the idea that if the United States was going to compete in the international marketplace, the quality of education in the entire country would have to improve. They also concluded that such improvement would only occur if students were held to high academic standards.

In 1989, President George Bush Sr. hosted an education summit for the nation's governors on academic standards and assessment. A charismatic governor from Arkansas named Bill Clinton took the lead in crafting a set of goals for increasing academic achievement in America. And when Clinton defeated Bush for the presidency three years later, the new president used these goals to craft his signature education policy known as Goals 2000.Goals 2000 provided money for each state to develop its own standards based on a national template. Critics of this initiative claimed that this effort violated the longstanding principle established by the 10thAmendment of the U.S. Constitution that education is the responsibility of the states. But the Clinton administration countered that the national standards were meant to be only a template for the states to follow and that each state was ultimately responsible for its own standards. Interestingly, Goals 2000 also authorized the creation of an approval board which would certify that states standards had indeed matched the national template. This approval board, however, never materialized because in the 1994 midterm election, Republicans gained the majority in Congress and quickly abolished it.

Even without the federal board, the effort to create state standards based on a national template continued, and in the mid--1990sprofessional subject--specific organizations released national standards for history, English, and math. The general public assumed that these standards would represent the basic knowledge and skills that students would need to know in a particular subject, but they soon discovered that these professional organizations had used this federally funded project to push unproven and, in a few cases, radical ideas within academic fields. Public opposition to these national standards spread quickly. Most states avoided the controversy of the national standards by creating their own unique standards. If there was one thing in *common* across state standards it was their emphasis on less controversial skills—such as "critical thinking," "cooperative learning," and "shared understanding"—rather than more concrete statements about specific ideas, people, and books that students should read.

In 2001, President George W. Bush pushed his education policy—known as No Child Left Behind (or NCLB)—which—like those before it—promised to increase student achievement by encouraging states to set high standards and to develop assessments based on those standards. But unlike the initiatives before it, NCLB required states to test all students in particular subjects and at particular grade levels in order to receive federal funding.

Looking back, most education experts—on both right and left—concluded that NCLB had failed to deliver real and lasting success. NCLB created an environment where "teaching to the test" became status quo. And what made matters worse is that from state--to--state, the tests were all different. Under NCLB, each state had its own academic standards that it was expected to meet. And because federal money was based on each state meeting its own standards, there was little incentive for states to keep the academic bar high. In an effort to show higher proficiency in student achievement, states began lowering proficiency levels in what Secretary Duncan referred to as a "race to the bottom." By the end of the decade, many in the education community were looking for an alternative to the "separate--and--unequal" approach to standards of NCLB.

Common Core

In 2007, two national trade organizations—the National Governors Association and the Council of Chief State School Officers—started work on a common set of curriculum standards in English language arts and mathematics. In December of 2008, these two groups produced a document on national education standards that would guide the Obama Administration during its transition into office. Two months later, the Secretary of Education announced a federal education grant program known as "Race to the Top" (the name is an obvious nod to the failures of No Child Left Behind). This program included money from the 2009 "Stimulus Bill," which was to be used by states to improve academic standards and assessments. In order to receive Race to the Top grants, state had to commit to "a set of content standards that define what students must know and be able to do and that are substantially identical across all states in a consortium." In 2011, the Obama administration made the decision to adopt common standards even easier. Most states were still obligated to meet onerous NCLB requirements. The U.S. Department of Education promised NCLB waivers to states that adopted a common set of college--and career--ready standards and assessments. And while the U.S. Department of Education did not require states to adopt the Common Core specifically, these standards were—and still are—the only standards that met the Education Department's criteria.

Forty--five states and the District of Columbia adopted the Common Core standards. Minnesota adopted the English language arts standards, but it rejected the math. Initially, only Alaska and Texas rejected Common Core, but in the end, Virginia and Nebraska did too.

Arguments FOR Common Core

The idea of common academic standards across all states is quite appealing to many in the field of education because it seems to cure some obvious and longstanding problems. Allow me to highlight two of the most important.

First, our mobile society makes it easy for families to pick up and move. As E.D. Hirsch points out in his book *The Knowledge Deficit* (2006),

> In a typical American school district, the average rate at which students transfer in and out of schools during the academic year is about one third. In a typical inner--city school, only about half of the students who start in September are still there in May—a mobility rate of 50 percent. (111)

When students move from school to school—especially when these moves are across state lines, they often experience a fractured education filled with huge gaps or boring repetitions. However, if all schools are meeting the same academic standards, the students have a greater chance of finding a relatively consistent education experience regardless of where they move within the country. In theory a student should be able to move from Maine to California with little disruption in his education.

Second, for years, the United States has lagged behind many industrialized nations in key academic areas such as math and science. Since Sputnik, policymakers have tried to craft a coherent plan to improve our country's standing in these subjects areas, but they have struggled to do so in light of the "patchwork of state standards." Pointing to the failures of NCLB, proponents of Common Core argue that having a common set of academically rigorous standards for the entire country would allow policymakers to craft a coherent plan for improving American education. Many corporate leaders and politicians argue that we are unable to compete as a nation in a global society if every state is doing its own thing.

Arguments AGAINST Common Core

As you can probably guess, Common Core has its critics, who typically focus one or more of the following concerns.

1.   **Cost**

Critics claim that Common Core will be very expensive to implement and maintain. The only study on the cost of implementing Common Core standards and assessment nationwide estimated a price tag of about $16 billion over seven years. But the truth of the matter is that no one really knows what the final price tag for Common Core will be. For this reason—and others—critics have already labeled this initiative Obama Core. Critics of Common Core charge that most states acted irresponsibly when they adopted the standards because they did not first have a firm understanding of its price tag. Many states saw the Race to the Top funds as a way to pay for immediate education expenses and failed to see that they were signing on to something that would be far more expensive.

2.   **Quality**

Critics argue that rather than pushing all states toward high standards, Common Core is encouraging a coalescence in the mediocre middle—so, for example, while Mississippi's standards appear to get stronger by adopting Common Core, the standards in Massachusetts get weaker. Several curriculum experts—including Ze'ev Wurman, Sandra Stotsky, and James Milgram—have examined the math and English language arts standards very carefully, and they have discovered some alarming concerns. In fact, because of these concerns and others, both Stotsky and Milgram—who served on the Common Core's validation committee—refused to sign the final validation report.

3.   **Privacy**

The 2009 "Stimulus Bill" required states to begin tracking students in a database—starting in their preschool years to their entry into the workforce. This database will link students' results on Common Core--related assessments to other private personal information. This database will be available to a wide variety of departments within the federal government. While supporters of Common Core claim that the system employs measures to protect the anonymity of students, critics have pointed to studies that demonstrate how these measure might not be as secure as supporters assume. But the larger issue remains about whether collecting such private information is consistent with the role of government expressed by the Founders.

4.   Constitutionality

The biggest concern of Common Core critics to date has been the federal government's ever--increasing role in education. The 10thAmendmentof the U.S. Constitution established the principle that the "power" to oversee education belongs to the states. This longstanding principle of local control of education is reiterated throughout our laws and government codes. For generations, Americans have understood that the constitutional authority for education rests with the states, not the federal government. Critics of Common Core see these standards as federal overreach and a violation of both the letter and spirit of federal education law and the U.S. Constitution.

Supporters of Common Core like to portray these critics as far--right extremists who are paranoid about a government takeover. But this is not true. Diane Ravitch, a respected historian of American education, is hardly a darling of the far right—especially in recent years. On Feb. 26th of this year, Ravitch wrote the following in a piece titled "Why I Oppose Common Core Standards." Her comments below summarize many of the central concerns that most critics have.

> I have long advocated for voluntary national standards, believing that it would be helpful to states and districts to have general guidelines about what students should know and be able to do as they progress through school.

> Such standards, I believe, should be voluntary, not imposed by the federal government...

> For the past two years, I have steadfastly insisted that I was neither for nor against the Common Core standards. I was agnostic. I wanted to see how they worked in practice...

> After much deliberation,...I have come to the conclusion that the Common Core standards effort is fundamentally

flawed by the process with which they have been foisted upon the nation. [153]

Ravitch then goes on to explain her opposition to Common Core:

> Their creation was neither grassroots nor did it emanate from the states. In fact, it was well understood by states that they would not be eligible for Race to the Top funding ($4.35 billion) unless they adopted the Common Core standards. Federal law prohibits the U.S. Department of Education from prescribing any curriculum, but in this case the Department figured out a clever way to evade the letter of the law. Forty--six states and the District of Columbia signed on, not because the Common Core standards were better than their own, but because they wanted a share of the federal cash. [154]

The response from Common Core supporters regarding federal overreach has been surprising weak. Michelle Rhee, the former chancellor of the D.C. public schools and a well--known education reformer, is a strong supporter of Common Core. In a speech last Thursday to political and business leaders in my home state, she said,

> The vast majority of states have adopted the standards. I've heard some rumblings from folks who say we don't like it when the federal government is telling us what to do. We don't like that. You know what you should not like? The fact that China is kicking our butts right now. Get over feeling bad about the federal government and feel bad that our kids are not competing. [155]

I certainly hope that this country's commitment to the Constitution does not simply hang on something as fragile as a

---

[153] Strauss, Valerie, "Why I Oppose Common Core Standards: Ravitch," *The Washington Post*, https://www.washingtonpost.com/news/answer-sheet/wp/2013/02/26/why-i-oppose-common-core-standards-ravitch/, Feb 26, 2013
[154] Ibid.
[155] https://www.democraticunderground.com/1014496942, (May 30, 2013)

"feeling" that we need to "get over." Rhee's cavalier critique of those who are concerned about federal overreach is troubling, but I—for one—appreciate her honesty. Most supporters of Common Core try to hide behind words like "state--led" and "voluntary." But anyone willing [to] take an honest look at what transpired between 2009 and 2011 would conclude that many of these cash--strapped states already under the burden of budget shortfalls and expensive NCLB requirements were seduced by a high pressured, time sensitive sales pitch for adopting the standards that included relief in the form of money and waivers. Yes, the states are ultimately responsible for selling their constitutional birthright for a bowl of porridge, and given more time, perhaps many more states might have rejected such a poor bargain. But perhaps, it's not too late.

The Retreat

Initially, Common Core experienced widespread bi--partisan support. Even some prominent Republican politicians—such as Jeb Bush of Florida, Chris Christie of New Jersey, and Mitch Daniels of Indiana—were strong supporters of Common Core. But support for Common Core seems to be weakening, and some states that originally adopted the standards are starting to take a second look.

This spring, the Michigan House of Representatives voted essentially to defund the implementation of Common Core standards and their related tests. In Indiana, the State Senate voted to delay implementation of Common Core so that the State Board of Education could get a better understanding of the quality, cost, and loss of local control associated with implementation of the standards and related assessments. In April, Indiana's new governor, Mike Pence, agreed to take "a long, hard look" at Common Core and quickly added that he was one of a only few politicians initially to oppose No Child Left Behind.

Other states are considering legislative action to delay or defund Common Core standards and assessments. Within the last nine months, the following states have held public forums or formal legislative hearings to discuss delaying or defunding Common Core: South Carolina, North Carolina, Georgia, Florida, Alabama,

Louisiana, Missouri, Kansas, Colorado, Utah, Idaho, South Dakota, Ohio, Pennsylvania, and Wisconsin.

In April, The Republican National Committee passed an anti--Common Core resolution stating that the RNC "rejects the [Common Core] plan which creates and fits the country with a nationwide straitjacket on academic freedom and achievement."

Never to be outdone, Texas boldly reiterated its opposition to the Common Core standards. In early May, the Texas House of Representatives formally rejected the standards by a margin of 140--2.

Last month, a poll of "education insiders," which included national and state education leaders, found that support for Common Core is beginning to fade. The poll showed that 63% of those polled believe that states will implement some sort of moratorium on Common Core.

And it would be wrong to assume that opposition to Common Core is coming only from the right. Recently, Randi Weingarten, president of the nation's second largest teachers union with about 1 million members, called for a moratorium on the use of standardized tests based on Common Core standards. Ms. Weingarten, initially a strong supporter of the Common Core standards, is concerned that aspects of Common Core have been poorly implemented and that without a "mid--course correction," the entire effort will fall apart. She said recently that "The Common Core is in trouble. There is a serious backlash in lots of different ways, on the right and on the left."

Something Much More Fundamental

The idea of common, nationwide standards is appealing, and as I mentioned above, the benefits of such standards should not be ignored. But the concerns over Common Core—and especially its implementation—are real and troubling. Any of these concerns—cost, mediocrity, and federal overreach—are serious enough that states should consider pausing and, perhaps, ultimately repealing their adoption of these standards. But a much more fundamental concern exists about Common Core that goes to the heart of any educational experience.

Recall Secretary Duncan's comments from the beginning of my talk. He said, "We want common, career ready...standards." The phrase "career--ready" or "college--and career--ready" appear throughout the Common Core standards. The opening page of the Common Core document includes eight references to "college--and career--" readiness. If any other goal is mentioned, such as literacy, it is subservient to this overarching goal. The catchphrase for the Common Core—printed below its logo—is "Preparing America's Students for College & Career." Common Core's mission statement reflects this notion as well. Here is the entire mission statement:

> The Common Core State Standards provide a consistent, clear understanding of what students are expected to learn, so teachers and parents know what they need to do to help them. The standards are designed to be robust and relevant to the real world, reflecting the knowledge and skills that young people need **for success in college and careers**. With American students fully prepared for the future, our communities will be best positioned **to compete successfully in a global economy.** [156]

With such a mission, it is easy to see why so many politicians and business leaders support Common Core. Even critics of Common Core have adopted the "college--and career--ready" mantra and now spend much of their time arguing how Common Core will *not* prepare students for the working world. I understand that this line of attack is necessary if they have any hope of stopping Common Core. But what I would like for us to consider here today is whether or not career preparation for a "global economy" should be the ultimate educational goal in America.

In the 1920s and 30s, progressive educators tried to devalue an impractical liberal arts education and saw schools as mechanisms for preparing students for particular roles within the social structure. During this era, schooling became job preparation.

---

[156] Blumenfeld, Sam, "Who's Behind the Common Core Standards," *The New American,* https://www.thenewamerican.com/reviews/opinion/item/13412-whos-behind-the-common-core-curriculum, (Oct 29, 2012)

But in the ancient world, job preparation was known as "servile education" because it prepared the student to "serve" a master in a particular kind of work. Modern theorists would say that I am being ridiculous to associate the ancient notion of "servile education" to "skills for the 21st century" which will allow students to adapt to an ever--changing society. But as long as students are told that the end of education is a job or career, they will forever be servants of some master.

Joy Pullman, an education policy analyst for the Heartland Institute (and a Hillsdale graduate), recently won the Robert Novak award to study and write about Common Core. Pullman is quickly becoming one of the nation's experts on Common Core. At a recent hearing in Wisconsin on Common Core Standards, Ms. Pullman addressed Common Core's misguided focus.

> [I]n a self--governing nation we need citizens who can govern themselves. The ability to support oneself with meaningful work is an important part, but only a part, of self--government. When a nation expands **workforce training** so that it crowds out the other things that rightly belong in education, we end up turning out neither good workers nor good citizens. [157]

The ancients knew that in order for men to be truly free, they must have a liberal education that includes study of literature and history, mathematics and science, music and art. Yes, man is made for work, but he is also made for so much more. Education should be about the highest things. We should study these things—stars, plant cells, square roots, Shakespeare's *Hamlet*, Mozart's *Requiem*, Lincoln's *Gettysburg Address*—not simply because they will get us into the right college or a particular line of work; rather, we study these noble things because they can tell us who we are, why we are here, and what our relationship is to each other as human beings and to the physical world that surrounds us.

---

[157] Farmer, Brian, "Common Core is Rotten to the Core," *The New American*, https://www.thenewamerican.com/culture/education/item/18437-common-core-is-rotten-to-the-core, (Jun 9, 2014)

Commenting on the Common Core standards, Anthony Esolen, English professor at Providence College, said,

> [W]hat appalls me most about the standards...is the cavalier contempt for great works of human art and thought, in literary form. It is sheer ignorance of the life of the imagination. We are not programming machines. We are teaching children...We are to be forming the minds, and hearts of men and women...[and we should] raise them to be human beings, honoring what is good and right, cherishing what is beautiful. [158]

If education in America has become—as Common Core openly declares—preparation for work in a global economy, then the situation is far worse than Common Core critics anticipated, and the concerns about the cost, the quality, and, yes, even the constitutionality of Common Core pale in comparison to the concern for the hearts, minds, and souls of America's children.

---

[158] Shaw, Jerry, Newsmax, "Common Core: 5 Quotes from University Officials on Heated Debate," https://www.newsmax.com/FastFeatures/common-core-quotes-university-officials-debate/2015/04/20/id/639571/, Apr 20, 2015

Appendix 3

A Classical Education for Modern Times [159]

Dr. Terrence O. Moore, PhD

Doctrina sed vim promovet insitam,rectique cultus pectora roborant.[160]

The Hillsdale College Barney Charter School Initiative has deliberately taken a classical approach to education. By "classical," we mean a form of education that could be called classical, civic, and liberal but in the school reform movement these days most often goes by the designation "classical." Some might call it "conservative," but we prefer the term "traditional." That is, we adhere to an ancient view of learning and traditional teaching methods. Such a choice might at first seem paradoxical or even out-of-touch with reality. Why, at the beginning of the twenty-first century, in the age of the internet, in a country that has long been addicted to the revolutionary and the novel, when almost everyone in the world of K-12 education is singing the chorus of "critical thinking skills for a twenty-first-century global economy," should cutting-edge schools root themselves so deeply in the past? Is not newer always better? What could today's young people learn from old books? We must answer these questions clearly from the outset.

Classical education has a history of over 2500 years in the West. It began in ancient Greece, was adopted wholesale by the Romans, faltered after the fall of Rome, made a slow but steady recovery during the Middle Ages, and was again brought to perfection in the Italian Renaissance. The classical inheritance passed to England, and from the mother country to America through colonial settlement. At the time of this nation's founding classical education was still thriving. Jefferson heartily recommended Greek and Latin as the

---

[159] https://www.hillsdale.edu/wp-content/uploads/2016/02/Charter-School-2016-A-Classical-Education-for-Modern-Times.pdf
[160] "Yet learning increases inborn worth, and righteous ways make strong the heart." Horace

languages of study for early adolescence. One of the Founding Fathers' favorite books was Plutarch's Lives of the Noble Greeks and Romans. Eighteenth-century Americans venerated and trusted George Washington in large part because he reminded them of the Roman patriot Cincinnatus. So important has classical education been in the history of the West that it would only be a slight exaggeration to say that the march of civilization has paralleled the vibrancy of classical schools. Unlike the old classical schools, today's classical schools do not make the medium of instruction Latin and Greek (though to be classical they must require the study of Latin at some point). Nonetheless, the Hillsdale-sponsored charter schools will remain classical by upholding the same standards of teaching, of curriculum, and of discipline found in the schools of old. Indeed, in these schools English will be taught using methods derived from centuries of teaching and learning the classical languages. Hillsdale thus takes stock in the tried and true rather than in the latest fads frothing forth from the schools of education.

Apart from this impressive history, Hillsdale has embraced classical education as the surest road to school reform for at least four reasons. These reasons constitute a clear break from modern, progressive education and a return to traditional aims and methods. Classical education:

- values knowledge for its own sake

- upholds the standards of correctness, logic, beauty, weightiness, and truth intrinsic to the liberal arts;

- demands moral virtue of its adherents;

- and prepares human beings to assume their places as responsible citizens in the political order.

We shall discuss each of these characteristics of classical education in turn.

Knowledge and Core Knowledge

The classical view of education holds that human beings are thinking creatures. Unlike other living beings, humans live by their intelligence. We want to know things. Specifically, we want to know what the things around us are and how they operate. We want to know who we are, where we come from, and what is expected of us. In short, we want to know the truth. From birth, the curiosity of children is astounding. Children observe everything around them. They pick up language at an astonishing rate. As soon as they begin to speak, they ask the question "What is it?" of everything that catches their attention. Children demonstrate what is true of all people: we are all natural learners. Any plan of education, therefore, should take advantage of young people's natural curiosity. Schemes that stall children in their learning because "they are not ready for it" or it is not "age appropriate," or that use various gimmicks that sugar-coat learning as though children regard their books as they do their medicine, are not only unnecessary but counterproductive and insulting to the human mind.

While children are naturally disposed to learning, everything we need to know does not come to us unaided from nature. Children need explicit instruction to understand the world around them, whether in language, the operations of physical nature, or the relations among human beings. As children grow, their questions become increasingly complex and their abilities to assimilate their observations more advanced. At every child's disposal is a veritable arsenal of mental capacities: memory, reason, imagination, a sense of beauty, a facility for language. Classical education does not simply leave children to their own mental urges and inclinations. Rather, it feeds and directs and strengthens children's mental capacities in the same way that sports exercise their physical abilities. The mind, like the body, atrophies when not well-trained. The emphasis on rigorous mental training is an important difference between classical education and modern, progressive education. By stressing childhood "creativity" and "spontaneity," while at the same time denigrating "mere rote learning" (and therefore human memory itself), without making children do much work or work on anything important, the modern school takes bright young children and puts them on a path to becoming bored adults who do not know very much. It is the old story of the tortoise and the hare. Falling in love with our talents— without making any substantial effort to improve them—causes one

214

to lose the race. In this case, it is the all-important race towards becoming informed, moral, thinking citizens.

So classical education puts young minds to work. It leads young people to understand themselves and the world around them. Students do not learn in the abstract. They must acquire concrete skills and gain knowledge in certain disciplines to participate fully and effectively in human civilization. To this end, Hillsdale, though it does not require the *Core Knowledge* curriculum in its schools, does embrace E. D. Hirsch's idea of "cultural literacy." For people to communicate effectively, according to Hirsch, they must not only use the same language. To express and understand complex ideas, they must possess a reservoir of common facts, ideas, and references known to all in a given social and political order. Abraham Lincoln is perhaps the best example of a leader who relied on cultural literacy to convey his ideas. Like other Americans on the frontier, he had little formal schooling. Yet he read intensively the works of Shakespeare, the King James' Bible, the fables of Æsop, Euclid's geometry, and the documents of the American Founding. Few men in our history have been able to express so forcefully and with such economy the principles of freedom and human dignity:

> Four score and seven years ago our fathers brought forth
> on this continent a new nation, conceived in liberty, and
> dedicated to the proposition that all men are created
> equal.

Lincoln's audience at Gettysburg instantly knew that he referred to the "proposition" of the Declaration of Independence. For this reason, the *Gettysburg Address* is not only one of the greatest speeches in our history; it is the shortest. Lincoln did not have to retell the history of the Revolution. His fellow Americans already knew it.

One of the great dangers we presently face as a nation is that, in the words of Hirsch, "many young people today strikingly lack the information that writers of American books and newspapers have traditionally taken for granted among their readers from all generations." The same observation applies to the realm of politics, the financial and industrial world, and all other facets of American

215

life. Employers are constantly amazed at what their employees do not know and therefore cannot do. In politics, the poignant allusions of a Lincoln would fall upon deaf ears. Indeed, most citizens and most elected officials are alarmingly ignorant of the basic facts of American history and constitutional government. Make no mistake. Cultural literacy is not merely ornamental trivia. Our purpose is not to make Jeopardy champions. Rather, cultural literacy is essential to a nation and its citizens. A culturally illiterate America cannot live up to the demands placed upon us by history and the present condition of the world. A culturally illiterate individual cannot comprehend and navigate the vast areas of human knowledge essential to his political, economic, and moral well-being.

By endorsing the idea of cultural literacy (and civic literacy), Hillsdale's charter school initiative has resolved to break out of the cycle of ignorance that modern culture and modern educational theories and practices perpetuate. The students of these schools will study the traditional liberal arts—language and literature, history and government, mathematics and the sciences, music and art—in a coherent and orderly program. Each curriculum will run from the rudiments of basic literacy and math skills to the higher orders of thought and expression. All students will be required to complete this classical curriculum. Admittedly, different children have different talents. Some students "catch on" more quickly than others. We shall always seek to challenge every student all the time. Yet Hillsdale regards any system of tracking that relegates certain students to an inferior curriculum as nefarious. Not all students will learn at the same speed, but all will complete the course.

Upholding Standards

In addition to requiring students to know certain things, a classical education also teaches young people judgment according to certain standards. To be "classical" means to uphold a standard of excellence. The classical works of Greece and Rome are not great simply because they are old. They are great because they employ harmonious language to depict remarkable human events and to explain the transcendent ideals of human existence. Each of the liberal arts has its own standard of correctness, logic, beauty, weightiness,

216

and truth. The study of a language offers perhaps the best example, especially since human beings live by communicating. Everyone can talk, and most people can read and write on a "functional" level. A classical education requires more than functional literacy, however. It teaches students from an early age high standards of grammar, precision in word choice, and an eloquence that can emanate only from a love of the language. Throughout his education, the student will be exposed to the highest examples of eloquence attained by the greatest writers and speakers of the language.

"... I come to bury Caesar, not to praise him." Shakespeare

"There is a tide in the affairs of men ..." Shakespeare

"We few, we happy few, we band of brothers." Shakespeare

"These are the times that try men's souls." Paine

"Never in the field of human conflict was so much owed by so many to so few." Churchill

These sentences are entirely grammatical. They could just as easily be used to teach grammar as "I come to help Jane, not to hurt her." By preferring Shakespeare to an anonymous "See Jane" sentence (usually not well written) we teach three things rather than one. We teach grammar. We teach cultural literacy. We also teach beauty. Our purpose is to introduce young people to the masters of the language so they themselves learn to employ the force and the beauty of the spoken and written word.

Young people today are particularly in need of standards of thought and of real beauty. Their speech ranges from the sloppy to the vulgar. The person whose only expressions of approval and disapproval are "that's cool" and "that sucks" lacks not only a copious vocabulary but also the ability to judge events according to their nature and gravity. Teachers at Hillsdale schools will not fail to teach students the standards that lift them out of the formless dross of the culture. Music is another area in which students are in dire need of high standards. The logical thinking that comes from mathematics and the sciences is no less important. Upholding standards is a principle of exclusion as much as of inclusion. Hillsdale does not pretend that all writing is equally good, that all human endeavors are equally important or beneficial to human life, or that all scientific theories are equally true. In choosing the elements of the curriculum—works of literature and art, events in history—our motto is that of Churchill: "I shall be satisfied with the very best."

Moral Virtue

Education is a moral enterprise. Young people are put into moral situations constantly. "Should I tell Mom that I broke her favorite vase or pretend like nothing happened?" "Should I copy the answers of the person sitting next to me?" "Should I smoke the cigarette and drink the beer my friend just gave me?" "Should my boyfriend and I have sex since we love each other?" These are the timeless moral questions youth face today and have always faced. Anyone who thinks they are new should read the Confessions of St. Augustine. This patriarch of the church stole apples as a child and as a teenager impregnated a woman to whom he was not married. His knowledge of sin came from his own inner struggle. Schools can approach the moral lives of children and youth in three ways. They can try to ignore moral issues altogether. They can open up moral questions for students to explore in a "non-judgmental" and noncommittal environment. Or they can teach classical views of self-command using traditional teaching methods.

The first approach is simply impossible. All schools must maintain an atmosphere of order and decorum for learning to take place. Schools that try to ignore the character of their students either end up with major discipline problems or teach some forms of character without claiming to do so. As soon as a school says "this is right" and "this is wrong" it is teaching character in some form. The second approach might seem the most worthy of reasonable people. "Let us talk about morality in a non-judgmental way and let students come up with their own answers," say the advocates of moral reasoning and values clarification. They even make moral discussion a part of the curriculum. What happens in these discussions is that teachers open up pre-marital sex, drug use, and other illicit activities as plausible "life choices" so long as students can explain those choices in terms of "their own values." Predictably, research has

218

indicated that students who are exposed to open-ended discussions of moral issues are far more likely to engage in vice. (See William Kilpatrick, *Why Johnny Can't Tell Right from Wrong*, ch. 4).

In contrast to the first two approaches, Hillsdale advocates the teaching of the classical virtues using traditional methods. ***In the public charter school setting we leave questions of faith up to the students and their parents.***[161] [Emphasis and footnote added by Editor] But we agree with Aristotle's dictum that one becomes virtuous by practicing the virtues. We believe that every young person has a conscience. It may be a conscience embattled against the individual's own passions and the allurements of the culture, but it is a conscience nonetheless. Like the capacities of the mind, the conscience must be educated or it will lapse into lethargy. We insist that students always be attentive and polite. We insist that schools inculcate core virtues at all levels of learning. When students become capable of discussing virtue, we do not present them with moral conundrums that seemingly have no right or wrong answers. Instead, we confront them with the great stories of self-command and self-sacrifice found in literature and history. These narratives show that actions have consequences, and that there is a clear difference between right and wrong. Just as we encourage students to emulate the intellectual virtues of writers and scientists, so we lead them to emulate the moral virtues of heroes and heroines. The history of classical education is quite simply a history of the conjunction of learning and morality. The Roman teacher Quintilian made the connection explicit:

My aim, then, is the education of the perfect orator. The first essential for such a one is that he should be a good man, and consequently we demand of him not merely the possession of exceptional gifts of speech, but all the excellences of character as well.

The Hillsdale model schools expect no less of their students.

---

[161] The difference between the classical liberal arts education based on the Western Civilization worldview and a classical Christian worldview education is the depth of theological study. Both programs are pro-Christian while the classical Christian worldview education focuses extensively on God's nature and character through His Word.

Civics and Citizenship

Classical education has always been concerned with the political order. Aristotle defined man as "by nature an animal intended to live in a polis." Accordingly, for the Greeks education was essentially political. All free citizens bore the responsibility and the privilege of voting in the assembly and defending the polis from invasion. Young boys were taught from an early age how to speak and how to fight. The American Founders similarly hoped that schools would teach young people how to preserve the constitutional republic they would inherit. The Founders knew that free government depends not on the decisions of a few politicians but on the wisdom and virtue of a people. Political wisdom and virtue do not come easily. More than two centuries of American history have confirmed that this nation can be sustained only by citizens who understand, serve, and defend America's founding principles. As much as they embraced free, constitutional government, the Founders feared the unchecked passions of an uninstructed multitude. In this light, Hillsdale regards the decline in political knowledge in our day as portending untold compromises on the safety and happiness of our people.

Hillsdale-sponsored schools will provide a political education reaffirming our nation's founding principles. They will exalt the inalienable rights of life, liberty, and the pursuit of happiness as guaranteed by and realized through the American frame of government. They will ensure that their students enter the world as citizens fully cognizant of their rights and responsibilities. They will teach students that true freedom and happiness are to be obtained through limited, balanced, federal, and accountable government protecting the rights and liberties of a vibrant, enterprising people. Such political knowledge can only be gained by a thorough study of American history and government: that study to consist principally in the reading of primary sources. If such explicit political instruction appears to some too patriotic, we must remember that James Madison, the father of the Constitution, considered a "reverence for the laws" a "prejudice" which even the most enlightened nations cannot afford to be without.

The End in View

Contrary to popular opinion, classical education is far from arcane, irrelevant, dull, and unimaginative. Rather, the classical view understands that a human being without knowledge of the past, without reverence for his inheritance, and without a judgment formed by the standards of true greatness, is much like a man with amnesia. He does not know who he is or where he comes from. He does not know his rights or his duties. He knows neither his debts nor his debtors. Worse, he may easily become the pawn of the first person he runs into, so unfamiliar and mysterious will his surroundings seem to him. A true classical, liberal, civic education recognizes with Lincoln that if we know where we are, by knowing where we have been, we shall then know "whither we are tending." While Hillsdale College worries that today's educational practices shortchange young people and fail to provide them with the cultural, moral, and civic literacy necessary to live a productive and happy life, it sees great opportunity in the resurgence of classical schools. Indeed, the demand for traditional education on the part of students and parents alike promises to be one of the surest methods of reacquainting today's citizens with the nation's Founding principles. Another way of saying this is that an increasing number of people today, even young people, demonstrate a longing for the good and the beautiful and the true. And such a longing is the first step on the road to true happiness.

Appendix 4

Further Readings on the Frankfurt School

William S. Lind

This is the sixth and final chapter in the Free Congress Foundation's book on Political Correctness, or – to call it by its real name – cultural Marxism. It is a short bibliographical essay intended not as an exhaustive resource for scholars but as a guide for interested citizens who want to learn more about the ideology that is taking over America.

As readers of the earlier chapters in this book already know, to understand Political Correctness and the threat it poses it is necessary to understand its history, particularly the history of the institution most responsible for creating it, the Frankfurt School. The Frankfurt School, or the Institute for Social Research as it was formally known, was established at Frankfurt University in Germany in 1923. This fact alone is important, because it tells us that Political Correctness is not merely a leftover of the American student rebellion of the 1960s.

Another fact from that long-ago year, 1923, is equally significant: the intended name for the Frankfurt School was the Institute for Marxism. The Institute's father and funder, Felix Weil, wrote in 1971 that he "wanted the Institute to become known, and perhaps famous, due to its contributions to Marxism as a scientific discipline..."[162] Beginning a tradition Political Correctness still carries on, Weil and others decided that they could operate more effectively if they concealed their Marxism; hence, on reflection, they chose the neutral-sounding name, the Institute for Social Research (Institut für Sozialforschung). But "Weil's heartfelt wish was still to create a foundation similar to the Marx-Engels Institute in Moscow – equipped with a staff of professors and students, with libraries and

---

[162] Martin, Jay. *The Dialectical Imagination: A History of the Frankfurt School and the Institute for Social Research*, 1923 – 1950 (University of California Press, Berkeley, 1996) p. 8.

archives – and one day to present it to a German Soviet Republic."[163] In 1933, this disguised "Institute for Marxism" left Germany and reestablished itself in New York City, where in time it shifted its focus to injecting its ideology into American society.

The most readable English-language history of the Frankfurt School is Martin Jay's book, The Dialectical Imagination: A History of the Frankfurt School and the Institute for Social Research, 1932 - 1950 (University of California Press, Berkeley, CA, 1973 – new edition in 1996). This book is in print in paperback and can be ordered through any bookstore. The reader should be aware that Jay's book is, in the words of another work on the Frankfurt School, a "semiofficial" history[164], which is to say that it is largely uncritical. Like virtually all other English-language authors on the Institute, Jay is on the political left. Nonetheless, the book provides a solid factual introduction to the Frankfurt School, and the reader should have little trouble discerning in it the roots and origins of today's Political Correctness.

In his first chapter, "The Creation of the Institut für Sozialforschung and Its First Frankfurt Years," Jay lays bare the Institute's Marxist origins and nature, and equally its efforts to conceal both: "The original idea of calling it the Institut für Marxismus (Institute for Marxism) was abandoned as too provocative, and a more Aesopian alternative was sought (not for the last time in the Frankfurt School's history)."[165] Of the Institute's first director, Carl Grünberg, Jay writes, "Grünberg concluded his opening address by clearly stating his personal allegiance to Marxism as a scientific methodology. Just as liberalism, state socialism, and the historical school had institutional homes elsewhere, so Marxism would be the ruling principle at the Institut."[166] Jay's first chapter also introduces the Institute's critical shift that laid the basis for today's Political Correctness, a.k.a. cultural Marxism: "if it can be said that in

---

163 Rolf Wiggershaus, The Frankfurt School: Its History, Theories, and Political Significance, trans. By Michael Robertson (The MIT Press, Cambridge, Massachusetts, 1995) p.24.
164 Andrew Arato and Eike Gebhardt, ed., The Essential Frankfurt School Reader (Continuum, New York 1997) p. vii.
165 Jay op. cit., p. 8.
166 Ibid., p. 11.

early years of its history the Institut concerned itself primarily with an analysis of bourgeois society's socio-economic substructure, in the years after 1930 its prime interest lay in its cultural superstructure."[167]

The second chapter, "The Genius of Critical Theory," gets at the heart of the "Critical Studies" departments that now serve as the fronts of Political Correctness on American college campuses. All of these are branches and descendants of the Critical Theory first developed in the 1930s by the Frankfurt School. The term "Critical Theory" is itself something of a play on words. One is tempted to ask, "OK, what is the theory?" The answer is, "The theory is to criticize." Jay writes, "Critical Theory, as its name implies, was expressed through a series of critiques of other thinkers and philosophical traditions...Only by confronting it in its own terms, as a gadly of other systems, can it be fully understood."[168] The goal of Critical Theory was not truth, but praxis, or revolutionary action: bringing the current society and culture down through unremitting, destructive criticism. According to Jay, "The true object of Marxism, Horkheimer argued (Max Horkheimer succeeded Carl Grünberg as director of the Institute in July, 1930), was not the uncovering of immutable truths, but the fostering of social change."[169]

The central question facing the Institute in the early 1930s was how to apply Marxism to the culture. The title of Jay's third chapter gives the answer: "The Integration of Psychoanalysis." Here, Jay's book falls down to some extent, in that it does not offer a clear understanding of how the Institute integrated Marx and Freud. The answer appears to be that Freud's later critiques were made conditional on a capitalist, bourgeois order: a revolutionary, post-capitalist society could "liberate" man from his Freudian repression. Here again one sees key aspects of Political Correctness emerging, including a demand for sexual "liberation" and the attack on "patriarchal" Western culture.

---

167 Ibid., p. 21.
168 Ibid., p. 41.
169 Ibid., p. 46.

If the precise nature of the blending of Marx and Freud is left open by Jay, his next chapter makes the blend's application clear: "The Institute's First Studies of Authority." The Institute left Germany for New York in 1933 because the Nazis came to power in Germany. Not surprisingly, one of the Institute's first tasks in New York was to oppose Nazism. It did so largely by concocting a psychological "test" for an "authoritarian personality." Supposedly, people with this authoritarian personality were likely to support Nazism. Both the concept and the methodology were doubtful at best. But the Institute's work laid down an important tool for the left, namely a notion that anyone on the right was psychologically unbalanced. And it marked a key turning for the Institute in the birth of Political Correctness in America, in that the empirical research the studies demanded was done on Americans. Ultimately, the result was Institute member Theodor Adorno's vastly influential book, The Authoritarian Personality, published in 1950.

Jay's fifth chapter, "The Institute's Analysis of Nazism," continues the theme of the "authoritarian personality." But his sixth, "Aesthetic Theory and the Critique of Mass Culture," provides an answer to the question of why most "serious" modern art and music is so awful. It is intended to be. Theodor Adorno was the Institute's lead figure on high culture – he began life as a music critic and promoter of Schönberg – and his view was that in the face of the "repressiveness" of bourgeois society, art could only be "true" if it were alienating, reflecting the alienated society around it. Jay quotes Adorno: "A successful work...is not one which resolves objective contradictions in a spurious harmony, but one which expresses the idea of harmony negatively by embodying the contradictions, pure and uncompromised, in its innermost structure."[170]

Adorno despised the new mass culture – film, radio, and jazz – in what seems to be a case of missed opportunity: today, the entertainment industry is the single most powerful promoter of Political Correctness. Another key Frankfurt School figure, Walter Benjamin, did see the potential: "he paradoxically held out hope for

---

[170] Ibid., p. 179.

the progressive potential of politicized, collectivized art."[171] At some point, someone – the question of who lies beyond the boundaries of Jay's book – put Benjamin's perception together with the Frankfurt School's general view, which Jay summarizes as "the Institut came to feel that the culture industry enslaved men in far more subtle and effective ways than the crude methods of domination practiced in earlier eras."[172]

In the remainder of the book, Jay traces the (sort of) empirical work of the Institute in the 1940s, which was beset by the same problems as their earlier survey "research," and follows the Institute in its return to Frankfurt, Germany after World War II. But by this point, the reader will already have the picture. He will have seen how Marxism was translated from economic into cultural terms; discerned the themes of sexual liberation, feminism, "victims" and so on that make up today's Political Correctness; and found in Critical Theory the origins of the endless wailing about "racism, sexism and homophobia" that "PC" pours forth. One key piece of history is missing: "an analysis of Marcuse's influential transmission of the Frankfurt School's work to a new American audience in the 1960s,"[173] as Jay puts it in his epilogue. Also, Jay curiously passes over with only the most minimal discussion the effective move of the Institute, in the persons of Horkheimer and Adorno, to Los Angeles during the war. Did the connections they built there play any role in injecting the Frankfurt School's philosophy into American film and, after the war, television? Jay does not touch upon the subject.

But for the reader new to the Frankfurt School as the source of today's Political Correctness, Jay's The Dialectical Imagination offers a solid base. The book concludes with an extensive (though not annotated) bibliography of works by and about the Frankfurt School.

As to other accessible works about the Frankfurt School, the definitive modern work in German has recently been translated into English: The Frankfurt School: Its History, Theories and Political

---

[171] Ibid., p. 211.

[172] Ibid., p. 216

[173] Ibid., p. 287; Herbert Marcuse joined the Institute for Social Research in 1932.

<u>Significance</u> by Rolf Wiggershaus, (translated by Michael Robertson, The MIT Press, Cambridge, MA, first paperback edition 1995). This covers much of the same ground as Martin Jay's book, although it also follows the Institute from its post-war return to Germany up to Adorno's death in 1969. Wiggershaus is more detailed than Jay, and, although he too is on the left politically, he is more critical than Jay. In the book's Afterword, Wiggershaus offers a brief look (and a hostile one) at some German conservative critiques of the Frankfurt School. A picture emerges that will seem familiar to Americans entrapped in the coils of Political Correctness:

> Since the publication in 1970 of his book The Poverty of Critical Theory, Rohrmoser has promulgated, in constantly varying forms, the view that Marcuse, Adorno, and Horkheimer were the terrorists' intellectual foster-parents, who were using cultural revolution to destroy the traditions of the Christian West. Academics such as Ernst Topitsch and Kurt Sontheimer, who saw themselves as educators and liberal democrats, followed in Rohrmoser's footsteps. In 1972 Topitsch, a critical rationalist who was Professor of Philosophy in Graz, had stated that behind the slogans of "rational discussion" and "dialogue free of domination" there was being established at the universities "a distinct terrorism of political convictions such as never existed before, even under Nazi tyranny."[174]

Additional works on the Frankfurt School include:

- <u>The Frankfurt School</u> by T.B. Bottomore (Tavistock, London, 1984). Another history written by a sympathizer; you are better off with Jay or Wiggershaus.

- <u>"The New Dark Age: The Frankfurt School and 'Political Correctness'"</u> by Michael Minnicino, in Fidelio, Vol. 1, No. 1, Winter 1992 (KMW Publishing, Washington, DC) One of the few looks at the Frankfurt School by someone not a sympathizer, this long journal article explains the role of the

---

[174] Wiggershaus, op. cit., p. 657.

Institute for Social Research in creating the ideology we now know as "Political Correctness." Unfortunately, its value is reduced by some digressions that lack credibility.

- <u>Angela Davis: An Autobiography</u> by Angela Davis (Random House, New York 1974) Angela Davis, a leading American black radical and Communist Party member, was described by Frankfurt School member Herbert Marcuse as "my best student." She also studied in Frankfurt under Adorno. This book shows the link between the Institute for Social Research and the New Left of the 1960s through the eyes of a key participant.

- <u>The Young Lukacs and the Origins of Western Marxism</u> by Andrew Arato (Seabury Press, New York, 1979). The author is, as usual, a sympathizer, but this work shows the key role Lukacs played in the thinking of the Frankfurt School and, later, the New Left.

- <u>The Origin of Negative Dialectics: Theodor W. Adorno, Walter Benjamin and the Frankfurt Institute</u> by Susan Buck-Morss (Free Press, New York, 1977). An important book on the relationship of the Frankfurt School and Critical Theory to the New Left.

- <u>Introduction to Critical Theory: Horkheimer to Habermas</u> by David Held (University of California Press, Berkeley, 1980). Yet another history by a fan of the Frankfurt School, but valuable for its discussion of the impact of Nietzsche on key Frankfurt School figures.

- <u>Adorno: A Political Biography</u> by Lorenz Jager (translated by Stewart Spencer, Yale University Press, New Haven, 2004) This recent study of Theodor Adorno, the Frankfurt School's most important "creative spirit," offers a highly readable introduction to the origins of Political Correctness, perhaps the best available to the layman. Lorenz Jager is an editor of the <u>Frankfurter Allgemeine</u>, one of Germany's most influential newspapers. He is no uncritical admirer of the Frankfurt

School, and thus offers a balanced treatment of Adorno instead of the usual hagiography.

Beyond these secondary works lies the vast literature produced by members of the Frankfurt School itself. Some key works were written in English, and many of those written in German are available in translation. As is usually the case with Marxist works, the prose style and vocabulary are often so convoluted as to make them almost unreadable. Further, the refusal of the Frankfurt School to make its own future vision plain led many of its members to write in aphorisms, which adds yet another layer of impenetrableness.

One work, however, is of such importance that it must be recommended despite its difficulty: <u>Eros and Civilization</u> by Herbert Marcuse (Beacon Press, Boston, first paperback edition in 1974 and still in print). Subtitled <u>A Philosophical Inquiry into Freud</u>, this book holds center stage for two reasons. First, it completes the task of integrating Marx and Freud. While the Marxism is *sotto voce*, the whole framework of the book is in fact Marxist, and it is through the framework that Freud is considered. Second, <u>Eros and Civilization</u> and its author were the key means of transmission by which the intellectual work of the Frankfurt School was injected into the student rebellion of the 1960s. This book became the bible of the young radicals who took over America's college campuses from 1965 onward, and who are still there as faculty members.

In brief, <u>Eros and Civilization</u> urges total rebellion against traditional Western culture – the "Great Refusal" – and promises a Candyland utopia of free sex and no work to those who join the revolution. About two-thirds of the way through the book, Marcuse offers this summary of its arguments:

Our definition of the specific historical character of the established reality principle led to a reexamination of what Freud considered to be universal validity. We questioned this validity in view of the historical possibility of the abolition of the repressive controls imposed by civilization. The very achievements of this civilization seemed to make the performance principle obsolete, to make the repressive utilization of the instincts archaic. But the idea of a non-repressive civilization on the basis of the achievements of the performance principle encountered the argument that instinctual liberation (and consequently total liberation) would explode civilization itself, since the latter is sustained only through renunciation and work (labor) – in other words, through the repressive utilization of instinctual energy. Freed from these constraints, man would exist without work and without order; he would fall back into nature, which would destroy culture. To meet this argument, we recalled certain archetypes of imagination which, in contrast to the culture-heroes of repressive productivity, symbolized creative receptivity. These archetypes envisioned the fulfillment of man and nature, not through domination and exploitation, but through release of inherent libidinal forces. We then set ourselves the task of "verifying" these symbols – that is to say, demonstrating their truth value as symbols of a reality beyond the performance principle. We thought that the representative content of the Orphic and Narcissistic images was the erotic reconciliation (union) of man and nature in the aesthetic attitude, where order is beauty and work is play.[175]

Marcuse continues after this summary to lay out the erotic content of the "reality beyond the performance principle," i.e., a new civilization where work and productivity were unimportant. "The basic experience in this (aesthetic) dimension is sensuous rather than conceptual,"[176] that is, feelings are more important than logic: "The discipline of aesthetics installs the *order of sensuousness* as against the *order of reason.*"[177]

"In German, *sensuousness* and *sensuality* are still rendered by one and the same term: *Sinnlichkeit*. It connotes instinctual (especially sexual) gratification…[178] No longer used as a full-time instrument of labor, the body would be resexualized… (which) would first manifest itself in a reactivation of all erotogenic zones and, consequently, in a

---

[175] Herbert Marcuse, Eros and Civilization: A Philosophical Inquiry into Freud (Beacon Press, Boston, 1955), p. 175-176.
[176] Ibid., p. 176.
[177] Ibid, p. 181.
[178] Ibid., p. 182

resurgence of pre-genital polymorphous sexuality and in a decline of genital supremacy. The body in its entirety would become an object of cathexis, a thing to be enjoyed – an instrument of pleasure. This change in the value and scope of libidinal relations would lead to a disintegration of the institutions in which the private interpersonal relations have been organized, particularly the monogamic and patriarchal family."[179]

This in a book which Marcuse dedicated to Sophie Marcuse, his wife of fifty years!

It is easy to see how this message – "If it feels good, do it" – published in 1955 resonated with the student rebels of the 1960s. Marcuse understood what most of the rest of his Frankfurt School colleagues did not: the way to destroy Western civilization – the objective set forth by George Lukacs in 1919 – was not through abstruse theory, but through sex, drugs, and rock 'n' roll. Marcuse wrote other works for the new generation that spawned the New Left – One Dimensional Man (1964), Critique of Pure Tolerance (1965), An Essay on Liberation (1969), Counterrevolution and Revolt (1972). But Eros and Civilization was and remains the key work, the one that put the match to the tinder.

Other central works by members of the Frankfurt School include:

- The Authoritarian Personality by Theodor Adorno (Harper, New York, 1950). This book is the basis for everything that followed that portrayed conservatism as a psychological defect. It had enormous impact, not least on education theory.

- Dialectic of Enlightenment by Theodor Adorno and Max Horkheimer (trans. By John Cumming, Verso, London, 1979). A complex philosophical work written during World War II largely in response to Nazism (and extensively devoted to discussions of anti-Semitism), this work seeks to find a kernel of "liberating" reason in the ruins of the Enlightenment.

- Minima Moralia: Reflections from a Damaged Life by Theodor Adorno (trans. E.F.N. Jophcott, New Left Books, London, 1974).

---

[179] Ibid., p. 201.

A book of aphorisms, almost entirely incomprehensible, but the effective conclusion of Adorno's work.

- <u>Escape from Freedom</u> by Erich Fromm (Farrar & Rinehart, New York, 1941, still in print in paperback) Fromm was the Institute's "happy face," and this book was often required reading at colleges in the 1960s. The thesis is that man's nature causes him to throw his freedom away and embrace fascism unless he "masters society and subordinates the economic machine to the purposes of human happiness," i.e., adopts socialism. At this point Fromm was in the process of breaking away from the Institute and his subsequent works cannot be considered as part of the Frankfurt School corpus.

- <u>Eclipse of Reason</u> (Oxford University Press, New York, 1947). Essentially a sequel to <u>Dialectic of Enlightenment</u>, the book is heavily the work of Adorno and other Frankfurt School personages, although only Horkheimer's name appeared on it. Its contents are based on a series of lectures Horkheimer gave at Columbia University in 1944. The prose style is surprisingly readable, but the contents are odd; there is throughout a strong nostalgia, which was normally anathema to the Frankfurt School. The key chapter, "The Revolt of Nature," reflects a strange Retro anarchism: "The victory of civilization is too complete to be true. Therefore, adjustment in our times involves an element of resentment and suppressed fury."

- <u>Critical Theory: Selected Essays</u> by Max Horkheimer (trans. Matthew O'Connell, Seabury Press, New York, 1972). The essay, "Traditional and Critical Theory" is especially important.

- <u>The Essential Frankfurt School Reader</u>, ed. By Andrew Arato and Eike Gebhardt (Continuum, New York, 1982, in print in paperback) Not an introduction to the Frankfurt School, but rather a reprinting of Frankfurt School essays not available elsewhere, this book is more useful to the specialist than the novice. Nonetheless, both the editors' lengthy introductions and some of the essays are useful (once again, the editors are solidly on the Left politically, and their style is as heavy as that of the Frankfurt School's members).

This small bibliography will be enough to get an interested reader started; the full literature on and by the Frankfurt School is immense, as the bibliographies in Jay's and Wiggershaus's books attest. What has been missing from it, at least in English, is a readable book, written for the layman, that explains the Frankfurt School and its works in terms of the creation of Political Correctness. This short volume is at least a start in filling that gap.

INDEX

Who's Who of Cultural Marxism

Bios of the Contributing Authors

Richard W. Hawkins was born (May 27, 1949) and raised in the Santa Monica/West Los Angeles area of California. After earning a BS in Engineering from California State University, Northridge, he earned an MBA from Chapman University while serving in the Air Force.

Richard retired active duty as Lt. Col. with over 20 years military service in the USAF and the Air National Guard. He served as Civil Engineering Officer, Assistant Base Civil Engineer and Base Civil Engineer at numerous bases as well as Squadron Commander for a Prime BEEF squadron. Richard was also a staff officer with the Air National Guard headquarters both at Andrews AFB, MD and the Pentagon.

After his military retirement Richard had some time to be Mr. Mom with his three school aged children. It was at this stage he became aware of the politically correct indoctrination conducted in public education which sparked his quest for truth against the world's lies. Richard has been leading Focus on the Family's *The Truth Project* since 2007, has taught adult Sunday school and was manager of the church's Bible Study programs.

Richard and wife Pamela now reside in Lake Havasu City, AZ. Richard has three children and five grandchildren and Pamela has two children, one grandchild and one great grandchild.

William S. Lind (born July 9, 1947) is an American conservative author of several books and one of the first proponents of fourth generation warfare (4GW) theory. William S. Lind is a columnist for *The American Conservative* magazine, the agent for Thomas Hobbes' novel *Victoria* and a member of St. James Anglican Catholic Church in Cleveland, Ohio. His latest book, *Retroculture,* is available from Arktos Books.

Mr. Lind graduated from Dartmouth College in 1969 and from Princeton University in 1971, where he received a master's degree in history. In 1973, having grown tired of doctoral work at Princeton, Lind wrote to his Senator Robert Taft, Jr. requesting his help in securing a job with Amtrak. In response, Taft instead offered Lind a job in his office, where he eventually began analyzing defense policy (Taft being a member of the United States Senate Committee on Armed Services.

Mr. Lind was the Director of the Center for Cultural Conservatism at the Free Congress Foundation (renamed the American Opportunity Foundation). The foundation believes that the American economy has been the engine driving both freedom and prosperity in the world since 1945 and American prosperity must exist so that our national security can protect our country. Additionally, the Foundation is focused on developing and advocating a new approach to American foreign policy that rejects unwise military intervention that is not designed to protect or achieve vital national security interests.

Raymond V. Raehn earned an M.A. degree in International Affairs from The George Washington University and is a graduate of the U.S. Naval War College. He flew Navy fighter planes during World War II and became the Commander of a fighter squadron some years later. After serving on the staff of the Chief of Naval Operation, he retired to head a real estate development company. In 1981, he [helped] found the United States Global Strategy Council, a conservative think tank, and served as its president as an advocate of a comprehensive U.S. national security strategy which became law in 1986. He was also a member by invitation only of a very elite corps of conservatives on the Council for National Policy. He operated a family cattle ranch in South Texas in 2016. On 10/25/2016, Raymond V. Raehn passed away and was 92 at the time. Raymond Raehn had lived in George West, TX; in the past Raymond has also lived in Mc Lean VA.

T. Kenneth Cribb, Jr. is a native of South Carolina. He received a B.A. from Washington and Lee University and a J.D. from the University Of Virginia School Of Law. He also has honorary doctorate degrees from Thomas Aquinas College, Oklahoma Christian University, and Universidad Francisco Marroquín.

Mr. Cribb was deputy to the chief counsel of the 1980 Reagan campaign. During the Reagan transition, he was deputy director of the Legal and Administrative Agencies Group, Office of the Executive Branch Management. He went on to serve the Reagan administration for almost the entire eight years of its existence, beginning in 1981 as assistant director for the Office of Cabinet Affairs.

He served next as assistant counselor to the President, in which capacity he assisted Counselor Edwin Meese. When Mr. Meese became attorney general, Mr. Cribb accompanied him to the Justice Department where he became counselor to the attorney general of the United States. In 1987, Mr. Cribb returned to the White House as assistant to the President for domestic affairs, serving as President Reagan's top advisor on domestic matters, supervising four White House offices: policy development, cabinet affairs, public liaison, and welfare reform. He served in this position until the fall of 1988.

Other Presidential appointments include vice chairman of the Fulbright Foreign Scholarship board from 1989 to 1992, governor of the American Red Cross, and councilor of the Administrative Conference of the United States.

He has served in many other leadership positions over the years. From 1971 to 1977, Cribb served as national director for the Intercollegiate Studies Institute (ISI). He became president of ISI and served from 1989 to 2011. He was also the founding publisher of ISI Books. Mr. Cribb retains the title of president emeritus of ISI.

He is the past president of the Collegiate Network, the Council for National Policy, and the Philadelphia Society and a former senior fellow of the Heritage Foundation.

Mr. Cribb has received numerous awards, including the Edmund Randolph Award, the highest honor given by the U.S. Department of Justice, and the Charles H. Hoeflich Lifetime Achievement Award, an honor rarely awarded by the Intercollegiate Studies Institute.

Currently, Cribb is a trustee and counselor to the Federalist Society, chairman of the board of trustees for the Brevard Music Center, and a trustee of the Sarah Scaife Foundation. He also serves on Young America's Foundation's Board of Directors and as the chairman of YAF's National Journalism Center Board of Governors.

Dr. Gerald L Atkinson, PHD, CDR, USN (Ret), is a retired executive of several high-technology research and development corporations which specialized in national security studies, applied artificial intelligence, alternative future energy technologies, terrorism assessments and nuclear non-proliferation studies. Concurrently, he served as Assistant Professor of Computer Science in a Masters' Degree Graduate Program at the Naval Air Test Center, teaching the Artificial Intelligence track.

From 1972-1976, Dry Atkinson served in the Office of the Secretary of Defense and as a member of the U.S./Soviet Standing Consultative Commission on the SALT I agreements. Dr. Atkinson worked under the direction of Hon. Paul H. Nitze, representing the Office of the Secretary of Defense at Interagency Staff conferences on SALT, including the National Security Council's Verification Panel Working Group. H authored classified studies assessing the impact on national security of strategic arms limitation measures. He negotiated directly with Soviet representatives on the procedures related to U.S./Soviet compliance with the ABM Treaty and Interim Agreement. In this connection, he was directly responsible for the negotiating tactics which led to Soviet acceptance of the U.S. proposed SSBN dismantling procedures.

Dr. Atkinson is a former Navy carrier aviator, Vietnam War combat veteran, Navy Test Pilot, and Landing Signal Officer. He was awarded the Legion of Merit, the Distinguished Flying Cross, Air Medal (4 stars), and the Navy Commendation Medal with Combat V. He performed the flight demonstration of the RA5C Vigilante in the 1965 Paris Air Show.

Dr. Atkinson earned a BS in Physics at Central Michigan College. He then earned a BA in Aeronautical Engineering at the Naval Postgraduate School in Monterey, CA. He finally earned two more degrees from the University of Michigan; a BS in Aeronautical Engineering and a PhD in Nuclear Engineering.

Dr. Paul Kengor, PhD is professor of political science at Grove City College and chief academic fellow of the college's Institute for Faith & Freedom. A New York Times bestselling author of over a dozen books. Kengor is also a visiting fellow at the Hoover Institution at Stanford University

Paul Kengor is author of over a dozen books, including several bestsellers. Kengor is an internationally recognized authority on the presidency, the Cold War, and communism, with extensive experience in Soviet archival research, particularly the Comintern Archives on Communist Party USA. Dr. Kengor's articles have appeared in numerous publications: the New York Times, USA Today, CNN.com, FoxNews.com, Washington Post, American Spectator, Wall Street Journal, The Guardian, Christianity Today, World, National Catholic Register, Crisis, Jewish Press, Jewish World Review, and many others. He has published articles in top refereed, scholarly journals, such as Political Science Quarterly and Presidential Studies Quarterly, and has been an editor or contributed chapters to books published by Harvard University Press, Columbia University Press, Oxford University Press, and other academic houses. Kengor has appeared on MSNBC, C-SPAN, NPR, BBC, and FoxNewsChannel, and has done many TV and radio shows, including "The O'Reilly Factor," "Hannity," Mark Levin, Michael Medved, Glenn Beck, and Bill Bennett.

Kengor received his doctorate from the University of Pittsburgh's Graduate School of Public and International Affairs and his master's degree from American University's School of International Service. He holds an honorary doctorate from Franciscan University (Steubenville, Ohio), where he was the commencement speaker in May 2009. Kengor, a native of Western Pennsylvania, lives with his wife Susan in Grove City, Pa., along with their eight children.

Two of Kengor's recent books that compliment this book are:

- *Dupes: How America's Adversaries Have Manipulated Progressives for a Century*, and
- *Takedown: From Communists to Progressives, How the Left Has Sabotaged Family and Marriage*

Rev. John P. Thackway was born in Ilfracombe, north Devon, in 1950. From an unchurched background, the Lord called him by grace through the ministry of a local evangelical church. The call to the ministry soon followed, and after graduating from the Bible Training Institute, Glasgow, he became pastor of Maryport Street Baptist Chapel, Devizes, Wiltshire. Married to Margaret in 1977, they have four children and seven grandchildren. In 1991, they moved to his present charge here, at the Holywell Evangelical Church. John Thackway has also been editor of the Bible League Quarterly since 1993. He is vice-chairman of the General Committee of the Trinitarian Bible Society and a committee member of Christian Worship Publishing Trust. He is also a visiting lecturer at the London Reformed Baptist Seminary and has spoken at a number of conferences in the UK and abroad. Mr. Thackway is also a signatory to the Affirmation 2010. He is a trustee of the Salisbury Reformed Seminary, and a visiting lecturer there.

Dr. David Randall, PhD, is the Research Director of The National Association of Scholars. David earned a Ph.D. in history from Rutgers University, an M.F.A. in fiction writing from Columbia University, a master's degree in library science from the Palmer School at Long Island University, and a B.A. from Swarthmore College. Prior to working at NAS he was the sole librarian at the John McEnroe Library at New York Studio School.

Dr. Marlene McMillan, PhD has been teaching Christians and non-Christians how to apply the Bible to daily life and influence our culture for over 20 years. Earning a D.Min. with an emphasis in Church and State Relations has opened doors for town hall debates, media interviews, and a greater level of cultural impact. She has become one of the most highly trained business consultants available, with an established reputation in the areas of Branding and Internet Marketing, Media Interview preparation and Niche Celebrity development. In addition to being in demand as a business speaker, she continues an active teaching ministry and is known as the Nations Expert on the Principles of Liberty. Dr. McMillan resides in Texas.

Dr. McMillan teaches about the power of your words, the power of ideas, and the power of forgiveness. She is considered an overcomer by those who know her because of the tragedies in her life. Dr. McMillan learned to press into the Lord and stand on God's word when all else failed.

Dr. Marlene McMillan is the author of _Mountains of Deceit: How the Dialectic Process has Infected the Culture_. It is a book about the language of the culture war and what you can do about it. Dr. Marlene is an author and international speaker known as the "Lady of Liberty and Forgiveness."

Many people ask how those subjects relate to liberty. As she has taught study groups for over 25 years, homeschooled her children and worked on her doctorate, she developed a philosophy of education and of life. (Philosophy means "why?") **Every subject ties back to liberty because liberty is the opportunity to assume responsibility for your life and accept the consequences.**

She can be reached at www.DrMarleneMcMillan.com and www.WhyLibertyMatters.com.

Janie B. Cheaney was born 1950, in Dallas, TX. Janie is married and has two children, Aquila and Tielman. She attended Abilene Christian College (now Abilene Christian University). Janie lives in Missouri, is a columnist for WORLD, writes novels for young adults, and is the author of the Wordsmith creative writing series. She also reviews books at RedeemedReader.com. Follow Janie on Twitter @jbcheaney.

Janie B. Cheaney has always loved literature but never wanted to be a writer until her mid-twenties. Twelve fiction manuscripts and untold magazine articles later, it appears she changed her mind. Her first published books were the _Wordsmith_ series, a creative writing program which grew out of her experience teaching writing to homeschoolers (including her own two children). She is the author of several novels for middle-grade readers, including _The Playmaker, The Middle of Somewhere, Somebody on this Bus is Going to Be Famous,_ and _I Don't Know How the Story Ends_. In 1992 her first World Magazine article appeared, and she and the respected Christian news journal have been privileged to grow up together. She's now a regular columnist at World, writing on aspects of culture and faith. She founded Redeemed Reader with a fellow World staffer, Emily Whitten, in 2011. Find more on her website, http://www.jbcheaney.com/.

Tom DeWeese is one of the nation's leading advocates of individual liberty, free enterprise, private property rights, personal privacy, back-to-basics education and American sovereignty and independence. A native of Ohio, he's been a candidate for the Ohio Legislature, served as editor of two newspapers, and has owned several businesses since the age of 23. In 1989 Tom led the only privately-funded election-observation team to the Panamanian elections. In 2006 Tom was invited to Cambridge University to debate the issue of the United Nations before the Cambridge Union, a 200 year old debating society. Today he serves as Founder and President of the American Policy Center and editor of The DeWeese Report. Tom also heads up an Internet news site calledFreedom21.com.For 40 years Tom DeWeese has been a businessman, grassroots activist, writer and publisher. As such, he has always advocated a firm belief in man's need to keep moving forward while protecting our Constitutionally-guaranteed rights

Dr. Daniel B. Coupland, PhD is a Professor and Chairman of the English Department and Dean of the Faculty at Hillsdale College. He earned a B.A. in Spanish from Liberty University, an M.A. in Linguistics from Oakland University, and a Ph. D. in curriculum, teaching, and education policy from Michigan State University. Before teaching in higher education, he taught Spanish at a public high school in southeast Michigan. At Hillsdale College, he teaches courses on English grammar and classic children's literature. In 2013, Dr. Coupland was named Hillsdale's "Professor of the Year." In 2016, he was a resident scholar at the C.S. Lewis Study Centre (The Kilns) in Oxford, UK. In 2017, Dr. Coupland received the Emily Daugherty Award for Teaching Excellence. His research focuses on classic children's literature and English grammar instruction. He is the co-author of an English grammar curriculum titled Well-Ordered Language: The Curious Child's Guide to Grammar (published by

Classical Academic Press). Dr. Coupland also serves on the board of directors for the Society for Classical Learning. He and his wife, Kari, live in Jonesville, Michigan, with their three children.

Dr. Terrence O. Moore, PhD has been the founding principal of three other classical schools and was the architect of the Barney Charter School Initiative at Hillsdale College.

A native of Texas, Dr. Moore earned a B.A. in history from the University of Chicago and a Ph.D. in history from the University of Edinburgh. He also served as a lieutenant in the U. S. Marine Corps from 1990-1993.

Dr. Moore taught at Ashland University in Ohio for two years.

For seven years he was the founding principal of Ridgeview Classical Schools in Fort Collins, Colorado, whose high school during his time there was twice ranked the number- one public high school in the state and also ranked fourth in the nation for open- enrollment schools, according to U.S. News and World Report.

From 2008-2014 Dr. Moore was a professor of history at Hillsdale College and helped to launch the Barney Charter School Initiative, which assists in the founding of classical charter schools across the country. At Hillsdale, Dr. Moore taught Western Heritage, American Heritage, The Enlightenment, and The Nature and History of Manhood. He also received the Emily Daugherty Award for Teaching Excellence. From 2014 to 2017 he was the founding principal of Atlanta Classical Academy and in 2018-19 the founding principal of Ascent Classical Academy of Douglas County, Colorado.

Dr. Moore has written frequently on school reform and other cultural and political topics, his most popular article being "Wimps and Barbarians" in the Claremont Review of Books. He has also written articles, editorials, and book reviews for The Claremont Review, The Washington Times, HumanEvents.com, Big Government, Townhall.com, Touchstone, The Family in America, and The Wall Street Journal.

Dr. Moore, has also written the excellent book *The Story-Killers: A Common-Sense Case Against the Common Core.*

Made in the USA
Columbia, SC
05 May 2020

95338796R00137